The Major
Shakespearean Tragedies

The Major Shakespearean Tragedies

A Critical Bibliography

Edward Quinn

James Ruoff

Joseph Grennen

The Free Press ❄ New York
Collier-Macmillan Publishers ❄ London

Library of Congress Catalog Card Number: 72–77284

printing number

1   2   3   4   5   6   7   8   9   10

Contents

Preface   vii

Hamlet
    Edward Quinn   1

Othello
    James Ruoff   77

King Lear
    Edward Quinn   147

Macbeth
    Joseph Grennen   211

General Works Related to Shakespeare   279

Preface

This book has a twofold purpose. The first is to provide reasonably detailed, accurate accounts of the most important statements in the history of the criticism and scholarship of *Hamlet, Othello, King Lear,* and *Macbeth.* The second hopefully emerging as a consequence of the first, reflected in our own critical remarks and in the individual introductions, is to offer a selective overview of the criticism of these plays. To that end we have arranged our material chronologically, beginning with writings from the late seventeenth century and proceeding to the most recent significant publications. In making our selections we have tried to remain as flexible as possible, and in our critical comments have attempted to restrain, but not altogether suppress, our own partisanship.

The book as a whole is designed for advanced undergraduate and graduate students and general readers who have a good acquaintance with the plays and who are now beginning their assault on the mountainous bulk of Shakespearean commentary. In addition, we feel the book will be of use and interest to the specialist, whether he be in the field of Shakespearean studies or simply an instructor of literature who teaches a course in which those plays are included.

Within chronological organization we have divided the work on each play into five categories: Criticism, Editions, Text, Sources, Staging. Of these, however, the section on criticism constitutes the overwhelming majority of entries. This emphasis on critical studies does not reflect a disparagement of noncritical scholarship. Rather, it is a recognition that whereas scholarship progresses in an orderly, linear fashion, the history of criticism is a much more untidy and complex affair. The god of criticism is Proteus, constantly shifting and changing, assuming all sorts of shapes and forms, many of them grotesque. Little wonder that many people regard it as a hopelessly subjective business, an example of human vanity dressed in a little brief authority looking into a mirror and declaring that what it sees there is a work of art. This is particularly true of Shakespearean criticism, which from one perspective often appears at best to be nothing more than a record of concerns and limitations of a particular historical epoch. Witness the *fin de siècle* Hamlet or the "unact-able" *King Lear*. How easy is a bush suppos'd a bear?

And yet, having granted the worst, we can still see the importance of critical history. For one thing, the discovery of the partial perspectives of past ages should help us to discover our own, or at least to acknowl-edge that they must be there even if we are not able to recognize them. For another, it should keep us respectfully alert to the power that these plays have to tell us more about ourselves as we attempt to say something about them. Finally, there is the consideration that the sum total of these partial perspectives adds up to something of great constancy.

We may not be willing to go as far as René Wellek and Austin Warren, who, in *Theory of Literature* (New York: Harcourt Brace, 1941), offered the thesis that "the meaning of a work of art is the history of its criticism"—but we do assert the proposition that extensive com-mentary on a work over a reasonably long period constitutes a very real and vital extension of that work. The demonstration of this fact re-quires a systematic consolidation of critical thought. Such a consolidation has been sadly lacking in relation to Shakespearean studies. The recent publication of Samuel Schoenbaum's *Shakespeare's Lives* (Oxford Uni-versity Press, 1970) has demonstrated the feasibility and value of such a consolidation in certain areas of scholarship. The need for a similar under-taking in critical history is even greater. Toward the achievement of that goal we offer this work as a modest but hopefully valuable contribution.

· Hamlet

Edward Quinn

✿ CONTENTS

Index to Critics Cited and Their Entry Numbers   *3*

Short Titles of Collections of Hamlet *Criticism*   *5*

The Criticism of Hamlet   *6*
    Introduction   *6*
    Entries for the Criticism of Hamlet   *11*

Sources and Date   *65*
    Introduction   *65*
    Entries for Sources and Date   *65*

Textual Criticism   *69*
    Introduction   *69*
    Entries for Textual Criticism   *70*

Editions   *74*

Staging   *76*

Index to Critics Cited
and Their Entry Numbers

Abel, Lionel 65

Adams, Joseph Quincy 27

Altick, Richard 54

Alexander, Nigel 81

Alexander, Peter 55

Auerbach, Eric 51

Babcock, Weston 62

Barker, Harley Granville 32

Booth, Stephen 76

Bowers, Fredson 56, T5

Braddy, Haldeen 66

Bradley, A. C. 19

Campbell, Lily B. 28

Charney, Maurice 77

Clemen, Wolfgang 46

Coleridge, Samuel T. 9

Craig, Hardin E3

Cruttwell, Patrick 67

Dowden, Edward 16

Draper, John W. 34

Duthie, G. I. T2

Eliot, T. S. 23

Elliott, G. R. 47

Empson, William 52

Fergusson, Francis 42

Flatter, Richard 43

Freudenstein, Reinhold T6

Furness, H. H. E1

Goethe, Johann Wolfgang von 7

Goldsmith, Oliver 4

Grebanier, Bernard 60

Gollancz, Israel S2

Greg, W. W. T4

Hankins, John Erskine 35

Hardison, O. B. 61

Hazlitt, William 11

Holmes, Martin 68

Honigmann, E. A. J. S3

Hoy, Cyrus E5

James, D. G. 48

Jenkins, Harold T6

Johnson, S. F. 49

Johnson, Samuel 5

Jones, Ernest 44

Joseph, Bertram 53

Joyce, James 26

Kaula, David S7

Kierkegaard, Sören 12

Kitto, H. D. F. 57

Kittredge, G. L. E4

Knight, G. Wilson 29

Knights, L. C. 63

Kott, Jan 69

Laforgue, Jules 18

Lamb, Charles 10

Levin, Harry 59

Lewes, George Henry 17

Lewis, C. M. 20

Lewis, C. S. 37

Mack, Maynard 50

de Madariaga, Salvador 39

Malone, Kemp S1

McFarland, Thomas 73

Morris, Harry 79

Murray, Gilbert   22
Newell, Alex   72
Nietzsche, Friedrich   15
Nosworthy, J. M.   T7
Olsson, Yngve   S6
Parrott, T. M.   E3
Prior, Moody E.   40
Prosser, Eleanor   74
Reid, B. L.   70
Richardson, William   6
Sanford, Wendy Coppedge   75
Santayana, George   21
Schlegel, W.   8
Schückling, L. L.   33
Sheridan, Thomas   3
Sister Miriam Joseph   64
Spencer, Theodore   38
Skulsky, Harold   80

Stabler, Arthur   S4
Stoll, E. E.   24
Taylor, Marion   S5
Tillyard, E. M. W.   45
Trilling, Lionel   44
Turgenev, Ivan   14
Voltaire   2
Waldock, A. J. A.   30
Walker, Alice   T3
Walker, Roy   41
Weitz, Morris   71
Werder, Karl   13
Wertham, Frederick   36
West, Rebecca   58
Wilson, J. Dover   31, T1, E2
Winstanley, Lillian   25
Zitner, S. P.   78

Short Titles of Collections of <u>Hamlet</u> Criticism

Many of the entries cited in this bibliography may be found in the following collections of Hamlet criticism. An asterisk(*) preceding a title means that the book is available in a paperback edition. Where both a hardcover and paperback edition are available, the paperback is listed second.

Bevington—*Twentieth Century Interpretations of Hamlet*, ed. David Bevington. Englewood Cliffs: Prentice-Hall, 1968.

Campbell—*Hamlet, ed.* O. J. Campbell, A. Rothschild, S. Vaughan. New York: Bantam Books, 1961.

Hoy—*Hamlet*, ed. Cyrus Hoy. New York: Norton, 1963.

Hubler—*Hamlet*, ed. Edward Hubler. New York: Signet, 1963.

Jump—*Hamlet: A Casebook*, ed. John Jump. London: Macmillan, 1968.

Leavenworth—*Interpreting Hamlet*, ed. Russell Leavenworth. San Francisco: Chandler, 1960.

Levenson—*Discussions of Hamlet*, ed. J. C. Levenson. Boston: D. C. Heath, 1960.

NV—*Hamlet: A New Variorum Edition*, ed. H. H. Furness [1877] New York: Dover Publications, 1963.

Sacks—*Hamlet: Enter Critic*, ed. Claire Sacks and Edgar Whan. New York: Appleton-Century-Crofts, 1960.

Williamson—*Readings on the Character of Hamlet*, ed. Claude C. H. Williamson. London, 1950.

The Criticism of <u>Hamlet</u>

INTRODUCTION

"A man who set out to read all the books about *Hamlet* would have time to read nothing else, not even *Hamlet*." These words were written by an eminent scholar, the late F. P. Wilson, over 25 years ago. They were true then; they are an understatement now. Since that time, the endless tide of articles and books on this, the most discussed work of literature in the history of western civilization, has been steadily increasing. A. A. Raven's *A Hamlet Bibliography and Reference Guide* (University of Chicago Press, 1936) covering the years 1877–1935, contained 2,167 items or an average of 37 a year. Gordon Ross Smith's *A Classified Shakespeare Bibliography* (Penn State University Press, 1962) covering the years 1936–1958, contains 933 items devoted to the play or an average of 42 a year. That these represent only a partial account of the output of critical material on the play is demonstrated by a glance at the annual Shakespeare bibliography published in the *Shakespeare Quarterly*. For the year 1969, the *Quarterly* lists no less than 134 items devoted to *Hamlet*. The result is a body of criticism so large that a mere listing of it, the Polish critic Jan Kott tells us, would produce a book twice the size of the Warsaw Telephone Directory.

Faced with these staggering statistics, the student beginning a serious study of the play might well be tempted to despair. What has not been said? What is there new to add to that verbal avalanche emanating for the past two centuries from the scholars and actors and artists, the amateurs and professionals, the lunatics and lovers and poets? The answer is, nothing and everything—nothing if your aim is to solve all of the play's puzzles, to pluck out the heart of its mystery and thereby to record for all time the "correct" interpretation; everything if your aim is to explore its inexhaustible vitality, to observe with a mixture of wonder, delight and occasional exasperation the profound attraction it has held for over three hundred years. For *Hamlet* has long since ceased to be just a famous play, just a part of our literature; it is a part of our lives and as such, it has the quality of an historical event or a cultural phenomenon.

This of course has its negative aspects. The danger is always present that our response to the play will become purely honorific and that we will transform it into a kind of national monument. The nineteenth century came dangerously close to doing just that. However, the saving grace of *Hamlet*, the evidence of its continuing vigor, is that it resists everyone's categories—the idolators' as well as the iconoclasts'.

Neo-Classical Criticism

Recorded comments about *Hamlet* are as old as the play itself. About 1600, probably the year in which the play was first produced, Spenser's friend, Gabriel Harvey, cited it along with *The Rape of Lucrece* as the two works of Shakespeare that "have it in them to please the wiser sort." A few years later (1604), a contemporary poet recorded the hope that his work would "please all, like Prince Hamlet." Its popularity continued throughout the century. In his Diary for August 31, 1668, Samuel Pepys noted that Thomas Betterton's performance in the title role was "the best part that ever yet man acted." Formal criticism, however, did not begin until the early eighteenth century when the patient work of editors such as Nicholas Rowe and Lewis Theobald introduced Shakespeare to a large reading public. Criticism in this period was based generally, but not exclusively, on neo-classical principles. English critics in particular, although still using the "rules of art" as a touchstone of judgment, began to see in the plays of Shakespeare an art that transcended the rules. Critics such as the anonymous author of *Some Remarks on the Tragedy of Hamlet* (1) were prepared to admit that the play's intellectual and emotional power more than overcame its occasional lapses in decorum or violations of the unities. [NOTE: Numbers in parentheses refer to entry numbers.]

Considerably less flexible and responsive were the French critics, notably Voltaire (2), who dismissed the play as inspired barbarism, "the work of a drunken savage." The French attack on Shakespeare was brilliantly refuted by Dr. Johnson. Johnson's admiration for *Hamlet*, however, was not entirely unreserved (5). He noted that, for all the play's excellencies, there were structural flaws, not the least of which was the violation of poetic justice represented by the death of Ophelia. His analysis marks the end of the first period of the play's critical history. It was a period that applauded the play's theatrical effectiveness and its emotional range and variety, while generally criticizing Shakespeare's failure to provide an explanation for Hamlet's delay in killing the King. This last point proved to be crucial, for it was precisely on this issue that a new response was to dominate critical reaction to the play for the next century and a half.

Romantic Criticism

The new attitude is reflected in the remarks of Thomas Sheridan (3) and in the more detailed criticism of Henry Mackenzie and William Richardson (6). It dealt with the problem that had disturbed earlier critics—Hamlet's delay—by assuming that the delay was consistent with the character of the hero. The age of the psychologizing of Hamlet had begun. It achieved its best known expression in Goethe's picture of the hero as a delicate vase (7) and in Coleridge's extraordinarily influential view of him as the reflective intellectual (9). As was later realized, both of these interpretations were more accurate as self-portraits of their originators than as objective analyses of the Hamlet of the play. Nevertheless Coleridge, Goethe and, to a lesser extent, Schlegel (8) struck a profoundly sensitive chord in the minds of their contemporaries. When Hazlitt (11) declared "We are Hamlet" and, even more startlingly, when the German poet, Ferdinand Freiligrath, announced "Deutschland ist Hamlet," they spoke for the nineteenth century. Implicit in these responses was the belief in Shakespeare as a type of prophet and in Hamlet as the prototype of the nineteenth century intellectual. It was at this point that the character of Hamlet began to be abstracted from the play, to assume an independent existence. The Prince's much-debated delay was seen to be the inevitable consequence, as Turgenev pointed out (14), of the divorce between will and reason.

Even then, however, there were dissenting voices. In 1859, Karl Werder (13), acting on an earlier suggestion of L. Klein, argued that the cause of Hamlet's delay was not internal but external. Hamlet's task is not mere revenge but the public unmasking of his father's murderer. Both Werder's analysis and those of Goethe and Coleridge were reviewed by another great critic of the play, A. C. Bradley (19). Bradley pointed out the weaknesses in all of these views before advancing his own. He saw the delay as internally motivated, a result of the "profound melancholy" into which Hamlet has been cast by his mother's remarriage.

Historical Criticism

Although Bradley was to remain the dominant figure in Shakespearean criticism for many years, his eminence was not undisputed. The first reaction against him was largely American in origin and reflected a distinctly American philosophical orientation. The pragmatism of John Dewey and William James, impatient of nineteenth-century metaphysical abstraction, found its scholarly equivalent in the work of E. E. Stoll (24) and his disciples. Stoll insisted that the nineteenth century had converted "structure into psychology," that is, had misinterpreted conventions of the Elizabethan theatre as insights into the psychology of the play's characters. Thus, argued Stoll, the nineteenth century had failed to see that Hamlet's delay—even his self-accusations—were merely *données* of the Elizabethan revenge play, to be accepted, not analyzed. *Hamlet* was, before everything else, a play designed by a busy man of the theatre to last two hours' traffic on the stage; Bradley had treated it as if it were a psychological novel. Stoll's analysis ushered in the era of historical criticism, reflected in the work of Campbell (28), Draper (34), Hankins (35), Elliott (47) and Bowers (56).

Modern Critical Approaches

In the meantime the reaction against Bradley was taking another form. In 1930 G. Wilson Knight presented the first of his "symbolic" interpretations of the play. Knight argued that character criticism as practiced by the nineteenth century and by the historical critics was fragmentary and superficial. *Hamlet* and all of Shakespeare's plays had to be seen as integrated, harmonious syntheses of character, action and poetry. The plays were themselves metaphors of the mystery of life: "revelations of profundity and grandeur. . . ." Although Knight's interpretation of *Hamlet* (29) was thought inadequate by many critics, his critical technique proved enormously influential. His influence was given added impetus by the imagery studies of Caroline Spurgeon and Wolfgang Clemen (46) and by the close textual analyses of the new critics on both sides of the Atlantic.

All this time a third approach to the play was provoking much discussion. This was the psychoanalytical interpretation initiated by Freud himself but skillfully developed at much greater length by his English disciple Ernest Jones (44). If Bradley had looked upon the play as a psychological novel, Jones went a step further to view it as a psychological case-history. The result was a fascinating, if finally inadequate, interpretation of Hamlet's character.

In the middle 1930's, two important studies appeared: J. Dover Wilson's *What Happens in Hamlet* (31) and Harley Granville-Barker's *Preface to Hamlet* (32). These two works have been particularly influential on modern stage productions. Granville-Barker's analysis of the "three act structure" and Wilson's clarification of some of the play's seeming inconsistencies have been adapted by contemporary directors with considerable success.

By 1940 the objections to character criticism—whether of the Stoll or the Bradleyan variety—became more pronounced. The title of C. S. Lewis's British Academy Lecture, *Hamlet: The Prince or the Poem* (37) accurately reflected the new tendency to shift the focus away from the hero, to see *Hamlet,* in Caroline Spurgeon's words, "not as the problem of an individual at all but as . . . a condition which . . . strikes and devours innocent and guilty alike." This emphasis on the play's thematic values, anticipated by Knight was skillfully developed by Walker (41) and Fergusson (42). Fergusson synthesized the play's imagery with the mythic interpretation first suggested by Gilbert Murray (22). The result was a convincing and comprehensive view of the play from the standpoint of plot (in the Aristotelian sense) in place of character.

At this time, too, the historical critics were focusing more on thematic values than on character. S. F. Johnson's 1952 essay (49) began as a defense of E. E. Stoll but ended with a good deal more flexibility and critical eclecticism than the latter had ever demonstrated. Fredson Bowers' 1955 essay (56) crystallized this tendency by demonstrating that the delay problem that had vexed so many of the character critics could be explained by an Elizabethan understanding of the terms "scourge and minister."

There also began in this period the critical "regeneration" of *Hamlet,* a counterattack against those who, echoing the eighteenth century view, had decided, in the face of the play's seemingly irresolvable difficulties, that the flaw was in the play itself. Chief among these were Eliot

(23), who had declared it "almost certainly a failure," Tillyard (45), who demoted it to the rank of problem play, and Waldock (30), who explained the delay as an authorial lapse. These objections were brilliantly refuted by Mack (50), Levin (59), Booth (75) and Alexander (81). These critics demonstrated that the play's puzzling qualities, the variously defined mysteries that lie at its heart, are in fact its defining distinctions. Its mysteriousness has become an image of our new sense of "the problematic nature of reality."

In thus testifying to the play's function as a symbol of a universal human experience, the critics now joined the long list of thinkers such as Kierkegaard (12) and Nietzsche (15), and artists such as Laforgue (18), Mallarmé, Mann, and Joyce (26), who have always seen *Hamlet* as representing, in Mack's phrase, "a paradigm of the life of man."

ENTRIES FOR THE CRITICISM OF *HAMLET*

1. *Some Remarks on the Tragedy of Hamlet Prince of Denmark.* London, 1736. 52 pp. Excerpted in Hoy, Jump, NV, and Williamson.

This remarkable essay, the first full-length critical discussion of the play, was published anonymously in 1736. The essay commends the play for the variety and consistency of its characters, for its "sublimity of thought," its "comprehensiveness of diction" and for the credibility of the ghost scenes. The criticisms it notes are the violations of the unity of time, minor inconsistencies in the action and the injudicious mixture of comic scenes in the play. The author is also disturbed by Hamlet's refusal to kill Claudius during the prayer scene for fear of sending him to heaven: "To desire to destroy a Man's Soul, to make him eternally miserable, by cutting him off from all hopes of Repentance; this surely, in a Christian Prince, is such a Piece of Revenge as no Tenderness for any Parent can justify."

This essay is in the best tradition of enlightened neo-classical criticism. It invokes the rules as guidelines, not as pigeonholes, always mindful of "the absurdity of such arbitrary rules . . . established by dogmatizing critics." The essay anticipates many of Dr. Johnson's points in his criticism of the play.

2. Voltaire (François Marie Arouet). *Oeuvres complètes de Voltaire.*
Paris: Lefèvre-Deterville, 1817. (Voltaire's Shakespearean criticism
is treated in T. R. Lounsbury's *Shakespeare and Voltaire* [London,
1902]. 463 pp. Excerpted in Campbell, Jump, NV, and Williamson.)

Voltaire alluded to *Hamlet* on a number of occasions between 1733
and 1776. His varying responses to the play provide a record of increasing
censoriousness and disapprobation. In his earliest allusion in *Lettres Philo-
sophiques* (1733), he is mildly critical but regards the play as the work of
genius. As the reputation and influence of both the play and its author
began to grow, Voltaire became increasingly negative in his response.
In his "Dissertation on Tragedy" (1752) he characterized the play as "a
vulgar and barbarous drama which would not be tolerated by the vilest
populace of France or Italy." In subsequent works (*Appel à toutes les
Nations*, 1761 and *Théâtre Complet*, 1768) he intensified his attack, although even here acknowledging that for all its "barbarity," the play contained passages of "sublime genius."

The rigidity of Voltaire's position must be seen against the background
of eighteenth-century rationalism and the aesthetic creed that was its
handmaiden. To Voltaire, Shakespeare and his hero, Hamlet, represented
the uncontrolled anarchic forces in life which the rationalists had striven
to overcome. The neo-classical principles of decorum and restraint were
symbols of the triumph of reason. The enormous emotional power of
Hamlet and its great popularity were symbols of a basic threat to that
triumph. Despite his ideological commitment, however, Voltaire was always conscious of the play's greatness.

3. *Sheridan, Thomas. Conversation recorded in *Boswell's London
Journal. 1762–1763*, ed. F. A. Pottle. New York: McGraw-Hill,
1950, pp. 234–235

On April 6, 1763, James Boswell noted in his *London Journal* a
conversation between himself and Thomas Sheridan, a distinguished
Shakespearean actor and the father of the playwright, Richard Brinsley
Sheridan. The conversation is important because it is the earliest recorded
interpretation of the character of Hamlet as "studious, contemplative . . .
delicate and irresolute," incapable of carrying out the revenge because
of his "good heart and fine feelings." Sheridan's comments represent the
first attempt to locate the reason for Hamlet's delay within the character
of the hero. Thus to Sheridan falls the distinction of being the forerunner

of the Romantic critics of the play (see Introduction). Equally interesting is the fact that Sheridan was, after Garrick, the greatest Shakespearean actor of his time. Thus his interpretation, unlike those of many of the Romantic critics, derived not from isolated literary study of the play but from the experience of having performed the role many times. (A discussion of Sheridan's interpretation is contained in J. Yoklavich's "Hamlet in Shammy Shoes," *Shakespeare Quarterly*, III [1952], 209–218.)

4. Goldsmith, Oliver. "The Use of Metaphors" [1765] in *The Miscellaneous Works of Oliver Goldsmith*, ed. James Prior. Philadelphia, 1875. Excerpted in NV, Sacks, and Williamson.

Goldsmith's essay contains some surprising comments on the "To be or not to be" soliloquy. He denounces the speech as "a heap of absurdities, whether we consider the situation, the sentiment, the argument, or the poetry." He argues that the dramatic situation does not justify Hamlet's desire for death; rather he has every motive—"revenge toward the usurper, love for the fair Ophelia, and the ambition of reigning" —for living. Secondly the speech itself is "inconsistent and incongruous." Its logic is confused, its syntax obscure and its metaphors "jumbled." The result is a speech that is "a strange rhapsody of broken images."

Goldsmith is the first of a long line of commentators who have had difficulty with this famous speech. His comments, viewed from a strictly logical, literal standpoint, have some validity. Even here, however, his objections are not unanswerable (see 72). More serious is his failure to see the value of the speech not as a logically organized syllogism, but, to use his own well-chosen phrase, as "a strange rhapsody."

5. Johnson, Samuel, *"Hamlet"* [1765] in *Samuel Johnson on Shakespeare*, etc., ed. W. K. Wimsatt. New York: Hill and Wang, 1960. 115 pp. Excerpted in Campbell, Hoy, Levenson, NV, Sacks, and Williamson.

Johnson's *Hamlet* criticism is contained in the notes to his edition of Shakespeare (1765). He praises the play's "variety," its mixture of the comic and tragic, its diversified scenes and its wide range of characters. His objections to the play are based on the presence of superfluous scenes, the passivity of the hero and the neglect of poetic justice. This last objection arises from the fact that although the villain is destroyed, the innocent, particularly Ophelia, suffer and die.

Johnson's notes also include his famous description of Polonius, summarized in the phrase "dotage encroaching upon wisdom."

Johnson's criticism of *Hamlet* is an excellent example of the difference between his approach to literature and that of the Romantic critics. Johnson is primarily concerned with character as it is reflected in situations. The actions of the character, as opposed to his thoughts and impressions, together with the moral implications of those actions, are his chief concern. Thus, on one of the great questions that was to concern the Romantic critics—Hamlet's madness—Johnson provides a characteristically straightforward, empirical response: "Of the feigned madness of Hamlet there appears no adequate cause."

6. Richardson, William. *A Philosophical Analysis and Illustration of Some of Shakespeare's Remarkable Characters.* London [1774], 203 pp., and *Essays on Shakespeare's Dramatic Characters* [1784], 170 pp. Excerpted in NV and Williamson.

Richardson's essays are important as one of the earliest of the long line of psychological analyses of the hero that has since dominated criticism of the play. He conceives of Hamlet's nature as scrupulously moral and deeply sensitive, paralyzed by the conflict between his sense of morality and his desire to inflict vengeance. His extreme sensitivity both to virtue and to vice accounts for his violent passion towards his enemies and his resolute fidelity towards his friends. He himself is dominated by a fine moral principle, "a sense of virtue," that renders him unable to fulfill the ghost's command: "he thus becomes an object not of blame but of genuine and tender regret."

Although there had been earlier allusions to Hamlet's delay, Richardson's essays were among the first sustained attempts to offer an explanation for it. In choosing to look within the character, he was responding to the emerging Romantic revolution which attempted to locate reality within the mind of the individual and which saw in Hamlet an image of that process.

7. Goethe, Johann Wolfgang von. *Wilhelm Meister's Apprenticeship,* trans. by Thomas Carlyle [1824]. New York: 1882. 596 pp. Reprinted in NV, Sacks, Hoy, Campbell, Williamson, and Jump.

Goethe's famous description of Hamlet is part of an elaborate discussion set down in the middle of his autobiographical novel, *Wilhelm Meister's Apprenticeship* (1796). The description itself has become the *locus classicus* for what has been called the sentimentalist view of the play. Ever since its appearance it has been subjected to almost as much comment as the play itself. Its most famous passage is as follows:

> The time is out of joint: O cursed spite,
> That ever I was born to set it right!

In these words, I imagine, will be found the key to Hamlet's whole procedure. To me it is clear that Shakespeare meant, in the present case, to represent the effects of a great action laid upon a soul unfit for the performance of it. In this view the whole piece seems to me to be composed. There is an oaktree planted in a costly vase, which should have borne only pleasant flowers in its bosom; the roots expand, the jar is shivered.

A lovely, pure, noble and most moral nature, without the strength of nerve which forms a hero, sinks beneath a burden which it cannot bear and must not cast away.

The image of Hamlet as "a costly vase" has evoked a great deal of negative criticism, but the idea behind the image—that of a beautiful, fragile nature subjected to an intolerable fate—has had a tenacious hold on subsequent criticism, and was particularly popular throughout the nineteenth century with critics and actors.

The inadequacy of Goethe's view has been effectively demonstrated by A. C. Bradley (19). Bradley pointed out that the Hamlet who stabs Polonius and then jokes about the body, who leaps on board the pirate ship and into Ophelia's grave, who sends Rosencrantz and Guildenstern to their death without a moment's qualm—this Hamlet hardly qualifies for the epithet "costly vase." Nevertheless, despite its obvious inadequacies, Goethe's analysis has called attention to an undeniable aspect of Hamlet's character.

8. Schlegel, Augustus William. *A Course of Lectures on Dramatic Art and Literature* [1808], trans. John Black and A. J. W. Morrison. London: G. Bell and Sons, 1876. 535 pp. Excerpted in Hoy, Jump, and NV.

Tragedy for Schlegel is the record of a conflict between man and a hostile universe. In Hamlet's case, this antagonism is further exacerbated by the hero's highly intellectual character, a character. that has rendered action repugnant to him. Thus *Hamlet* is a "tragedy of thought inspired by continual and never-satisfied meditation on human destiny . . ." Its moral "is intended to show how a calculating consideration which aims at exhausting . . . all the relations and possible consequences of a deed, cripples the power of acting."

Schlegel's view was adopted and elaborated by Coleridge and, in its Coleridgean form, became for many years the dominant view of the play and of its chief character. Its chief weaknesses lie in its failure to perceive the emotional aspect of Hamlet's character and its attempt to reduce his complex and vital nature to a formula.

9. Coleridge, Samuel Taylor. "Lectures and Notes on *Hamlet*," in *Coleridge's Shakespearian Criticism*, ed. Thomas M. Raysor. 2 vols. Harvard University Press, 1930. Reprinted or excerpted in Campbell, Hoy, Hubler, Levenson, NV, Sacks, and Williamson.

Easily the most influential criticism ever made about the play, Coleridge's view of Hamlet is still the most popular and prevalent conception of the character. His remarks appear in a series of fragmentary notes, the best known of which contains his description of Hamlet as exemplifying "great enormous intellectual activity and a consequent aversion to action." In short, Hamlet is a symbol of the paralyzed intellectual whose inability to avenge his father's murder is a result "of thinking too precisely on the event."

Derived largely from Schlegel, Coleridge's view of the play as the tragedy of the intellectual dominated much nineteenth-century and some early twentieth-century thinking about the play. Its chief weakness lies in its narrowly subjective, psychological bias; every aspect of the character is determined by his inward disposition. Coleridge never indicates how that disposition is affected by the external events in the play. In fact he presents a Hamlet "abstracted from the world without." The result implies the *reductio ad absurdum* of Romantic criticism: the Prince of Denmark without *Hamlet*.

10. Lamb, Charles. *On the Tragedies of Shakespeare, Considered with Reference to their fitness for Stage Representation*. London, 1811. Excerpted in Williamson and Jump.

The thesis of Lamb's essay is the paradoxical one that "the plays of Shakespeare are less calculated for performance on a stage than those of almost any other dramatist whatever." The reason for this, he asserts, is that Shakespeare's plays are filled with a profound, meditative wisdom which cannot be realized in performance. No actor, for example, can even approximate the true character of Hamlet, "the shy, negligent, retiring Hamlet." For the essence of Hamlet is his subjective musing, too private for public representation.

Lamb's analysis represents a further step in the Romanticizing of Hamlet since it takes him off the stage and into the closet. Having removed him from the theatre, Lamb thus made it possible for succeeding critics to remove him from literature altogether and to treat him as an historical human being.

11. Hazlitt, William. *Characters of Shakespeare's Plays* [1817]. London: Oxford University Press, 1929. 229 pp. Reprinted or excerpted in Campbell, Hoy, Jump, Hubler, NV, Sacks, and Williamson.

Hazlitt's critical indebtedness to Coleridge is nowhere better illustrated than in his essay on *Hamlet*. Like Coleridge, his Hamlet is "the prince of philosophical speculators" paralyzed by the habit of reflection. He differs from Coleridge, however, in focusing not on the mind of Hamlet but of the audience. "It is we who are Hamlet." The universality of the character's appeal derives from the fact that there is a little of Hamlet in all of us, and that little bit is the best part of us. The play does not abide our critical questioning, revealing as it does "a prophetic truth."

Hazlitt, a distinguished theatrical critic, admitted that his conception of *Hamlet* could never be realized on the stage. Indeed, his intensely subjective, impressionist conception of the play could not be objectively realized even in his criticism. The result is that his essay lacks coherence and unity, having the character more of an emotional outburst than of reasoned reflection.

12. Kierkegaard, Sören. "A Side Glance at Shakespeare's Hamlet," A Supplement to "Guilty?"/"Not Guilty?" [1845] in *Stages on Life's Way*, translated by Walter Lowrie. Princeton University Press, 1940. 472 pp.

"Guilty?"/"Not Guilty?" is the story of Kierkegaard's unhappy love affair and an account of one of the three "stages" of human existence. These stages are characterized by Kierkegaard as the aesthetic, the ethical and the religious. *Hamlet* is essentially a "religious" drama. The perplexing quality of the play arises from the attempt to interpret the character of the hero in "aesthetic" terms. From an aesthetic perspective, Hamlet's "procrastination and delay, his postponement and his self deceitful pleasure in renewing his purpose . . . merely abase him." In religious terms, on the other hand, the hero's delay is explained as "the collapse within himself in the religious experience. . . ." However, the problem here is that such an experience cannot be rendered dramatically. Thus the play's failure lies in its inability to operate simultaneously in two existential spheres—the "aesthetic" and the "religious."

An interesting supplement to Kierkegaard's remarks on *Hamlet* is contained in Denis De Rougemont's essay "Kierkegaard and Hamlet: Two Danish Princes" (*The Anchor Review*, I, 1955). De Rougemont points up some striking parallels between the play and Kierkegaard's own biography. Kierkegaard, like Hamlet, is "a deeply melancholic young man . . . given a dreadful mission over which he hesitates a long time." Finally Kierkegaard exposes the "usurper" (in Kierkegaard's case, the false and sanctimonious "Christendom" of nineteenth-century Europe) and dies as a result. As with Hamlet, the progression towards this fate is marked by the rejection of his beloved, the recourse to irony and indirection and the assumption of presumed madness. Both lives provide profound witness to the ennobling reality of suffering.

13. Werder, Karl. *The Heart of Hamlet's Mystery*, tr. from the German (*Vorlesungen über Hamlet* [1875]). New York: G. P. Putnam's, 1907. 223 pp. Excerpted in NV, Sacks, and Williamson.

Originally a series of lectures delivered in 1859, this book is remarkable in its anticipation of a prominent twentieth-century view of the problem of Hamlet's delay. Hamlet delays because his task is "not to crush the King at once . . . but to bring him to confession, to unmask and convict him." Thus Hamlet is far from being the procrastinator pictured by Goethe and others. He is a man of action, assigned the extraordinarily difficult task of bringing Claudius to public justice. The turning point of the play is the killing of Polonius, the act which precipitates all the subsequent tragic events.

The objections to Werder's position have been summarized by Bradley: Hamlet never alludes to the difficulty pointed out by Werder; in fact he says just the opposite ("I have cause and will and strength and means to do it"); secondly, the Laertes uprising in Act IV is designed to show by implication the comparative ease with which Hamlet might have carried out his revenge. Despite Bradley's objection, Werder's position, with some modification, has become the accepted view of many recent scholars (see 47, 56, 64).

14. *Turgenev, Ivan. "Hamlet and Don Quixote—The Two Eternal Human Types" [1860]. *Current Literature*, 42 (January, 1907), pp. 290–93, 349–52. Reprinted in *Shakespeare in Europe*, ed. Oswald Le Winter. Cleveland: Meridian Books, 1963.

Turgenev's thesis is that Hamlet and Don Quixote represent two antithetical types of human behavior. Don Quixote is the representative of faith, self-sacrifice and idealism. He is the exemplar of the man who lives for others, who endures the blows of fortune with humility and patience and who retains untarnished the perfection of his moral ideal.

Hamlet on the other hand is the embodiment of scepticism, self-absorption and introspection. He is the supreme egoist, offering his fellow man nothing, unsuited to any practical task, incapable of love. Although he hates evil he has lost all faith in the existence of good. As a result, his impact is negative, his impulses self-destructive.

Turgenev's essay is less a criticism of Hamlet than it is an attempt to deliver a moral critique of modern sensibility. For Turgenev inherent disaster lay in the fact that "thought and will have separated and are separating more and more." He uses the character of Hamlet, or rather the

Schlegel-Coleridge conception of Hamlet as a paralyzed intellectual, as an example of this process. In so doing he foreshadows the anti-Hamlet reaction of later critics such as Salvador de Madariaga (39) and Rebecca West (58).

15. *Nietzsche, Friedrich. *The Birth of Tragedy* [1872]. New York: Doubleday Anchor Books, 1956, pp. 51–52.

In his long philosophical essay on the origins and nature of Greek tragedy, Nietzsche records only one passing allusion to *Hamlet*. However, it is an extraordinary one in its anticipation of the view of the play that a number of modern critics, notably G. Wilson Knight (29), now share. The allusion occurs during his famous description of the Dionysiac principle, the dark, mysterious, irrational agent of the will:

> In this sense Dionysiac man might be said to resemble Hamlet: both have looked deeply into the true nature of things, they have *understood* and are now loath to act. They realize that no action of theirs can work any change in the eternal condition of things, and they regard the imputation as ludicrous or debasing that they should set right the time which is out of joint. Understanding kills action, for in order to act we require the veil of illusion; such is Hamlet's doctrine, not to be confounded with the cheap wisdom of John-a-Dreams, who through too much reflection, as it were a surplus of possibilities, never arrives at action. What, both in the case of Hamlet and of Dionysiac man, overbalances any motive leading to action, is not reflection but understanding, the apprehension of truth and its terror.

Thus Hamlet's failure to act is rooted in his awareness of the absurdity of any action, his perception in fact of "the ghastly absurdity of existence."

Nietzsche made one other allusion to *Hamlet* in *Nietzsche Contra Wagner* (1876) where he speaks of Hamlet as an example of the "fiery insolent spirits" who attempt to conceal the fact that they are "at bottom broken, incurable hearts." Both of these allusions are all the more striking when it is realized that they were made at a time when Coleridge's "Apollonian" view of Hamlet was dominant.

16. *Dowden, Edward. *Shakespeare: A Critical Study of His Mind and Art* [1875]. New York: G. P. Putnam, 1962. Excerpted in NV, Jump, and Williamson.

For Dowden the play eludes any final solution. Its mystery is an aspect of the mystery of existence itself and cannot be "contained in cognitive language." Hamlet himself Dowden sees in essentially Coleridgean terms as an example of the will paralyzed by intellect. He differs from Coleridge, however, in emphasizing the emotional side of Hamlet's character. This conflict of thought and feeling, intellect and will is never resolved. It is a mistake, he argues, to accept Hamlet's comment about Providence as a resolution. Hamlet goes to his death with the heart of his mystery unrevealed.

Dowden's presentation represents the most polished and sophisticated version of the Coleridgean interpretation. As such, it constitutes a formidable argument, but one that has been largely discredited by subsequent critics. Its weakness for modern readers lies in its mistaking the one character for the entire play. Nevertheless, Dowden's emphasis on the element of mystery as lying at the heart of the drama is an important perception, one that has been utilized by many later critics.

17. *Lewes, George Henry. *On Actors and the Art of Acting* [1875]. New York: Grove Press, 1957. Excerpted in NV and Williamson.

Lewes directs his attention to the vexed problem of Hamlet's madness—"whether it be real or assumed." Lewes argues that Shakespeare has erred in failing to make the matter very clear. Hamlet may not be mad, but the language of the play indicates that he has been severely unsettled by the ghost's revelation, leaving him in a state of "intense cerebral excitement. . . ." Also, the view that Hamlet only assumes madness has resulted in the misreading by many actors of certain key passages in the play. Chief among these is the "To be or not to be" soliloquy, which is usually rendered in a state of reflective calm. If the speech were read as the wildly passionate declamation of a haunted man, its "dramatic force" would be infinitely more effective.

A distinguished dramatic critic, Lewes never loses sight of the theatrical aspect of the play. The question of Hamlet's "insanity," which in non-theatrical criticism is little more than a semantic problem, is an important one when the staging of the play is being considered. Thus, Lewes' explanation of the problem provides some valuable insights for actors and directors.

18. Laforgue, Jules. "Hamlet, or the Consequences of Filial Piety" [1887] in *Selected Writings of Jules Laforgue*, ed. William Jay Smith. New York: Grove Press, 1956. 287 pp.

Laforgue recast this play as a modern narrative viewed from the consciousness of its acutely self-conscious hero. Laforgue's Hamlet is a portrait of the artist-manqué, self-mocking, ironic, bored, and omniscient. He is the embodiment of late nineteenth-century Romanticism, the aesthete who takes nothing seriously as he waits for death.

Laforgue's hero is of course not a representation of Shakespeare's Hamlet but of "Hamletism," his term for the frustration and ennui that the sensitive man experiences in his encounter with life. Clearly a development of Goethe's romantic view, Laforgue's Hamlet differs from the early Romantic position in its emphasis on irony and mockery.

A detailed account of the historical and literary significance of Hamletism is given by Helen Phelps Bailey in *Hamlet in France from Voltaire to Laforgue* (Geneva: Librarie Droz, 1964).

19. *Bradley, A. C. *Shakespearean Tragedy* [1904]. New York: Meridian Books, 1955. New York: Fawcett, 1966. 432 pp. Excerpted in Bevington, Campbell, Hoy, Jump, Leavenworth, Levenson, Sacks, and Williamson.

Bradley begins his essay with an account of the various theories of Hamlet's "delay." After demonstrating the inadequacies of these theories, including those put forth by Werder, Goethe, Schlegel and Coleridge, he provides his own explanation of the delay. According to Bradley, Hamlet's inability to avenge his father's murder is caused by "a state of mind quite abnormal and induced by special circumstances—a state of profound melancholy." The event that plunged Hamlet into melancholy was the hasty remarriage of his mother. Thus, when he receives the Ghost's command, he is already victimized by the paralyzing malady. Hamlet's doubting of the ghost and his failure to kill Claudius at prayer are conscious rationalizations, designed to disguise his native inability to kill Claudius.

Bradley's presentation has been disputed on a number of points. He has been accused of treating characters as if they were actual people with living histories, of over-psychologizing in his analysis and of being ignorant of Elizabethan thought and of Shakespeare's stage. In his almost exclusive preoccupation with character, Bradley has been dismissed as irrelevant by some modern critics. Yet it is clear that he represents the last great, possibly the greatest, expression of the nineteenth-century view of Shakespeare as the master creator of character.

20. Lewis, C. M. *The Genesis of Hamlet.* New York: Henry Holt, 1907. 133 pp. Excerpted in Williamson.

Lewis approaches the play by attempting to make some clear distinctions "between Shakespeare's original contributions to the story and the legendary materials he inherited." Lewis's procedure in determining the Shakespearean element in the play is to examine closely the pirated First Quarto of *Hamlet*, the seventeenth-century German version, *Der Bestrafte Brudermord*, and the French story as given in Belleforest's *Histoires Tragiques*. Then, operating on the assumption that the author of the *Ur Hamlet* was Thomas Kyd, he attempts to reconstruct that lost play.

His conclusion is that *Hamlet* as we know it is an imperfect fusion of the Kyd and the Shakespeare plays. Kyd is responsible for the plot, Shakespeare for the characterization: "Kyd's Hamlet does most of the deeds of the play, and Shakespeare's Hamlet thinks most of the thoughts." The results are the irreconcilable characteristics of the hero that have puzzled the critics. The solution to the critical problem is to recognize that "the composite Hamlet is not an entity at all, and therefore not a subject for psychological analysis."

The chief objection to the Lewis analysis is that it presupposes that the play lacks a unified, coherent structure. A few critics following Lewis (see 23, 30) have made precisely this claim. However, this judgment directly contradicts the view of most readers and playgoers that the puzzling quality of the play is not a flaw but, indeed, is its greatest virtue.

21. Santayana, George. "Hamlet" [1908] in *Obiter Scripta*. New York: Scribners, 1936. 319 pp. Excerpted in Williamson.

Santayana begins by accepting the premise that certain inconsistencies of plot and character are the result of Shakespeare's imperfect assimilation of material from his sources. Paradoxically, however, these very inconsistencies lend an even more profound dimension to the hero's already complex character. They "suggest a mind inwardly rent asunder, a delicate genius disordered." Hamlet's flaw is a self-destructive impulse that "pursues the good in a way especially designed never to attain it." His is the tragedy of the Romantic idealist, "of a soul buzzing in the glass prison of a world which it can neither escape nor understand. . . ." In the total experience of the play, however, his failure counts as nothing; all that finally matters is the moral triumph of his existence.

Santayana's essay is written with characteristic subtlety and grace. He anticipates a number of modern critics in his insistence that the inconsistencies deepen the experience rather than detract from it. At the same time his characterization of Hamlet looks back to that of Goethe and Coleridge. Thus his essay marks an interesting transitional point in the history of the criticism of the play.

22. *Murray, Gilbert. "Hamlet and Orestes" [1914] in *The Classical Tradition in Poetry*. Harvard University Press, 1927. 274 pp. Excerpted in Williamson.

First delivered in 1914 as the Annual Shakespeare Lecture of the British Academy, "Hamlet and Orestes" holds the distinction of being the earliest of the so-called mythic interpretations of Shakespeare, an attempt to explore the relationship between primitive myth and literature. Murray traces the development of both the Hamlet and Orestes stories, both of which have profoundly deep roots in the mythology of early Western civilization. He argues that both sagas are ultimately explained as re-enactments of the myth of the seasonal god "in that prehistoric and world-wide ritual battle of Summer and Winter, of Life and Death, which has played so vast a role in the mental development of the human race."

In presenting the argument for a mythic background to the play, Murray is careful not to claim too much. He does not suggest that the myth "explains" the play—merely that there is "a natural line of growth" between the two and that the connection accounts for the profound emotional impact that the play has always created. Murray's analysis has provided the basis for an entire school of Shakespearean criticism and for a number of interpretations of *Hamlet,* the most sucessful of which is that of Francis Fergusson (42).

23. Eliot, T. S. "Hamlet and His Problems" [1919] in *Selected Essays 1917–1932.* New York: Harcourt, Brace and Company, 1932. 415 pp. Excerpted in Bevington, Jump, Hoy, Leavenworth, and Levenson.

Eliot's celebrated essay begins with the assumption that the play is a "stratification," a series of visions and revisions, the last of which was Shakespeare's. The result is that the play as we have it contains a core of "intractable" old material that Shakespeare was unwilling or unable to absorb into the design of his revision. Thus Shakespeare's particular theme—"the effect of a mother's guilt upon her son"—is never fully realized. This artistic imbalance is heightened even further by the second major flaw in the play, the failure to provide an "objective correlative" for the emotion that dominates Hamlet. An "objective correlative" is any phenomenon in the play that is the external equivalent of a given emotion, so that when the external phenomenon is produced, the emotion is invoked. The objective equivalent of Hamlet's emotional state is the character of Gertrude, but Gertrude herself appears so banal and insipid as to be an entirely inadequate equivalent. Thus the play, "far from being Shakespeare's masterpiece . . . is almost certainly an artistic failure."

At the roots of Eliot's critique lie certain assumptions with which the reader should be familiar. The first of these is the work of the so-called "disintegrators," a group of late nineteenth- and early twentieth-century scholars who argued that a considerable portion of the 37 plays merely represents Shakespeare's revision of other men's work. (Disintegrators, by the way, should not be confused with Baconians and other fringe groups who claim that the plays were written by someone other than Shakespeare.) At the time Eliot's piece was written (1919), the "disintegrators," particularly Mr. J. M. Robertson, whom Eliot cites throughout the essay, were riding high. Since that time, however, most of their assumptions have been discredited by later scholars. Eliot's second assumption is that the play's theme deals with the effect of

Gertrude's behavior on Hamlet. This hypothesis, an inadvertent echo of the Freudian interpretation, fails to do justice to the richness and complexity of the play. That Eliot himself had second thoughts about the validity of his view is evidenced in his later remark that he was more dissatisfied with his Shakespearean criticism than with any other criticism he had written.

24. Stoll, Elmer Edgar. *Hamlet: An Historical and Comparative Study*. University of Minnesota Press, 1919. 75 pp. (Excerpted in Bevington, Levenson, Sacks, and Williamson); *Art and Artifice in Shakespeare* [1933]. New York, 1962. 178 pp.

One of the most important analyses in the history of the play, Stoll's essay inaugurates a new era of Hamlet criticism. Reacting sharply against the Romantic tradition, culminating in Bradley, that focused on psychological interpretations of Hamlet, Stoll contends that the play must be seen as a product of the Elizabethan theatre, reflecting the conventions, prejudices and methodology of that age. Stoll argues that once we have taken the trouble to understand these conventions, many of the play's problems will be solved. For example, the extant evidence makes it quite clear that the famous problem of Hamlet's delay was created by the Romantic critics. The delay was a convention, a feature which, in one form or another, is to be found in all classical and Renaissance revenge tragedies. It provided the play with a dramatic, not psychological, motive and maintained the audience's interest. Only when the play began to be treated as a novel or poem did the problem of the hero's delay arise—a problem that never would have occurred to the audience during the swift passage of events on stage.

Stoll's emphasis on the need to see the play through Elizabethan eyes has had a great influence on scholars and historical critics, particularly in the United States. Equally influential has been his insistence on the importance of *Hamlet* as a piece written for the theatre, not for the study. Despite these important contributions, his view of the play has been largely discredited as over-simplified and reductive. Having dwelt on the similarity of *Hamlet* to other Elizabethan revenge plays, he failed to develop sufficiently those characteristics that mark its surpassing excellence. *Hamlet* in Stoll's hands becomes just another revenge tragedy, a play more of its age than for all time.

25. Winstanley, Lillian. *Hamlet and the Scottish Succession.* Cambridge University Press, 1921. 188 pp.

Hamlet as a topical allegory. The play deals with the two most important political problems in England in the year 1601: the unsuccessful revolt of the Earl of Essex against the crown and the possible succession of James VI of Scotland to the English throne when Elizabeth's reign would end. Shakespeare avoided censorship by incorporating both of these incidents, cleverly disguised, into the old story of Hamlet. Thus the Prince combines characteristics both of James and of Essex.

Miss Winstanley's book is representative of the many attempts, dating back to the eighteenth century, to see the play as a political allegory. The view that the character of the brilliant, dashing, occasionally melancholic Earl of Essex provided Shakespeare with an imaginative model for his hero has been a particular favorite of those who view the play from this perspective. But there is a considerable difference between this view, endorsed by J. Dover Wilson and others, and that of Miss Winstanley, who attempts to see a point-by-point analogy between the play and certain historical events. Her determination to prove her case leads her to a number of excesses which finally undermine the occasionally convincing parallels she adduces.

26. *Joyce, James. *Ulysses* [1922]. New York: Random House, 1934, pp. 182–215.

The celebrated Library Scene in *Ulysses* is the occasion for a discussion of Shakespeare's life with particular reference to *Hamlet.* The discussion is led by Stephen Dedalus, who propounds the theory that sometime before writing the play, Shakespeare discovered he had been cuckolded by one of his younger brothers, either Richard or Edmund. Thus Shakespeare identified himself with King Hamlet, an identification aided by the fact that he had a son named Hamlet (Shakespeare's son, who died in 1598, was actually named *Hamnet* but the two forms of the name appear to have been interchangeable). Stephen later emends his theory to the point of admitting that both King Hamlet and Prince Hamlet represent a dual portrait of Shakespeare.

As biography or criticism, Stephen's argument represents pure unsubstantiated hypothesis. Its importance, however, lies in its highlighting of the *Hamlet* symbolism in the novel. Throughout the book, Stephen is consistently identified with Hamlet, who serves so often in modern literature as an image of the alienated artist.

Two excellent studies of the *Hamlet* theme in *Ulysses* are E. Duncan's "Unsubstantial Father," *University of Toronto Quarterly* XIX (1950), 126–140, and William Schutte's *Joyce and Shakespeare*, Yale University Press, 1957

27. Adams, Joseph Quincy. "Commentary" in *Hamlet: Prince of Denmark*, ed. Joseph Quincy Adams. Boston: Houghton Mifflin, 1929. Excerpted in Williamson.

Adams' edition contains the text of the play, a 163-page commentary and a 20-page discussion of the sources. His commentary is a scene-by-scene description of the characters and action of the play. Hamlet is presented as an idealist about human nature who, when disillusioned, is plunged into melancholy. Fortinbras, Laertes, and Horatio act as foils for the hero, each objectifying an aspect of his interior disposition. The climax of the play is the appearance of the ghost in the closet scene, for it marks the beginning of Hamlet's recovery from his melancholic inactivity. His recovery comes too late to save him but, though he loses his life, "the greatness of his . . ." character remains intact. His death is the triumph of the soldier who has died for a noble cause.

Adams' analysis owes much to Bradley (19) in its reliance on melancholy as an explanation of the hero's delay. Adams, however, provides a much more detailed working out of Bradley's thesis on the level of the dramatic action of the play. His presentation is logical, coherent and, as a result, slightly reductive.

28. *Campbell, Lily B. *Shakespeare's Tragic Heroes: Slaves of Passion* [1930]. New York: Barnes & Noble, 1960. 296 pp.

Miss Campbell's book is directed to the argument that Shakespearean tragedy is concerned with the catastrophe issuing from the dominance of passion over reason. In *Hamlet* this theme is particularized in the problem of grief—Hamlet is a victim of excessive grief. His reason has been overmastered by this emotion to the point that he is incapable of carrying out the rational command to kill the King. Analogous situations are seen in the lives of Laertes and Ophelia, Gertrude and Claudius. Aligned against them as examples of reason and passion in proper equilibrium are Fortinbras and Horatio, who dominate the end of the play. The moral points up "the lesson of tragedy" that "those who balance passion by reason are not Fortune's puppets."

Miss Campbell's analysis is an example of the radical oversimplification of which some historical critics are guilty. In attempting to see the play through Elizabethan eyes, she reduces it to a psychological case history and finally to a dramatized sermon.

29. *Knight, G. Wilson. *The Wheel of Fire* [1930]. Cleveland: World Pub. Co., 1962. 5th ed. revised. 343 pp. Meridian Books, 1957. Excerpted in Bevington, Hoy, Levenson, Sacks, and Williamson

For Knight, the theme of the play is death; its hero is death's ambassador, "a living death in the midst of life." Hamlet is a Nietzschean superman who, in absorbing the reality of death, has "seen the truth, not alone of Denmark, but of humanity, of the universe: and the truth is evil." Thus, Hamlet is the symbol of the negation of life, the embodiment of the sickness in Denmark. In opposition to him stand Claudius and his court representing life, optimism, and "the healthily second-rate." The conflict between these two forces is finally resolved by fate which puts an end to the spreading contagion, the source of which is the soul of Hamlet. This position is further elaborated by Knight in an essay on "life-themes" in the play which appeared in his *The Crown of Life* (London, 1931). *The Wheel of Fire* also includes an essay on "Hamlet's Melancholia." This essay makes the interesting, peripheral point that Hamlet's suffering, like Lear's, is given a grotesquely comic coloring.

Knight's analysis of the play—like most of his work—is distinguished by great imagination and originality. Unfortunately in his essays on *Hamlet*, his inventiveness is put to the service of a view of the play that can only be characterized as perverse. To see Hamlet as the source of the "rottenness" in Denmark is to fail to see the play that Shakespeare wrote.

Knight's more extreme views were later modified in "Hamlet Reconsidered," a "rough draft" appended to the fifth revised edition of

The Wheel of Fire. Here Knight suggests that to speak, as he has done, of the evil within *Hamlet* is to emphasize the principles of conventional morality where, in fact, moral considerations are not relevant. Hamlet operates in a Nietzschean realm beyond good and evil, striving to achieve an integrated, fully realized existence. His tragedy is that he just misses achieving this transcendent integration. "This troubled theme is . . . pushed to a ritualistic close; raised, that is, from intellect to life, from thought to being, and there we must leave it."

30. Waldock, A. J. A. *Hamlet: A Study in Critical Method*. Cambridge University Press, 1931. 99 pp. Excerpted in Williamson.

This small but important book contains a review of earlier critics, particularly Bradley and Jones, in connection with the problem of delay. Mr. Waldock's answer to the problem is that there is no answer. The fact is that although the delay is implied in the play, it is never demonstrated. We do not become aware of it until after our experience of the play when we are reflecting on its meaning. This is because the delay theme is simply not that important in the play. It is one of the play's minor discrepancies, resulting from Shakespeare's failure to incorporate every element into the total pattern. Undeniably great as it is, the play finally lacks the coherent, tight design that its critics have thought it contained.

Waldock's view is a more complex and detailed restatement of the early eighteenth-century position that the play's difficulties are the results of inherent flaws in its structure. It is a convincing argument and a brave attempt to be "realistic" about Shakespeare's limitations. In retrospect it fails to convince, however, because it does not see the underlying unity of the play's verbal design, a unity which subsequent critics such as Clemen (46), Fergusson (42), Mack (50), and Levin (59) have discerned.

31. *Wilson, J. Dover. *What Happens in Hamlet*. Cambridge, 1935; 3rd edition, 1951. Excerpted in Bevington, Jump, Campbell, Hoy, Levenson, Sacks, and Williamson.

Probably the best-known and most influential analysis of the play since Bradley, *What Happens in Hamlet* is unusual in that it attempts no broad aesthetic or philosophical interpretation of the play. It sets out simply—as its title suggests—to clarify the action and plot of the play. Such clarification, however, required an enormous preliminary undertaking: determining the correct text of the play. The fruits of this effort are to be found in Wilson's detailed textual analysis *The Manuscript of Shakespeare's "Hamlet"* (T1). Having established to his satisfaction a definitive text, Wilson then proceeds to discuss the many "problems" of the play, bringing to bear on them his detailed knowledge of the attitudes, events and language of Elizabethan England. Thus he reminds us frequently that Shakespeare's audience would have been intensely aware that Claudius was a usurper, that Gertrude was guilty of incest and that the Ghost might indeed be a diabolical spirit tempting Hamlet to an evil deed.

Wilson also offers solutions to several other of the play's problems. He argues that Hamlet's treatment of Ophelia in the Nunnery scene is explained by the fact that the Prince has previously overheard Polonius' plan to "loose his daughter." Claudius' failure to react to the Dumb show (III, ii) is explained by postulating that Claudius is talking to Polonius while the show is being performed. (It might be added that since the first appearance of the book in 1935, both of these suggestions have been frequently incorporated into productions of the play.)

The great virtue of Wilson's book is the combination of zest and wide knowledge that inform virtually every page. The years of frequently tedious research that formed the basis of his work have failed to blunt his enthusiasm for the play. Occasionally this enthusiasm leads him to critical judgments that fail to convince. It is a rare reader however, who will not be enlightened, entertained and edified by the love of learning and literature evidenced in this book.

32. *Granville-Barker, Harley. *Preface to Hamlet* [1936]. New York: Hill and Wang, 1957. Princeton University Press, 1965. 272 pp. Excerpted in Bevington, Jump, Campbell, Hoy, Hubler, and Williamson.

This detailed, thorough analysis is an account of both the action and the characters of the drama. The natural development of the play is not in the five acts created by later Shakespearean editors but in three movements. The first movement ends with the Ghost's revelation; the second with Hamlet's departure for England; the third begins with the madness of Ophelia and the revolt of Laertes, and it carries to the end of the play. The climax occurs when Hamlet postpones killing the King in the player scene. Each of these movements is carefully examined and clarified.

As for character, Granville-Barker succinctly analyzes every character in the play from Hamlet to Francisco, the guard. Hamlet is seen as a divided man, faced with irreconcilable alternatives. In this respect he is the representative of Shakespeare's technical problem in writing the play: "to reconcile the creature of his imagination with the figure of the borrowed story." In a larger sense this dilemma reflects the fundamental Renaissance conflict of faith and doubt, a conflict still present today and one that accounts for our identification with the hero.

This outline does no justice to the most valuable aspect of Granville-Barker's essay. That, of course, is his unexcelled ability to view the play with a theatrical director's eyes without losing sight of its literary values. His years of experience as a director of Shakespearean plays, in combination with a first-rate critical intelligence, left him uniquely qualified to synthesize the conflicting claims of poetry and drama. The essay on *Hamlet* is eloquent testimony to the success of that synthesis

33. Schücking, Levin L. *The Meaning of Hamlet.* Translated from the German by Graham Rawson. Oxford University Press, 1937. 195 pp. Excerpted in Jump and Williamson.

For Schücking, *Hamlet* is a work of art of a type best described as "baroque." Schücking uses the term to characterize the diversity and variety of the play, its heterogeneous mixture of seemingly contrasting elements. This baroque feature in *Hamlet* sometimes results in an absence of a harmonious, coherent relationship among the various parts of the play. But the triumph of the play is that its totality is somehow greater than the sum of its parts.

As for the character of the hero, Schücking views him as a study in the "humour" of melancholy. According to Schücking, Hamlet's irascible, erratic behavior immediately identifies him as the conventional stage type—"the melancholy man."

Many of Schücking's incidental comments are interesting and original. Too often, however, his presentation is marred by the assumption that Shakespeare's characters are simply conventional representations of type characters. The result—the opposite of the Romantic critics who *overemphasized* character—is to reduce Shakespeare's characterization to mere manipulation.

34. Draper, John W. *The Hamlet of Shakespeare's Audience.* Duke University Press, 1938. 254 pp. Excerpted in Williamson.

This book represents an attempt to judge the play in terms of the "social conditions" of Shakespeare's time. Using the criterion of the Elizabethan audience's social preconceptions, Draper analyzes all of the subsidiary characters in the play before proceeding to an interpretation of the hero and finally to the play's setting, style and theme. Thus he argues that the original audience's response to characters such as Polonius, Ophelia and Claudius would have been conditioned to a large degree by the knowledge of their social status. All of these characters, and Hamlet as well, must have been thought of as essentially dignified, in keeping with their public roles. Claudius would have been seen as a "noble" villain and Gertrude as a sympathetic, if somewhat misguided, "imperial jointress." Hamlet himself would have appeared "a perfectly integrated trinity of personalities," a combination of the ideal courtier, the feigning madman and the "all-too-human human being, struggling and suffering . . . pursuing his inevitable goal . . . to ultimate catastrophe."

The major weakness of Draper's presentation lies in the oversimplification of his basic premise: the notion that certain generalities about Elizabethan life can provide us with the proper focus for viewing the play.

35. Hankins, John Erskine. *The Character of Hamlet and Other Essays.* University of North Carolina Press, 1941. 264 pp.

An historical critic, Hankins is concerned to see what light can be thrown on the play by reference to Renaissance thought and learning. His book consists of a lengthy essay on the character of *Hamlet* and a number of supplementary essays dealing with such topics as politics, religion and suicide in the play.

The main essay contains a preliminary review of interpretations of Hamlet's character, particularly those of Bradley (19), Stoll (24) and Draper (34). On the question of Hamlet's delay, Hankins' position is that Hamlet delays because of an internal conflict between the code of "honor" (in the sense of "personal glory") and that of justice (identified in the play with the word "conscience"). In the course of the play Hamlet moves from the shallow, self-interested motives of "honor," represented by Laertes and Fortinbras, to that of justice, "perfect conscience." In support of his argument, Mr. Hankins draws upon a wide range of classical and Renaissance religious and philosophical authorities such as Plato, Aristotle, Aquinas, and Richard Hooker.

Hankins' essay is an example of historical criticism at its best, not content with purely external explanations of the play but willing to go beyond its surface in order to explore its ethical and philosophical foundations. His emphasis on the importance of the principle of justice has had a strong influence on later interpretations of the play.

36. Wertham, Frederic. *Dark Legend: A Study in Murder.* New York: Duell, Sloan and Pearce, 1941. 270 pp.

Wertham is a psychoanalyst, but one who takes exception to the thesis that Hamlet is the victim of an Oedipal fixation. His argument is based upon the case history of a young Italian boy who stabbed his mother to death. Wertham sees in the boy's history a strong parallel to Hamlet. Both are victims of an "Orestes complex," the desire to murder the mother dramatized in the story of Orestes' murder of Clytemnestra and given a number of explicit expressions in *Hamlet,* notably in the closet scene. This matricidal impulse is rooted in the same problem—excessive attachment to the mother—as the Oedipal fixation. In the case of the Italian boy and Hamlet, it expresses itself in Wertham's terms as a "catathymic crisis," the idea that a violent act is the only solution to a particular problem. The crisis develops in five stages: the initial thought, the formulation of a plan, the enactment of the plan, the restoration of superficial normality and the final stage of insight and recovery.

Wertham's theory is open to all the objections that have been lodged against Jones (44). It might also be criticized for the dubious value of its "bio-literary" approach, the comparison of a literary character with a living person. Nevertheless the presentation makes interesting reading and calls attention once again to the play's profound unconscious roots and to the seemingly inexhaustible ingenuity of its commentators.

37. Lewis, C. S. *Hamlet: The Prince or the Poem?* Annual Shakespeare Lecture of the British Academy. London, 1942. 18 pp. Excerpted in Bevington, Campbell, Hoy, Sacks, and Williamson.

Lewis begins his lecture by placing himself in opposition to criticism that focuses exclusively on character. Character criticism has distorted *Hamlet* by placing the mystery that pervades the play within the character of the hero. This misemphasis has resulted in a failure to see that the theme of the play is *death*—not dying but the state of being dead. It is death that creates the mystery lying at the heart of the play. The play describes a "spiritual region," the central figure of which is "man—haunted man—man with his mind on the frontier of two worlds, man unable either quite to reject or quite to admit the supernatural . . . ."

Lewis's effort to direct attention to the fundamental experience of the play was a necessary corrective to the character-oriented approach that was still dominant in 1942. Although not employing the methodology of the new critics or the symbolist interpreters such as G. Wilson Knight, he clearly aligned himself with those critics against the dominant schools of historical and character criticism. For these reasons, as well as for the intrinsic value of his speculation, Lewis's lecture remains one of the most important explorations of the play in recent years.

38. *Spencer, Theodore. *Shakespeare and the Nature of Man* [1942]. New York: Macmillan, 1961. Excerpted in Bevington and Williamson.

For Spencer the play is concerned with the conflict arising out of two divergent Renaissance views of the nature of man. These two views, the one "bright, orderly, optimistic . . . man as he should be," the other "full of darkness and chaos . . . man as he is"—converge in the consciousness of Hamlet. He becomes intensely aware of the difference between appearance and reality. In the play this difference is represented in the realization that the reality of evil underlies the appearance of good. Hamlet fights his way through this realization in order to reconcile and resign himself to "the world as it should be and the world as it is." His fifth act speeches—particularly the "readiness is all" speech—indicate that he has finally been successful. He has come to terms with life and emerged "exhausted, resigned and, in a way exalted . . . ."

One limitation of Spencer's view is his tendency to oversimplify the function of "appearance" or illusion in the play. As later critics have demonstrated (50), appearance and reality in Hamlet are much more complexly interwoven, suggesting that they do not function as simple opposites but as complementary features of a larger "reality."

39. de Madariaga, Salvador. *On Hamlet.* London: Hollis and Carter, 1948. 145 pp. Excerpted in Bevington.

Madariaga's essay begins with an attack on the sentimentalization of Hamlet by those who choose to conceive of him as a noble idealist when in fact he is nothing of the sort. The mind of Hamlet is that of a Renaissance aristocrat, ruthless and self-absorbed. As the Elizabethan version of Cesare Borgia, Hamlet is more Machiavelli's Prince than Denmark's. De Madariaga's Hamlet is immoral (he has seduced Ophelia) and "foul-mouthed" (his language is "fit only for the barracks or the brothel"); his real concern is not the death of his father but the fact that Claudius has robbed him of his kingdom. The sensitive, intellectual, gentle Hamlet is the creation of modern English critics. The real *Hamlet,* however, is the Hamlet of Shakespeare's time and "the era of Shakespeare is the era of Spain." Spanish values were dominant throughout the Renaissance and these values are reflected in the play and in its main character—who conceives of life and grapples with its most fundamental problems in absolute terms.

De Madariaga's analysis bears some resemblance to that of Rebecca West (58) in emphasizing the negative aspects of Hamlet's character. In so doing it errs on the side of overstatement, quietly ignoring the abundant evidence of Hamlet's admirable qualities. Similarly, his thesis about the dominance of Spanish values in sixteenth-century England is interesting, but fatally weakened by the author's penchant for unsubstantiated generalizations. Nevertheless, the book is of value in correcting some tacit "modern-liberal" assumptions about the play.

40. Prior, Moody E. "The Thought of Hamlet and the Modern Temper," *ELH, A Journal of English Literary History,* XV (1948), 261–285.

Prior argues that too often in discussion of the play, its philosophical aspects have been divorced from its dramatic development. What is needed, he suggests, is an increased awareness that the reflective element in the play is carefully keyed to the play's action. Thus Hamlet's speculations on the role of reason in human nature have their basis in his personal response to Gertrude's "frailty." From this starting point the speculations assume a universal significance: ". . . his search for the place of reason in man has ended in the conviction that if it does not make us like gods . . . it nevertheless distinguishes us as men."

In arriving at this perception, Hamlet experiences a profound doubt that mirrors the scepticism of the Renaissance and the anxiety of the modern world. Thus the play has continued to grow and change as long as succeeding ages respond to it as a symbol of their experience of life.

Prior's essay provides a valuable historical perspective that has too often been obscured by rival claims and conflicting interpretations. Ultimately the play's meaning is the accretion of meanings which it acquires in the course of its critical history.

41. Walker, Roy. *The Time Is Out of Joint: A Study of Hamlet.* London: Andrew Dakers, 1948. 157 pp.

Walker's analysis is the first of a number of modern interpretations that stress the hero's sacrificial role in the play. Hamlet is seen, according to this view, as the instrument and agent of Providence, "heaven's scourge and minister." To him has fallen the tragic task of cleansing the rottenness that infects all Denmark. In the course of assuming that role, Hamlet himself has become contaminated. The contamination expresses itself in the killing of Polonius, not in his delay. Indeed, the so-called delay is nothing more than Hamlet's intuitive awareness that the heaven-ordained time for the restoration of order had not yet arrived.

In emphasizing the redemptive and regenerative aspects of Hamlet's role, Walker set the tone for much subsequent criticism of the play. Many of his arguments, particularly those relating to Hamlet's self-doubt and his delay, lack conviction. Nevertheless the value of his analysis lies in its reminding us that tragedy is finally "a presentation of the dazzling vision of the pitiful state of humanity."

42. *Fergusson, Francis. *The Idea of a Theatre.* Princeton University Press, 1949. Excerpted in Leavenworth. 239 pp.

Fergusson's analysis is based upon the mythic interpretation of the play first suggested by Gilbert Murray (22). Fergusson, however, enlarges considerably upon Murray. He argues that Shakespearean drama is conceived in analogical terms. It has no linear logical construction; rather it is built on a series of analogous scenes and situations, all of which reflect the play's basic *action* (in the Aristotelian sense of the word). This basic action is best described by the phrase "to find and destroy the hidden 'imposthume' which is poisoning the life of Claudius' Denmark."

The rhythm of the play is created by the alternation of two theatrical experiences: ritual and improvisation. Ritual is reflected in the pageantry scenes, improvisation in the topical allusions and in the play's comic scenes. These reflect two aspects of the Elizabethan theatre, which in Shakespeare's time functioned both as a place of entertainment and as the locus of a ritual religious experience. The ritual aspect of the play is seen in Hamlet's role as "sacrificial agent," the scapegoat hero of ancient drama, fated to destroy the rottenness pervading Denmark and embodied by Claudius. Thus the play and the theatre for which it was written have deep roots in the collective experience of Western man.

A wide-ranging, provocative analysis contained within the limited space of an essay inevitably involves its author in presenting unsupported generalizations. Fergusson's analysis is not exempt from this flaw. He has not, for example, substantiated his theory of the ritualistic character of the Elizabethan theatre. Nevertheless his essay remains one of the most original and penetrating of modern studies of the play.

43. Flatter, Richard. *Hamlet's Father*. Yale University Press, 1949. 206 pp.

Hamlet's Father is an attempt to see the Ghost as the source and controlling power of the play. Viewed from this perspective, he becomes, in fact, one aspect of the divided self that is Hamlet, that aspect that knows he cannot fulfill the impossible dual task both of killing the king and sparing Gertrude (since she is implicated in the murder). The Ghost's intervention in the Closet makes it clear, that above all else, Gertrude must be treated with forgiveness and love. Thus the Ghost's action embodies the play's theme, "the triumph of even-handed justice and of all-forgiving love. . . ."

A professional director, Flatter interlards his presentation with a number of observations on theatrical aspects of the play. Among these is the hypothesis that the much-disputed Dumb Show was the first presented on the upper stage. Other theatrical remarks are contained in the Appendix, including notes on "Goethe as Producer of *Hamlet*" and "The Staging of the Play."

Flatter's book contains interesting and lively observations growing out of his practical experience in producing the play. As a serious thematic analysis of the drama, however, *Hamlet's Father* is radically wide of the mark. It would be difficult to conceive of two attributes more strikingly understated in the play than forgiveness and love.

44. *Jones, Ernest. *Hamlet and Oedipus.* New York: Doubleday, 1954. 194 pp. Excerpted in Bevington, Jump, Campbell, Hoy, Sachs, and Williamson.

The essay first appeared in the *American Journal of Psychology* (January, 1910). It was revised and expanded in 1923 and presented in its final form in 1949. Its thesis is by now a familiar one: Hamlet suffers from an Oedipal fixation, an unconscious desire to kill his father and marry his mother. His delay in killing Claudius is thus the result of an unconscious identification with the murderer.

Furthermore, the Oedipal motif in the play is a reflection of the same deeply rooted conflict in its author. The play was written in 1601, the year in which Shakespeare's father died and the year in which the Earl of Essex, Shakespeare's "father-substitute" was executed. Thus the new life which Shakespeare poured into the old story was the outcome of inspirations that took their origin in the deepest and darkest regions of his mind."

Jones' argument has provoked too wide a range of discussion for summary here. Probably the most objective and well-reasoned critique of his position is contained in Lionel Trilling's essay "Freud and Literature" (*The Liberal Imagination,* New York: Anchor Books, 1953). While acknowledging the illumination and insights that Jones provides, Trilling calls attention to the inadequate grounds upon which Jones relates the play to Shakespeare's life. He then goes on to demonstrate "that Freud and Dr. Jones . . . do not have an adequate conception of what an artistic meaning is." The meaning of a work of art cannot be reduced to the intention, conscious or unconscious, of its author, even assuming that one has proved, as Dr. Jones has not, that such an intention was there.

45. Tillyard, E. M. W. *Shakespeare's Problem Plays.* University of Toronto Press, 1949. 168 pp.

Tillyard argues that *Hamlet* is not, properly speaking, a tragedy at all: "though *Hamlet* is tragic in certain senses, that tragic quality is not the principal quality." Tragedy, according to Tillyard, is never ambiguous; character and action are presented in a clear, unmistakable form. In *Hamlet*, however, the tragic action has been clouded over by the pale cast of thought. ". . . the problems themselves, their richness, their interest and their diversity and not their solution or significant arrangement . . . come first." Thus it is that *Hamlet* is, like *Troilus and Cressida* or *Measure for Measure*, a "problem play," a play whose primary motive is the abstract analysis of subtle religious, philosophical or moral problems.

The proof of this thesis, Tillyard argues, lies in the absence in the play of one of the defining characteristics of tragedy: the final enlightenment or perception on the part of the hero which signals "a new order of things." Tillyard then proceeds to deny the view that Hamlet's speech on "readiness is all" (V, ii) is evidence of precisely this type of perception. This does not, however, diminish the play's greatness. It remains, despite the absence of a tragic essence, the supreme presentation of "the utmost variety of human experience in the largest possible cosmic setting."

The heart of Tillyard's argument is his reading of "the readiness is all" speech. His position was sharply contested by S. F. Johnson (49), who views the speech as evidence of Hamlet's insight into his fate. Tillyard's thesis is provocative and thoughtful, but its appeal is the appeal of novelty, not of truth.

46. *Clemen, Wolfgang. *The Development of Shakespeare's Imagery.* Harvard University Press, 1951. 236 pp. Reprinted in Hubler and Jump.

The most striking feature of the imagery in *Hamlet* is the vitality of the hero's language. "When he begins to speak, the images fairly stream to him without the slightest effort—not as similes or conscious paraphrases but as immediate and spontaneous visions." These image patterns demonstrate that Hamlet, far from being an abstract thinker, always has an intensely concrete vision of reality, enabling him to pierce the deceptive façade of appearance in order to confront tragic reality. Failure to perceive the nature of Hamlet's imagery has led to some notable distortions in interpreting his character. For example, Hamlet's remark that "the native hue of resolution is sicklied o'er with the pale cast of thought" has traditionally been interpreted to mean "reflection hinders action." The image, however, makes it clear that "reflection" and "action" are not conceived of as two opposing principles but as two aspects of human nature which together combine to erode and destroy that nature. Thus the line is related to the major image of the play—disease and sickness spreading in cancerous fashion throughout the body politic.

Apart from its many illuminating insights, Clemen's analysis is chiefly valuable for its demonstration of the play's organic unity and for the light it sheds on the relationship of the disease imagery to the language and character of the prince. Its significance is further enhanced by the author's awareness of the need to see imagery in relationship to the other elements in the play rather than as its sole determining factor.

47. Elliott, G. R. *Scourge and Minister: A Study of Hamlet as Tragedy of Revengefulness and Justice.* Duke University Press 1951. 208 pp.

Elliott's, book is designed to offer an alternative to two traditionally dominant views of Hamlet, that of the Romantic genius and that of the modern sceptic. According to Elliott, Hamlet is a Renaissance Christian gentleman, more like Hooker than Hazlitt, closer to Castiglione than to Camus.

The plot centers not just on Hamlet but on "Hamlet-and-Claudius," representatives of two radically different social orders. Hamlet's "delay" in killing Claudius is not in fact a delay but a gradually developing awareness of the inadequacy of personal revenge. Hamlet's pride causes him to falter, but ultimately he achieves the frame of mind wherein he can kill the king with a "perfect conscience" as an act of impersonal social justice. Hamlet therefore fulfills his role as divinely appointed "scourge and minister."

Elliott's basic position—that the play is less a character study than

an attempt to embody certain Renaissance abstractions—is, with qualifications, a sound one. His chief flaw, however, is that he does not do
justice to the complexity of Renaissance thought. He neglects to mention,
for example, the one major Renaissance thinker whose thought is most
pervasive in *Hamlet*, i.e., Montaigne, presumably because Montaigne's
thorny, ironic scepticism does not sit well with Elliott's view of a Renaissance Christian humanist. The result is that a facile optimism replaces the
play's keen sense of loss, pain and waste, of the presence of which even
the non-Romantic, non-modern Dr. Johnson was aware.

48. James, D. G. *The Dream of Learning: An Essay on the Advance-
    ment of Learning, Hamlet and King Lear.* Oxford: Clarendon Press,
    1951. 126 pp. Excerpted in Bevington and Jump.

A collection of lectures delivered at Oxford in 1950, *The Dream
of Learning* offers a theoretical comparison and contrast between Bacon
and Shakespeare. The mind of Shakespeare, in contrast to that of Bacon,
is seen to be pervaded by moral and metaphysical doubt. In *Hamlet* this
doubt is expressed by the hero's philosophical scepticism which Shakespeare had absorbed from reading Montaigne. But this intellectual position
is complicated by an imaginative commitment to Christian eschatology.
Hamlet is thus the image of the modern man, intellectually agnostic but
not emotionally ready or able to abandon the sustaining forms of the old
belief. His is "a mind arrested in dubiety before the awful problem of life."

While many of James' generalizations about Renaissance thought
might be questioned, his analysis of *Hamlet* is penetrating and thoughtful.
What is particularly valuable in his lecture is the demonstration of Shakespeare's use of Montaigne's reflections on death in the soliloquies. They
shed considerable light, although occasionally overemphasizing their importance, on the relationship of the soliloquies to the rest of the play.

49. Johnson, S. F. "The Regeneration of Hamlet," *Shakespeare Quar-
    terly*, III (1952), 187–207.

Johnson's thesis is conveyed by his sub-title "A Reply to E. M. W.
Tillyard with a counter-proposal." He is concerned to demonstrate that
Tillyard's view of *Hamlet* as a "problem play" (see 45) rather than a
tragedy is not only false but indicative of a tendency among certain modern

critics to look upon the play merely as a test of their own ingenuity. Johnson focuses specifically on Tillyard's argument that *Hamlet* is not a tragedy because the hero experiences no final enlightenment or perception about himself or about the nature of the universe. Drawing upon the insights of a number of other critics, Johnson argues that the "readiness is all" speech (V,ii,230–235) is evidence of Hamlet's final awareness that he is destined to be an "ordained minister of Providence." In this speech he recognizes the requirements of his role, "the heroic sacrifice, in setting right the time that was out of joint." His perception and acceptance of this role transform him from a mere victim into a tragic hero.

Johnson's thesis is often weakened by his attempt to make every aspect of the last act conform to his argument. The pattern of Hamlet's "regeneration" is never as clear as he claims. Nevertheless he is quite right in suggesting that his analysis is representative of a great many scholars of the time. As elaborated and corrected by Bowers (56), the conception of Hamlet as "scourge and minister" later becomes the dominant view of the play.

50. Mack, Maynard. "The World of Hamlet," *The Yale Review*, XLI (1952), 502–523. Reprinted in Hubler, Bevington, and Jump, and in *Tragic Themes in Western Literature*, ed. Cleanth Brooks (Yale University Press).

Mack's essay is an exploration of the "imaginative environment" of the play. Analyzing the verbal patterns that reveal this environment, he sees the play defined by three attributes: mysteriousness, the theme of appearance and reality, and mortality. The sense of mysteriousness is conveyed by the questions which resound throughout the play, ranging from the opening line's "Who's there?" to that most famous and fundamental question "To be or not to be." Behind all these questions lies the second major motif of the play—the attempt to pierce the curtain of appearance in order to arrive at reality. This theme is conveyed by the recurrent imagery of cosmetics and clothes, and principally by the multiple meanings which attach themselves to the words "act," "play," and "show." The third attribute of the play is "mortality," Mack's term for all the limiting conditions of human existence. The mortality motif is carried on by the sense of human instability, by the dominant imagery of infection and particularly by the radical sense of loss—that loss which is the indelible mark of human imperfection. In the graveyard scene, Hamlet finally learns to absorb and accept the reality of this loss and thus emerges as an "illuminated" hero.

Mack's essay has become, not without justice, a minor classic of Shakespearean criticism. It does not deal with the play as a drama; it suggests a verbal and textual coherence that many scholars would deny the play, and it is even possible to quarrel with the too seductive gracefulness of Mack's style. However, when all the criticisms have been registered, "The World of Hamlet" remains one of the finest critical statements ever made about *Hamlet*.

51. *Auerbach, Eric. "The Weary Prince" in *Mimesis: The Representation of Reality in Western Literature,* trans. by Willard Trask [1953]. New York: Doubleday Anchor Books, 1957. 498 pp.

"The Weary Prince" is an essay on the significance of the mixture of comic and tragic elements in Shakespearean drama. In this connection *Hamlet* is particularly interesting, for Hamlet combines within his own character, as does Shylock, both tragic and comic elements. This interpenetration of the tragic and comic, of the sublime and the low, is an outgrowth of the "cosmic drama of the story of Christ" as presented in the medieval Christian theater. By Shakespeare's time, the focus of this drama had shifted from God to man, but the medieval mixture of styles remained. It is this mixture that lends such vitality and flexibility to the character of Hamlet, who combines the functions of the tragic hero and the fool, ranging from the sublime to the ridiculous, from the noble to the grotesque. In so doing he provides a definition of man more complex and multi-layered than was realizable in later literature.

Auerbach's essay provides an important insight into the complex "comi-tragic" texture of the play and, incidentally, a valuable historical perspective on Elizabethan drama in general.

52. Empson, William. "*Hamlet* When New," *Sewanee Review,* XLI (1953), 15–42, 185–205. Excerpted in Levenson.

Empson argues with his customary ingenuity that by the time Shakespeare came to re-write *Hamlet,* the old play (the *Ur-Hamlet*) had come to be regarded as a laughable melodrama. The first audience would have come to see whether Shakespeare "could ravamp the old favorite without being absurd." Thus Shakespeare had to try to make "the old play seem real by making the hero seem life-like." This he accomplished by making Hamlet's delay a mystery. Other aspects of the complication of his character include his behavior towards Ophelia, which the audience, according to Empson, would have found shocking, and his almost Freudian relationship with his mother. A further complication was introduced in having Hamlet represent a "modern" attitude towards the feudal cult of revenge. In the best tradition of Empson's criticism, his essay on *Hamlet* is provocative and stimulating, studded with original insights. Equally representative on the negative side, however, is his tendency to disregard the facts, to oversimplify an opposing point and frequently to advance his own argument with tongue in cheek.

53. Joseph, Bertram. *Conscience and the King: A Study of Hamlet.* London: Chatto and Windus, 1953. 175 pp. Excerpted in Bevington.

Joseph's book is another excercise in historical criticism, the attempt to see the play "from the Elizabethan point of view." For Joseph the theme of the play is the "triumphant assertion that evil will always be defeated." Hamlet's delay is the result of his fear that the ghost may be a diabolical spirit luring him to damnation. Gertrude was not guilty of adultery in the modern sense of the word. Claudius would have been recognized by an Elizabethan audience as an arch-deceiver, a "white devil." In arguing these and other points, Joseph frequently cites contemporary sources, chiefly from sermons, homilies and other religious writings. In essence, then, his position is that the play is to be looked on as a dramatized homily: ". . . the Prince is brought to his death as a result of his own mistakes, yet the more we contemplate it, that tragedy . . . makes us aware of the hand of Providence destroying evil."

Mr. Joseph's book is a fair representative of the historical approach to the play. As such its chief virtue is its attempt to recreate the original experience of the Elizabethan audience upon seeing *Hamlet*. Its chief vice is the rather naive belief that because one contemporary source interprets a given situation a certain way, this is necessarily the way it should be interpreted in the play. The truth, of course, is that there was considerable divergence of opinion in Shakespeare's time on such problems as revenge, regicide, the meaning of adultery and a number of other matters that Joseph confidently "explains" by reference to a few contemporary sources.

54. Altick, Richard D. "*Hamlet* and the Odor of Mortality," *Shakespeare Quarterly*, V (1954), 167–176.

The dominant images of disease and corruption have often been noticed in studies of the play (see 46); disease and decay function as the sensory equivalents of the moral corruption that Claudius has unleashed in murdering King Hamlet. Altick focuses on two aspects of this disease imagery: corruption of the flesh and the association of that experience with offensive and foul odors. Behind the frequent and repeated allusions to cancerous growth and infection is the related suggestion of a foul odor that permeates and poisons the atmosphere. Altick argues that the association of infection with noisome stench would have been natural in Shakespeare's time when the "odor of mortality" from plague victims was a common experience. The effect of the image of foul smells serves to emphasize the theme that evil ". . . spreads into a whole society, just as the reek generated by a mass of putrid flesh bears infection to many who breathe it."

Generally the argument is cogently presented; particularly effective are the allusions to Claudius' prayer (III,iii): "O my offence is rank, it smells to heaven." Less credible are the attempts to see the words "offend" and "foul" as always having an olfactory association in the play or the suggestion that Hamlet's reference to Polonius as a "fishmonger" has malodorous overtones. This type of intellectual straining has, as Cranly tells Stephen Dedalus, "the true scholastic stink."

55. Alexander, Peter. *Hamlet: Father and Son.* Oxford: Clarendon Press, 1955. 189 pp. Excerpted in Bevington.

Hamlet: Father and Son focuses on the problem of the hero's "tragic flaw." Alexander takes as his starting point the epigraph to the Laurence Olivier film version of the play: "This is the story of a man who could not make up his mind." Here is a simplified version of Aristotle's *hamartia*, a term which has come to connote (erroneously) the idea of a deep-seated flaw within the hero that results in his downfall and thereby "justifies the gods in having visited on [him] their tragic fate."

This mistaken emphasis ultimately reduces the significance of tragedy. What the tragic artist is really concerned with are the virtues of the hero.

Hamlet "is a kind of consecration of the common elements of man's moral life." Its hero is a Pascalian blend of opposites, reconciling within himself the themes of "heroic passion" and "meditative wisdom." Hamlet's capacity to effect this reconciliation is the mark of his tragic greatness.

Alexander's argument is subject to some criticism. In dismissing the "tragic flaw" he overlooks all the hero's faults. He also never demonstrates how Hamlet finally achieves his reconciliation. Nevertheless, the book on the whole represents an important contribution not merely to *Hamlet* criticism but to speculation on the nature of tragedy in general.

56. Bowers, Fredson. "Hamlet as Minister and Scourge," *PMLA*, LXX (1955), 740–749. Reprinted in Bevington.

Bowers argues that the key passage of the play occurs in Hamlet's speech after the killing of Polonius.

> For this same lord,
> I do repent; but heaven hath pleased it so,
> To punish me with this, and this with me,
> That I must be their scourge and minister.

According to Bowers, Hamlet's reference to himself as both "scourge" and "minister" would have brought home to an Elizabethan audience a very precise and critical distinction. In the tradition of "revenge" tragedy, a "scourge" is one who engages in revenge to satisfy his personal vindictiveness, thereby incurring his own death. A "minister" on the other hand is one whose revenge, like Richmond's in *Richard III* or Macduff's in *Macbeth*, in accordance with divine providence, is an act of public justice. In the first three acts Hamlet sees himself in his ministerial role but is none too patient. He impulsively violates his ministerial role by slaying Polonius, an act which has a doubtly ironic impact: the wrong man is killed and Hamlet's doom is sealed. His remarks thus testify to his awareness of his role, an awareness made more explicit in the fifth act ("There's a divinity that shapes our ends," etc.).

Bowers, who is chiefly noted for his rigorous textual criticism (see

T5), brings here to the play his extensive knowledge of the revenge tragedy tradition. The result is an essay that has proved to be among the most influential of recent years and that seems to have put to rest, for the time being at any rate, the interminable problem of Hamlet's delay.

————. "The Death of Hamlet," in *Studies in the English Renaissance Drama in Memory of Karl Holzknecht*, eds. J. W. Bennett and Oscar Cargill. New York: New York University Press (1959), pp. 28–42.

In this essay Bowers focuses on what he characterizes as Shakespeare's extremely careful efforts to leave the audience with a positive impression of Hamlet at the play's conclusion. Thus the moral taint associated with the killing of Polonius is, if not removed, at least subordinated to the sense of the hero's vindication in the play's final scene.

————. "The Moment of Final Suspense in *Hamlet:* We Defy Augury," in *Shakespeare 1564–1964*, ed. Edward A. Bloom. Providence: Brown University Press, 1964.

Here Bowers argues that Hamlet's defiance of augury and acceptance of providence christianizes the moment that in classical drama would be used to exemplify the hero's *hubris*. The Christian *ethos* of Hamlet renders this moment not an ironic anticipation of disaster but the serene reconciliation of the individual to Heaven's ordinance. See also Bowers' "Dramatic Structure and Action: Plot in *Hamlet*," *Shakespeare Quarterly*, XV (1964), 207–218.

57. Kitto, H. D. F. *Form and Meaning in Drama*. London: Methuen, 1956. 341 pp. Excerpted in Jump and Sacks.

Kitto's essay points out a basic analogy between *Hamlet* and the drama of Aeschylus and Sophocles. Like Greek tragedy, Hamlet is a "religious drama," in the sense that it focuses on the *transcendent* principle that governs the play and its characters. Eight people die in the course of the play and in all their deaths one fact stands out: the role of Providence. In each case Providence directs the catastrophe. In the final analysis it does not matter whether the character is innocent, as is Ophelia, or guilty, as is Claudius. The important fact is that everyone is "brought to nothing by evil" and that in all of their deaths, "heaven is ordinant." The murder of King Hamlet is only one symbol of this evil—the impersonal rottenness that infects all of Denmark—an evil that must work itself out to its natural conclusion and, in so doing, destroy everyone with whom it comes in contact. In all of this "the real focus is not on the tragic hero but on the divine background" through which we are able to perceive the inscrutable design of Providence.

Kitto's essay represents another example of the tendency of modern critics to draw attention away from discussions of "character" in order to focus on the play's larger issues. In emphasizing a more comprehensive view, Kitto brings into prominence an important, often neglected dimension of the play. His emphasis on the transcendent principles that govern human life enlarges and enriches one's experience of the play.

58. West, Rebecca. *The Court and the Castle.* Yale University Press, 1957. 319 pp.

The essay on *Hamlet* contained in this book is part of a larger thesis concerning man's wilfulness and the nature of original sin. The argument in relation to *Hamlet* is sharply iconoclastic. According to the author, the character of the hero has been consistently misread by a modern mentality that has denied the reality of original sin. Identifying her position with those of de Madariaga (39) and Turgenev (14), she argues that Shakespeare has drawn in Hamlet the portrait of a Renaissance egoist, opportunistic and sceptical. Hamlet represents man cut off from God's grace, and as such he serves as a warning "against the theory that man is free equally to choose between good and evil . . . and that our race could be changed and made innocent without search for a higher authority and submission to it." Such a theory denies the orthodox Christian position that we are all radically, inherently flawed by original sin. In creating Hamlet as the spokesman for this theory, Shakespeare created the best possible proponent; however, there is no doubt that he wished to condemn the theory and "to present Hamlet as a bad man."

The author's argument is a necessary corrective to many of the romantic, uncritical responses to the character of Hamlet. Nevertheless, her sternly Calvinistic analysis overemphasizes his faults. In attempting to see Hamlet as "a bad man," she offers a view of his character not only at variance with the experience of the vast majority of readers but with the text of the play itself.

59. *Levin, Harry. *The Question of "Hamlet."* New York: Oxford University Press, 1959. 178 pp. Excerpted in Bevington and Jump.

Operating from the assumption that *Hamlet is* "primarily and finally a verbal structure," Levin offers a rhetorical analysis of the play. He sees embedded in its design three prominent rhetorical patterns, which he characterizes as Interrogation, Doubt and Irony. These three figures of speech and thought evolve in dialectical fashion. Interrogation, the thesis, is conveyed through the questioning tone that pervades the play. Doubt, the antithesis, is presented through the motif of choosing between alternatives. Irony, the synthesis, is present both as a verbal and mental characteristic of the hero and as a way of apprehending tragic reality, "the terror or the absurdity of existence."

Underlying this rhetorical design are the countless resonant verbal echoes and reduplicated motifs that create the unified literary experience of the play. Mr. Levin is a master of the art of making connections—the best example of which is his brilliant "Explication of the Player's Speech" included as an appendix in this book. Inevitably he establishes a connection or sees a significance that strains one's credulity. Inevitably, also, the reader is occasionally rankled by the Harvard *hauteur* that is a feature of his style. But these are minor blemishes in an otherwise flawless performance.

One further admonition: the student should not approach Levin's book until he has read the play a number of times and absorbed much of its language. This is wise procedure before consulting any criticism, but particularly in the case of a book which, to be most effective, depends upon the reader's intimate knowledge of the text.

60. *Grebanier, Bernard. *The Heart of Hamlet.* New York: Thomas Y. Crowell, 1960. 311 pp.

Grebanier's analysis is prefaced by a lengthy autobiographical discussion on how the author came by his interpretation of the play and a brief discourse on the nature of tragedy. These are followed by two long chapters in which the author reviews and sharply criticizes a large number of early interpretations. He then proceeds to his own interpretation. Briefly summarized, Grebanier's position is as follows: Hamlet is not mad nor pretending to be mad; neither does he delay—his tragic flaw, in fact, is rashness. The climax of the play is the killing of Polonius, " 'the rash and bloody deed' which will bring him [Hamlet] to catastrophe."

Some of this is interesting, none of it is new, and much of Grebanier's free-swinging, lively approach to the play and its criticism is just oversimplified. *The Heart of Hamlet* castigates virtually every important critic of the play and then proceeds to offer an eclectic collection of received opinions as a "new" interpretation.

61. Hardison, O. B. "The Dramatic Triad in *Hamlet,*" *Studies in Philology,* LVII (1960), 144–164.

Hardison argues that a characteristic feature of Shakespeare's plays, adapted from medieval drama, is a triadic structure in which the hero is seen as a mean situated between two extremes represented by two other characters. The determining situation in *Hamlet* is the death of the father. The two extreme reactions to this fact are represented by Laertes, who chooses revenge, and Ophelia, who chooses suicide. Hamlet is susceptible to both of these reactions but declines both in favor of an intermediate position, which Hardison characterizes as "forbearance." In the play "forbearance" is practiced not only by Hamlet but by Fortinbras who declines to go to war in order to avenge his father. Thus there is an identification between the two, Fortinbras representing "the ideal position towards which Hamlet is striving." Fortinbras' assumption of Hamlet's role of king at the end of the play is an indication that Hamlet has finally achieved his ideal.

Hardison is particularly good in demonstrating the relationship between the internal psychology of the hero and the external structure of the play. Less convincing are his attempts to show the consistent relevance of "forbearance" to the character of Hamlet.

62. Babcock, Weston. *Hamlet: A Tragedy of Errors.* Purdue University Press, 1961. 134 pp.

Babcock attempts "to examine the play scene after scene and to ask what a spectator uncoached by commentary would conclude . . .

from the words he had heard and the actions he had thus far seen." The result is a scene by scene analysis of the play as a tragedy of "errors," of misconceptions and misjudgments that move its chief characters toward disaster. He sees Hamlet's basic error to be his assumption of Gertrude's guilty complicity in the murder of his father. This error complicates his task of revenge, even leading him to suspect that Ophelia is Claudius' mistress.

This type of observation pervades the book, although generally Babcock's comments are better balanced. On the whole this is a lively and interesting account of the play but not a very important one.

63. *Knights, L. C. *An Approach to "Hamlet."* Stanford University Press, 1961. 90 pp. Excerpted in Jump.

For Knights, the play is a symbol of the "corruption of consciousness," of Hamlet's paralyzing inability to come to terms with reality. The Prince has fixed his gaze on human corruption so exclusively that his mind becomes as distorted and corrupt as the world he inhabits. His mind is arrested at the level of the knowledge "of evil seemingly inherent in human nature." He thus never achieves the breakthrough into the "purgatorial" self-awareness of King Lear.

Knights's view is, as he makes clear, designed more as a tentative "approach" than as a full-scale interpretation. As such, it is interesting and subtly argued. The inevitable distortions it invites, however, become only too clear in the course of his analysis of the play. Knights chooses to overlook the dramatic structure, devoting most of his attention to the soliloquies. The result is that his thematic treatment is divorced from the dramatic action of the play, a divorce which suggests that the two are incompatible.

64. Sister Miriam Joseph. *"Hamlet*: A Christian Tragedy," *Studies in Philology*, LIX (April, 1962), 119–140.

Sister Miriam's title states her thesis: the play is a Christian tragedy and "Hamlet is a Christian hero whose tragic flaw is his failure at the moment of crisis to measure up to the heroic Christian virtue demanded of him by the moral situation and by the ghost." The play is saturated with a Christian atmosphere and Christian values. Through the agency

of the Ghost, Hamlet has been given a special command by God "to exe-
cute justice . . . but he expressly forbade him ('Taint not thy mind')
to violate supernatural charity." However, in refusing to kill Claudius at
prayer, Hamlet violates this command, thereby capitulating to "personal
hatred." His moral failure at this, the climax of the play, is the core of
the tragedy and determines the succeeding tragic events. Ultimately Hamlet carries out the ghost's command but not before his failure to exercise
"heroic Christian charity" has precipitated the catastrophe.

Sister Miriam's position is similar to that of Fredson Bowers (56),
with the exception that it locates the climax at the prayer scene rather
than at the killing of Polonius. It differs from Bowers, also, in its rather
narrowly sectarian view of the action of the play. That there is a Christian
ethos in *Hamlet* is undeniable but to see it, and particularly the virtue of
charity, as the heart of the tragedy is a radical distortion. If Hamlet's
failure at charity is his fatal flaw, what are we to make of him in the fifth
act? According to Sr. Miriam, by this time he has seen the error of his
ways, yet he speaks of having sent Rosencrantz and Guildenstern to their
death with casual indifference and he finally kills Claudius in a spirit more
vindictive than anything else.

65. *Abel, Lionel. *"Hamlet* Q.E.D." in *Metatheatre.* New York: Hill
     and Wang, 1963. 146 pp.

Abel's thesis is that the play is not a tragedy but an example of
metatheatre. Metatheatre is Abel's term for a dramatic form, distinct
from tragedy, of which *Hamlet* is the earliest notable example. The
distinctive feature of this form is subjectivity; it locates its values
not in objective reality but in human consciousness—tentative, sceptical, improvisational and ironic. Its key feature is the "dramatic consciousness" of its characters, a consciousness, that is, of being characters in a play. In *Hamlet,* "for the first time in the history of drama,
the problem of the protagonist is that he has a playwright's consciousness."
Thus the metaphor Abel employs to analyze the play is that each of the
characters are writing a script for the other characters, all of them under
the illusion that they are writing the definitive version. The play finally
demonstrates that the definitive dramatist is Death.

Abel's argument is a provocative one. It rests upon the assumption that *Hamlet* exhibits a complex conception of the relation of illusion and reality, at the core of which is a loss of faith in the existence of objective values. In this respect, Abel's analysis is akin to Tillyard's view of *Hamlet* as a problem play (see 45).

66. Braddy, Halden. *Hamlet's Wounded Name*. El Paso: Texas Western Press, 1964. 82 pp.

Braddy identifies his goal as the restoration of Hamlet's good name. The latter it seems has been wounded by Freudians and other contemporary critics who have seen Hamlet as mentally unbalanced. Braddy vindicates Hamlet's extreme reaction to his mother's affection for Claudius by citing the folklore tradition of revulsion over "woman's perverse preference for the inferior man." Hamlet's antic disposition is merely the mask he adopts as "a wily man of parts" rooted in the Scandinavian myths of tricksters who triumph by the use of their wits.

Braddy's purpose is reasonable enough but his treatment of opposing points of view is oversimplified and his own arguments not sufficiently detailed to be convincing.

67. Cruttwell, Patrick. "The Morality of Hamlet—Sweet Prince or Arrant Knave," in *Hamlet*, Stratford-Upon-Studies, 5, ed. J. R. Brown and Bernard Harris. New York: St. Martins Press, 1964. Reprinted in Jump.

Cruttwell begins his essay by noting the mixed response to the character of Hamlet which has become increasingly more in evidence in modern criticism. The tendency of nineteenth-century criticism—Turgenev's essay (14) is a notable exception—was to see the hero as the "angel-borne prince of Horatio's farewell." Modern criticism, partly in reaction to this view, has come to look upon him as a morally dubious figure. However, this dubiety is not, according to Cruttwell, in the character but in the play: ". . . what we have in *Hamlet* is an extraordinary muddle of two moralities." These conflicting moralities are those of Christianity and the code of revenge. This conflict is one very much in evidence in 1600 and Hamlet is the image of the young intellectual of the time trying to serve two masters, a Christian conscience and an inherited pagan code of behavior. His seemingly dubious morality is actually the morality of the soldier during war. "He has done things, as we all do in wars, he would rather not have done; but he believes it to be a just war, and all in all, he has borne himself well."

Cruttwell's analysis of Hamlet's dilemma is similar to that of Hankins (35) and others who view the problem as a choice between opposing ethical alternatives. What is of particular value in his argument is the cogency with which he argues that Hamlet should be seen as a young Elizabethan intellectual such as John Donne; it reminds the reader of Bradley's casual remark that Hamlet's mind is similar to those of the metaphysical poets.

68. Holmes, Martin. *The Guns of Elsinore.* New York: Barnes & Noble, 1964. 188 pp.

The sub-title of this book might well have been "What Happened in Hamlet," since it sets out to reconstruct the original production of the play. Its first five chapters deal with the background conditions of the play: its audience, theatre, prompt book, actors and the Elizabethan knowledge of Denmark. Most of these comments are interesting and a few of them apparently new, although the author's cavalier attitude toward citation and documentation makes it difficult to distinguish just how many of his facts and insights are original. For example, his ideas about the expectations of the original audience of the play were anticipated by William Empson (52).

The second half of the book provides a scene-by-scene commentary on the play itself, marked by frequent allusions to contemporary attitudes and events. A number of intriguing suggestions are introduced, among them that the play that was "caviare to the general" was *Troilus and Cressida;* that Hamlet's fourth act soliloquy ("How all occasions . . .") is an interpolated allusion to English participation in the Siege of Ostend (1601); and that Laertes' rebellion had to be cut in performance because it bore an uncomfortable resemblance to the revolt of the Earl of Essex. These and many other suggestions provide an interesting insight into what the Elizabethan audience may have seen when they looked at the play. One would like to think, however, that, to those whom Gabriel Harvey called "the wiser sort," the profounder aspects of the play were not lost.

69. *Kott, Jan. "Hamlet of the Mid-Century," in *Shakespeare Our Contemporary*, trans. Boleslaw Taborski. New York: Doubleday Anchor Books, 1964. 241 pp. Reprinted in Jump.

Kott analyzes the play in the light of "our modern experience, anxiety and sensibility." One modern aspect of the play is its political character; it is a play full of political intrigue, its hero a "youth, deeply involved in politics, rid of illusions, sarcastic, passionate and brutal. . . . Action, not reflection, is his forte. He is wild and drunk with indignation." Profoundly aware of the absurdity of action, committed only to his own "inner freedom," he is thrust into a political conspiracy, the chief agent in a *coup d'etat* that issues inevitably in his death.

Kott's analysis is an admittedly partial view, imposing a "forced modernity" on the play. Nevertheless, he does provide a number of interesting insights, provided one is aware of the narrowness of his perspective and of his penchant for quoting lines from the play out of context.

70. Reid, B. L. "The Last Act and the Action of *Hamlet*," *Yale Review*, LIV (Autumn, 1964), 54–80.

Reid's approach is Aristotelian. The last act is the "end," just as Act I is the "beginning" and Acts II–IV the "middle." The subject of the last act is death. Here we see Hamlet in a new mood, "a strange and beautiful detachment" growing out of his acceptance of life's limitations. He has become fully human, fully representative of tragic humanity in his encounter with inevitable death. We are left with a vision of "the woe and wonder of the human condition." The woe is conveyed in the events of the play; the wonder in the reshaping of those events by the tragic artist, offering us the only consolation that tragedy can offer—the knowledge that the terrible can be made beautiful.

Reid's essay—in addition to being both eloquent and perceptive—is also interesting as an example of the growing tendency to eschew any interpretation that settles for a view of the play as instructive or exemplary in any but the broadest possible sense. In this view, tragedy is not teaching us how to behave but showing us what it means to be.

71. Weitz, Morris. *Hamlet and the Philosophy of Literary Criticism*. University of Chicago Press, 1964. 335 pp.

Using the critical history of *Hamlet* as a "test case," Weitz sets out to provide a philosophical-linguistic analysis of literary criticism. Each critic of *Hamlet,* accordng to Weitz, has been engaged in one of four linguistic procedures: description, explanation, evaluation or poetics. Of these procedures only descriptions are verifiable, that is, capable of being shown true or false. However, many of the most famous problems posited by critics are not descriptions and therefore not subject to true and false answers. As a preface to his discussion, Weitz outlines the views of the most prominent critics of the play from Bradley (19) to Fergusson (42) in order to arrive at his categories of their critical procedures. Weitz's book is an important and penetrating critique of the attitudes and pre-suppositions implicit in literary criticism. Under the unsparing light of linguistic analysis many of the critics' logical fallacies are revealed. Particularly valuable is Weitz's Wittgensteinian analysis of "the classical theory of language" in his chapter "Philosophy and Criticism." However, the book is not free from the limitations of Weitz's own philosophical position. For example, he is unable to take Fergusson at his word when the latter suggests that various critics should be seen as "reflectors" illuminating partial aspects of the play. In his rigid adherence to "true-false" categories Weitz is confused by Fergusson's awareness of the incompleteness of his (Fergusson's) own view, an awareness that is shared by many modern critics of the play.

72. Newell, Alex. "The Dramatic Context and Meaning of Hamlet's 'To Be or Not To Be' Soliloquy," *PMLA,* LXXX (March, 1965), 38-50.

The best known single speech in all literature, Hamlet's "To be or not to be" soliloquy has been subject to a wide variety of interpretations. Of these the most common are those that see the speech as a reflection either on suicide or on the intended death of Claudius. Newell argues that both of these interpretations are not so much wrong as they are fragmentary and incomplete. Their chief flaw is that they ignore the dramatic context of the soliloquy, fail to see that it occurs just after Hamlet's decision to use the play within the play in order to "catch the conscience of the king." Newell's position is that the soliloquy grows out of Hamlet's attempt to confront the problem of action—specifically the action of putting on the play. Thus the celebrated opening line, in its dramatic context at least, is really a question as to whether the play is to be or not to be. Out of this question develops the possibility that such an action will lead to Hamlet's death (II.57-69), which in turn leads to a general reflection on death (II. 70–78) and which finally returns to Hamlet's specific problem of action (II. 79–88). In the conclusion Hamlet rededicates himself to the project at hand (the play within the play), this time from an intellectual, not merely emotional, basis. Encompassed within this problem of action are the suicide and Claudius interpretations, but they are merely constitutive aspects of the problem, not the problem itself.

The chief value of Newell's essay lies in its insistence on the dramatic appropriateness of a speech which, for all its fame, has often been treated as irrelevant or incoherent (see 4). His analysis restores the soliloquy to its central place in the drama as a vital, organic element of the play, not merely as an independent, spoken "aria."

73. *McFarland, Thomas. "Hamlet and the Dimension of Possible Existence," in *Tragic Meanings in Shakespeare*. New York: Random House, 1966.

McFarland's book brings to bear on the major tragedies the insights and terminology of certain Existentialist philosophers such as Martin Heidegger and Karl Jaspers. Thus *Hamlet* is analyzed in terms of the existentialist conception of the terms *possibility* and *decision*. Possibility is the defining characteristic of authentic existence, enabling one to transcend the limiting conditions of a particular time and place. Aware of the need to incorporate both the past and the future in order to establish authentic existence, Hamlet is "oriented toward transcendence." In asking the question "Ought I to kill Claudius?" Hamlet brings to birth an irreconcilable dilemma which leads him to a confrontation with the reality of nonbeing. His decision—the decision not to decide—is grounded in the absolute existentialist values of possibility and freedom, affirming them, as the gravedigger scene shows, in the face of the knowledge of the absurdity of life.

The major objection to McFarland's analysis is that it uses the play to illustrate a philosophical position rather than employing the philosophy to illuminate the play. His treatment is too general, his terms too universal in their applicability; the result is that we are left, as in the Freudian analysis, with the impression of *Hamlet* as the case history of a real human being, rather than as a work of art.

74. Prosser, Eleanor. *Hamlet and Revenge.* Stanford University Press, 1967. 287 pp.

This volume is divided into two sections. The first constitutes an admirable essay in historical scholarship in which Professor Prosser demonstrates that, in Elizabethan times, revenge, both on and off the stage, was denounced as immoral and self-destructive. The second section of the book is devoted to an analysis of Hamlet derived from this fact.

The thesis relates to the character of the Ghost. The author argues that he should be seen as evil in his insistence on revenge. Shakespeare's position is that of the Christian establishment. In other words a revengeful Ghost is "not honest but demonic." Once Hamlet capitulates to the Ghost's command (in the "To be or not to be" soliloquy), he begins a descent from grace that is not arrested until the fifth act. Although he himself is finally redeemed, his "savage course" of revenge "is intended to appall us." The context and ground of the play is "explicitly Christian," although those Christian values may be viewed as broadly humanistic, "the basic view of man held throughout the civilized world."

Professor Prosser anticipates the most serious objection to her analysis. "No work as universally appealing as *Hamlet* . . . can be tied up in a neat little package labeled Renaissance Christian Morality Play." She has anticipated the objection but not answered it. Despite some artful dodging—as well as some first-rate historical scholarship—her interpretation rests upon the confusion of an ethical dilemma as we might encounter it in life with the tragic experience as it engages us in great art.

75. Sanford, Wendy Coppedge. *Theater as Metaphor in "Hamlet."* The Le Baron Russell Briggs Prize Honors Essay in English. Harvard University Press, 1967. 51 pp.

The author argues that the theatrical metaphor is central to the structure and meaning of the play. Amplifying an observation of Abel (65), she notes the great number of staged scenes that occur in the play, focusing particularly on Hamlet and Claudius as "directors" of these scenes. In the fifth act, Hamlet emerges with an awareness of that "Other Director," the divinity who shapes our ends.

The theatrical metaphor is further developed in the image of Hamlet as actor, trying on roles in an attempt to achieve an integrated personality. His consciousness of his play-acting prevents him from making a permanent commitment to any one role. Thus he is at various times the clown, the madman, the lover, the cynic, the fawning courtier, and the ambitious prince. Nevertheless, the process itself finally results in personal integration, the achievement of wholeness; and this movement of encompassment mirrors the action of the play itself.

Perhaps inevitably the author tends to make too much of the theatrical metaphor (a more balanced view of its importance is reflected in Charney's analysis [77]). Her work would also have benefited by an awareness of the work of Anne Righter (*Shakespeare and the Idea of the Play*) and, more particularly, of C. R. Forker ("Shakespeare's Theatrical Symbolism and Its Function in Hamlet," *SQ*, XIV [1963]). She has provided, nevertheless, a lively and intelligent focus on an important area of the play.

76. Booth, Stephen. "On the Value of *Hamlet*," in *Reinterpretations of Elizabethan Drama*, ed. Norman Rabkin. New York: Columbia University Press, 1969, pp. 137–176.

"*Hamlet* is the tragedy of an audience that cannot make up its mind." This aphorism—a parody of the famous comment that precedes the Olivier film version of the play—summarizes Booth's striking analysis. He approaches the play phenomenologically, discussing it as "a succession of actions upon the understanding of an audience." His detailed analysis of the play's events is designed to point up a pattern of incoherence in the action which the audience absorbs and which is the source of the value with which the audience invests the play.

Viewed from this perspective, *Hamlet* both reveals itself and is experienced as a dilemma. The point, however, is that the attempts to resolve that dilemma invariably distort and reduce it. We must, says the author, learn to recognize that the play represents a movement toward *inclusion*, not *conclusion*. As a result, it stretches the mind of its audience by denying it the secure compartments of coherence and consistency. The play's value lies in its capacity to contain all its contradictions and to force its audience to confront those contradictions in an intense, unmediated fashion.

Booth's essay represents the culmination of a movement (beginning with Kenneth Burke's 1931 essay, "Psychology and Form") which attempts to see the play's mysteries not as problems to be solved but as experiences to be absorbed.

77. Charney, Maurice. *Style in Hamlet.* Princeton University Press, 1969. 333 pp.

In discussing style, Charney has in mind the broader meaning of the term—not just its verbal characteristics, but its theatrical images (gestures, sound effects, costumes, and music) and style—as an aspect of characterization. The latter represents an attempt to discuss characters not in terms of psychological motivation but as creations individualized for us in terms of their language and behavior.

The first section of the book is devoted to an extensive analysis of the play's major images. The author groups these under five headings. The first group, War, Weapons, and Explosives, focuses our attention on the play's public issues: the state of the nation, politics, and kingship. Secrecy and Poison, the second grouping of images, calls attention to the movement of dramatic action from darkness to light. Corruption imagery, the third category, intensifies the sense of human evil; the imagery of "Limit" crystallizes the conflict between unlimited possibility and the fact of "man's finiteness and mortality." Theatrical imagery, the fifth heading, is designed to elicit "a sceptical and ironical awareness" on the part of its audience.

In the second section the play's theatrical effects are discussed through an imagined early performance in the manner of Empson (52) and Holmes (68).

The concluding section of the book is devoted to a stylistic analysis of Polonius, Claudius, and Hamlet. The extraordinary virtuosity of Hamlet's style is catalogued by Charney as self-conscious, witty, passionate, and simple, adopting each to suit the particular moment, suggesting among other things that Hamlet "thinks of experience as a work of art that can only be mastered by aesthetic means."

Charney's study lacks a unifying view of the play. We never are allowed to see the forest, but the study is valuable nevertheless for its detailed examination of an extraordinary number of trees.

78. Zitner, S. P. "Hamlet, Duellist," *University of Toronto Quarterly,* XXXIX (1969), 1–18.

Zitner focuses on the use of weapons in the play both as verbal motif and dramatic device. He points out that during the 1590's the rapier had emerged as a weapon, and that the use of the rapier had complicated the practise of duelling by greatly increasing "the possibilities for serious violence among the court aristocracy." Furthermore the rapier contributed to an increased self-consciousness on the part of young aristocrats. The source of certain attitudes in the play may be reflected in a popular duelling manual, Vincent Saviolo's *Practice*, published in 1595. Saviolo's treatise contains comments on "just revenge," focusing particularly "on the self-consciousness of the avenger, on the disinterestedness that abandons private will to the will of God."

In *Hamlet* Shakespeare presents us with the dilemma of the Elizabethan aristocrat, alienated from society at large and attempting to weigh and formulate a code of behavior that is personally meaningful even though politically futile. Hamlet is among other things, "the tragedy of a self-tortured young swordsman moved by ambiguous injunctions to uphold a vanished glory."

An original and provocative study of the play, marred only by a tendency to offer untested generalizations about the divorce between public good and private conscience both in the play and in the age.

79. Morris, Harry. "*Hamlet* as a *Memento Mori* Poem," *PMLA* 85 (Oct. 1970), 1035–1040.

Focusing on the graveyard scene, Morris enumerates the various characteristics of the play that entitle it to be characterized as a *timor mortis–memento mori* poem: the fear of death, the meditation upon skulls and of the corruption of the body, the catalogue of famous men, the *ubi sunt* motif, and the concern for life after death. The last is particularly critical since that apprehension—reflected in the condition of the Ghost, Hamlet's refusal to kill Claudius at prayer, Ophelia's "maimed rites," and Hamlet's fear of the undiscovered country—is a prominent part of the entire play. All of this "argues strongly for an eschatological reading of the play. . . ." Hamlet's "readiness" is thus an expression of his belief that he is in the state of grace.

Morris presents a number of interesting observations and helps to establish the importance of the graveyard scene. His conclusion, however, rests upon a willingness to accept these parallels as literal adaptations of the *memento mori* form. More probably, Shakespeare adapted the form in order to register the particular variations on it that suited his specific purposes. It remains open to question whether those purposes were as narrowly religious as Morris suggests.

80. Skulsky, Harold. "Revenge, Honor and Conscience in *Hamlet*," *PMLA*, 85 (1970), 78–87.

Skulsky sees Hamlet divided between two opposing definitions of revenge, the law of the talon and the code of honor "—between the unrestrained, bloody vengeance embodied in the figure of Pyrrhus and the "young man's game" of courtly vindictiveness exemplified by Laertes and Fortinbras. Both of these positions are repudiated in the play. Hamlet himself, however, maintains an ambivalent posture toward them. On the one hand, he remains committed to absolute revenge; on the other, he sets up in his soliloquy an identification between suicide and revenge and an opposing identification of conscience and cowardice. This argues a moral error on Hamlet's part, an error intensified in his image of himself as a "scourge of heaven." Thus the play is "a tragedy of spiritual decline arrested only by the brief madness of the Prince's last anger. . . . The . . . Prince, though he is saved, is no better than the rest of us."

Skulsky's is a subtle and complex argument. The problem with it is that it reads the play as though it were a Henry James novel: full of tricky, excruciatingly subtle ethical dilemmas. Like Tillyard (45), Skulsky sees *Hamlet* as a moral problem play rather than as a tragedy. In leveling Hamlet to "no better than the rest of us" he has ignored the tone of solemn ritual and nobility present throughout the play.

81. Alexander, Nigel. *Poison, Play and Duel.* Lincoln, Nebraska: University of Nebraska Press, 1971.

As his title indicates Alexander suggests that poison, play and duel constitute "the dominant symbols of the action of *Hamlet*." Using these terms as consistent frames of reference, he analyzes the play in terms of certain traditional Renaissance symbols: the art of memory (Hamlet and the Ghost), psychomachia (the soliloquies), the theatre of the world (the play within the play), the three graces (Ophelia and Gertrude), the *memento mori* (the graveyard scene). The pattern of poison, play and duel—constituting in effect the past, present and future of the play— culminates in the duelling scene. Along the way the play asks many questions which remain unanswered but those questions and doubts are precisely part of the results Shakespeare is working for. It is not his purpose to offer solutions but to confront the spectator with a powerful and recognizable image of the human situation. "The pattern of poison, play and duel reaches out beyond the stage and takes possession of the minds of its audience. It offers them growth in consciousness and understanding."

This is a sensitive, detailed and imaginative reading of the play. It is somewhat weakened by a conclusion that is too tentative and understated but is nevertheless an important and illuminating attempt to pluck out the heart of the mystery.

Sources and Date

INTRODUCTION

Rooted in primitive myth (see 22), the story of Hamlet is at least a thousand years old. The genesis of the Shakespearean play has been traced to Saxo Grammaticus' twelfth-century account in his *Historiae Danicae*. Saxo's version of the story was adapted by François de Belleforest and incorporated into his *Histoires Tragiques* (1576). Belleforest's narrative became in turn the source of an English play, probably by Thomas Kyd, sometime in the late 1580's. This play—the *Ur-Hamlet* as it is known—formed the source not only of Shakespeare's tragedy but of a seventeenth-century German play, *Der Bestrafte Brudermord* ("Fratricide Punished"). In addition to these direct sources, the play reflects the influence of a number of important theoretical works written during the Renaissance. The most important of these are Montaigne's *Essays*, translated by John Florio in 1603, and Timothy Bright's *A Treatise of Melancholy* (1586).

In addition to the works considered below, the sources of the play and the problems connected with them are treated in Kenneth Muir's *Shakespeare's Sources* (London: Methuen, 1957).

(Note: Geoffrey Bullough's *Narrative and Dramatic Sources of Shakespeare*, Vol. 7 [Columbia University Press, 1972] contains selections from the sources and a discussion of their relevance to Shakespeare's play.)

ENTRIES FOR SOURCES AND DATE

S1. Malone, Kemp. *The Literary History of Hamlet. I: The Early Tradition.* Heidelberg, 1923.

This book was to have been the first part of a three-part history of the Hamlet story, but it is the only volume that has been completed. It covers the earliest emanations of the tale up to its appearance in Saxo Grammaticus' *Historiae Danicae*. Malone traces the roots of the story to the legend of the Geats, the same tribe that originated the story of Beowulf. In fact, Malone argues, the original source of the Hamlet story is the legend of the Swedish King, Onela, who is treated in *Beowulf*. The story of Onela, which assumed different forms throughout northern Europe and Ireland, was transformed by the tribes on the Danish peninsula of Jutland into the story of Amleth as given in Saxo Grammaticus.

This brief outline does not begin to do justice to the complexity, ingenuity, and erudition of Malone's presentation. It is an extremely difficult book to read, recommended only to advanced students of the play and of Germanic philology.

S2. Gollancz, Israel. *The Sources of Hamlet*. London: H. Milford, 1926. 321 pp.

This book provides the texts of the major extant sources of the play together with a preliminary survey of the development of the Hamlet story in northern mythology. According to Gollancz, the story is Celtic in origin, later incorporated into Scandinavian mythology and first re-corded in Saxo Grammaticus. *Historiae Danicae* (History of the Danes), Saxo's account, was adapted by François de Belleforest, who incorporated it into his *Histoires Tragiques* (1576).

Saxo's version also seems to have borrowed from the story of Lucius Junius Brutus, the Roman hero. Gollancz discusses a number of other early analogues such as the Icelandic saga centering on the figure of Ambales. The texts consist of the relevant sections of Saxo in the original Latin with an English translation on facing pages, Belleforest's account with an early English translation, *The Hystorie of Hamblet* (1608); and an English translation of the first two chapters of the *Ambales Saga*.

Gollancz's collection of texts provides a valuable reference for the student interested in the development of the Hamlet story. As for his argument that the myth is of Celtic origin, most scholars have discarded that hypothesis in favor of the one put forth by Kemp Malone (70).

S3. Honigmann, E. A. J. "The Date of *Hamlet*," *Shakespeare Survey* 9 (1956), pp. 24–34.

Honigmann reviews all the extant evidence for the dating of *Hamlet*. The play is not mentioned by Francis Meres in his list of Shakespeare's plays in *Palladis Tamia* (September, 1598), and it was entered in the Stationers' Register in July, 1602. Therefore it must have been first produced between 1598 and 1602. The earliest extant allusion to the play is a marginal note by Gabriel Harvey (see Introduction to the Criticism of Hamlet) in a copy of a book first published in 1598. This same note also mentions the Earl of Essex in the present tense. Essex was executed in February, 1601. Furthermore the play itself contains a celebrated allusion to the so-called "war of the theatres," which did not begin until late 1599. The play also alludes to an "inhibition" (II,ii,346) against stage plays, which is generally regarded as a reference to an order from the Privy Council restricting stage performances, promulgated in June, 1600. After carefully weighing the conflicting interpretations of these events Honigmann concludes that "the most likely date of composition seems to be late 1599 to early 1600."

Honigmann's argument, if true, pushes the date of the play back a year earlier than generally assumed. Although far from conclusive, his thesis coincides with a growing tendency among Shakespearean scholars to assume that Shakespeare's plays were written somewhat earlier than formerly has been supposed.

S4. Stabler, Arthur. "King Hamlet's Ghost in Belleforest," *PMLA*, 77 (March, 1962), 18–20.

———. "Elective Monarchy in the Sources of *Hamlet*," *Studies in Philology*, 62 (1965), 654–661.

———. "Melancholy, Ambition and Revenge in Belleforest's Hamlet," *PMLA*, 81 (June, 1966), 207–213.

———. "The Source of the German *Hamlet*," *Shakespeare Studies*, V (1969), 97–105.

Stabler's studies provide a convincing demonstration that such features as the melancholy of the hero, the vindictive spirit of the ghost (see also Prosser [74]), the theme of frustrated ambition, and the conflict of private and public revenge are present in the French narrative source of the play.

S5. Taylor, Marion. *A New Look at the Old Source of Hamlet.* The Hague: Mouton, 1968.

Taylor's thesis is that the Amleth story is rooted in a ninth-century Varangian tale. The Varangians were Northmen who settled in Russia under Rurik, the alleged founder of the Russian monarchy. The Varangians derived their story from the Roman tale of Junius Brutus.

S6. Olsson, Yngve. "In Search of Yorick's Skull: Notes on the Background of Hamlet," *Shakespeare Studies*, IV (1968), 183–230.

Olsson offers another source for the original Hamlet play or for Shakespeare's revision. This would be a Latin history of Scandinavia, *Chronica Regnorium Aquilornarium Daniae Svetiae Norvagiae* by Albert Krantz, published in the 1540's. Olsson reprints the relevant sections of the Hamlet story in Krantz and provides an English translation.

S7. Kaula, David. *"Hamlet* and the *Sparing Discoverie,"* *Shakespeare Survey*, 24 (1971), 71–77.

Kaula points out verbal similarities between the play and a theological pamphlet titled *A Sparing Discoverie of our English Jesuits* published in 1601. The pamphlet involved a controversy among English Catholics. A few of the verbal echoes are striking. One point that Kaula doesn't make is that if Shakespeare read the pamphlet—as he certainly read Harsnett's *Declaration of Egregious Popish Impostures*—it argues an uncommon interest in Catholicism on his part.

Textual Criticism

INTRODUCTION

Three early printed versions of Shakespeare's play survive. The earliest was published in quarto size in 1603. This text, usually abbreviated as Q1, is a "bad quarto," a radically corrupt, pirated version of the play, published at a time when an author had no copyright privileges over his work. This badly botched text was reconstructed from memory by a former actor in Shakespeare's company, probably the one who had the minor role of Marcellus. In the following year, 1604, an authorized edition of the play was printed in quarto (Q2). This text, probably based on Shakespeare's own manuscript, is the most complete version of the play. The other authoritative edition was published in 1623 in the famous collection of Shakespeare's works known as the First Folio. The Folio text was printed from either an edited copy of Q2 or from the acting company's prompt-book. In any case it is some 200 lines shorter than Q2 while at the same time providing some 80 lines not found in that quarto.

Since Q2 derives from Shakespeare's manuscript there would seem to be no question but that a modern edition would be based on it. However, the problem is not that simple. Q2 is a poorly printed text containing many obvious misprints probably resulting from the compositors' inability to read Shakespeare's handwriting. On some occasions, particularly in setting the first act, the compositors were forced to consult Q1, a notoriously unreliable text.

Of course, the Folio text presents difficulties, too. It represents the play as it was performed on the stage and therefore contains a number of interpolations inserted by actors as well as many non-authorial changes that may have been dictated by the exigencies of theatrical production.

The result is that a modern editor must be extremely selective in establishing a text. Most modern editions (i.e., since 1934) are based primarily on Q2, after it has been carefully collated with the Folio text.

To the general reader many of the conjectures of textual scholars must appear as scholarly hair-splitting of little or no importance. On the contrary, these studies are rooted in the most fundamental scholarly problem: the attempt to reconstruct to the fullest extent possible the text that Shakespeare finally intended.

ENTRIES FOR TEXTUAL CRITICISM

T1. Wilson, J. Dover. *The Manuscript of Shakespeare's Hamlet and the Problems of Its Transmission.* 2 vols. Cambridge University Press, 1934. 437 pp.

This two volume study is the most extensive textual analysis of the play ever undertaken. It argues that the Second Quarto (1604) is the most authoritative edition because it was printed from Shakespeare's own manuscript. The Folio text on the other hand was printed from a transcript of the prompt-book and thus represents the acting version of the play. All of the errors in Q2 can be explained as the mistakes of the compositor who had difficulty reading Shakespeare's handwriting as he set the type for this edition.

The second volume is devoted to editorial principles and problems. Among other points it argues that Shakespeare's punctuation is revealed in the Second Quarto and puts forth an effective case for a number of emendations in the accepted text. Among the latter is Wilson's well-known argument for the validity of the quarto reading "sallied" against the Folio reading "solid" in the line "O that this too, too sallied flesh" (I,ii,129).

Although many of Wilson's arguments have been modified or refuted by later scholars, the bulk of this work is of indisputable value. Taken together with his edition of the play (E2) and his *What Happens in Hamlet* (31) it reveals him as the twentieth-century's most significant contributor to our knowledge of *Hamlet*.

T2. Duthie, G. I. *The "Bad" Quarto of Hamlet.* Cambridge University Press, 1941. 279 pp.

Duthie's book is a careful study of the origins of the pirated 1603 edition of the play. Duthie noted that while most of the text is corrupt, occasional passages, particularly those that feature Marcellus, are reprinted with considerable accuracy. On this basis he concluded that the 1603 quatro was printed from a text reconstructed from memory by the actor who played Marcellus. When the actor's memory failed him, as it frequently did, he patched it together with half-remembered lines from the pre-Shakespearean *Hamlet*. This version was probably produced by an unauthorized road company touring in English country towns. This hypothesis of "memorial reconstruction" made for a touring company probably also accounts for the origins of *Der Bestrafte Brudermord*, the seventeenth-century German play that bears strong resemblances to *Hamlet*.

Duthie's explanation of the genesis of the bad quarto has received general acceptance. His is the only hypothesis that satisfactorily accounts for all the features of the text.

T3. Walker, Alice. *Textual Problems of the First Folio.* Cambridge University Press, 1953, pp. 121–137.

Miss Walker's thesis concerning *Hamlet* is that the text of the Folio version was not based, as Dover Wilson argued (T1), on a transcript of the acting company's prompt-book but on a copy of the Second Quarto which had been collated with the prompt-book. The significance of this argument lies in the fact that it undermines the Folio's authority as an independent text. The practical effects of such an argument is that it would lead to more eclecticism on the part of modern editors of the play. For if Q2 and Folio are independent of each other and they both agree on a given passage, then the reading must be kept regardless of how puzzling it appears to be. If, however, Folio is derived from Q2, then a puzzling passage may be explained as an initial error in Q2 which was merely repeated in F.

Miss Walker elaborated this thesis in a subsequent article, "Collateral Substantive Texts (With Special Reference to *Hamlet*)," *Studies in Bibliography*, VII (1955), 51–67. The thesis was disputed in the same issue by Harold Jenkins ("The Relation Between the Second Quarto and the Folio Text of *Hamlet*," *Studies in Bibliography* [VII], 1955, 69–83).

T4. Greg, W. W. *The Shakespeare First Folio*. Oxford: Clarendon Press, 1955, pp. 299–333.

Greg's essay contains a careful review of the play's major textual problems. He examines and accepts, with a number of important qualifications, Duthie's thesis that the bad quarto is a memorial reconstruction (T2) and Wilson's argument that Q2 is based on Shakespeare's manuscript (T1). On the important question of the origin of the Folio text, Greg is undecided. He acknowledges the cogency of the contrasting views of Walker (T3) that the Folio was printed from an edited copy of Q2 and of Wilson that it was printed from a transcript of the prompt-book.

Greg's essay offers no new or conclusive textual evidence. Its importance derives, rather, from the fact that it represents the carefully considered judgment of a great scholar who devoted his entire life and his extraordinary critical acumen to the analysis of Shakespeare texts.

T5. Bowers, Fredson. "The Printing of Hamlet Q2," *Studies in Bibliography*, VII (1955), 41–50. "The Textual Relation of Q2 to Q1 Hamlet," *Studies in Bibliography*, VIII (1956), 39–66.

In the first of these two essays Bowers, in conjunction with John Russell Brown, demonstrates through a rigorous textual analysis that the Second Quarto of the play was not set in type, as J. Dover Wilson had argued, by a single careless compositor. Rather it was set by two compositors, the same two, to judge by their spelling habits, who set the 1600 Quarto version of *The Merchant of Venice*, a text with comparatively few errors. The importance of these facts is that they undermine Wilson's theory about an incompetent compositor and they enable an editor to make a more educated guess as to the reliability of a given passage in the Quarto.

Bowers' second essay explores the relationship between Q1 and Q2 and shows that Act I of Q2 may have been set from an annotated copy of the bad quarto. At the very least it appears likely that Q1 was consulted when Q2 was being set in type.

T6. Freudenstein, Reinhold. *Der Bestrafte Brudermord: Shakespeares Hamlet auf der Wanderbühne des 17. Jahrhunderts.* Hamburg: Cram, de Gruyter, 1958.

A German study of the problems connected with the relationship between the Hamlet text and this seventeenth-century German version. *Der Bestrafte Brudermord* was derived either from the *Ur-Hamlet*, the bad quarto (Q1),or the good quarto (Q2). The author argues that the German play is based on both Q1 and Q2 and is not dependent on the *Ur-Hamlet*.

T7. Jenkins, Harold. "Playhouse Interpolations in the Folio Text of *Hamlet*." *Studies in Bibliography*, XIII (1960), 31–47.

Jenkins argues that there are a minimum of 65 times when the Folio text, presumably derived from the actors' prompt-book, gives evidence of having been tampered with by the actors. Many of these interpolations take the form of repetitions, of the type that heighten the theatrical effect. None of these is to be found in the Quarto and therefore must be considered to have been added by the actors in Shakespeare's company. Furthermore, this characteristic is not unique to *Hamlet* but is present in a number of other plays published in the Folio. Thus an editor wishing to restore what Shakespeare wrote should carefully examine the possibility of playhouse contamination in the Folio text.

Jenkins' thesis is convincingly argued. An important peripheral aspect of it is the weight it lends to the view that the Folio text is derived from the prompt-book, not from Q2 (see T3).

T8. Nosworthy, J. M. *Shakespeare's Occasional Plays.* New York: Barnes and Noble, 1965, pp. 128–215.

Citing the title page of Q1 (". . . acted by his Highnesse servants in the Cittie of London: as also in the two universities of Cambridge and Oxford . . ."), Nosworthy argues that it was written with particular occasions in mind, one possibly before an aristocratic audience in London, another before a university audience. As a result, Q2 and F represent "two variously separated stages in the creation of a private occasional *Hamlet*." Q1 represents a memorial reconstruction of the abridged version that must have been adapted to the taste and time standards of the public theatre.

Editions

For *Hamlet*, as indeed for Shakespeare's plays generally, there is no such thing as a "definitive" modern edition. What there is, however, is a wide variety of texts, ranging from the scholarly to the popular, published in every conceivable format. The more important of these are given below:

E1.**Hamlet: A New Variorum Edition*, ed. H. H. Furness [1877]. 2 vols. New York: Dover Publications, 1963.

This edition is an invaluable repository of information on the play. Volume One contains the text of the play (running well over 400 pages), profusely annotated. Volume Two reprints the First Quarto, the major sources and a translation of the seventeenth-century German play, *Der Bestrafte Brudermord* ("Fratricide Punished"). It also contains a wide selection of eighteenth- and nineteenth-century criticism of the play.

E2. *Hamlet*. The New Shakespeare, ed. J. Dover Wilson. Cambridge University Press, 1934.

The first modern edition to be based primarily on the Second Quarto, it incorporates Wilson's conclusions about the play and its text that were presented in his major works (see 31 and T1). The Introduction also includes a valuable stage history of the play written by Harold Child.

E3. *The Tragedy of Hamlet: A Critical Edition of the Second Quarto, 1604*, eds. T. M. Parrott and Hardin Craig. Princeton University Press, 1938.

This is a critical edition of the Second Quarto. It is designed only for the student involved in textual study of the play: the spelling is not modernized and the introduction deals primarily with textual questions. In the main it agrees with Wilson's thesis that Q2 was derived from Shakespeare's manuscript.

E4. **Hamlet*, ed. George Lyman Kittredge. Boston: Ginn and Co., 1939. Revised by Irving Ribner (1967).

This conservative text has the benefit of Kittredge's lucid and learned notes. The unfortunate placement of the notes at the end of the text instead of on the relevant page is corrected in the revision of Kittredge's edition edited by Irving Ribner.

E5. **Hamlet*, ed. Cyrus Hoy. New York: W. W. Norton, 1963.

Easily the best of the school editions of the play. The text, based on the Second Quarto, is carefully edited and well annotated. This edition also contains extracts from the sources and from material, such as Montaigne's essays, that provided the intellectual background of the play. There is in addition a number of excerpts from critics from the eighteenth century to the present and a good bibliography.

(Note: The forthcoming New Arden *Hamlet*, edited by Harold Jenkins and to be published by Harvard University Press, promises to be one of the most important editions of the play in our time.)

Staging

Concise stage histories of the play are given in the New Cambridge edition (see E2), and in *The Reader's Encyclopedia of Shakespeare*, eds. O. J. Campbell and Edward G. Quinn (New York, 1966). Early performances are treated in the relevant sections of G. C. D. Odell's *Shakespeare from Betterton to Irving* (2 vols. New York, 1920) and in A. C. Sprague's *Shakespeare and the Actors* (Cambridge, Mass., 1944, 440 pp.). Recent productions are treated in E. Browne's "English Hamlets of the Twentieth Century," *Shakespeare Survey* 9 (1956, pp. 16–23), and in J. C. Trewin's *Shakespeare on the English Stage 1900–1964* (London, 1964, 328 pp.). Sir John Gielgud's memorable portrayal, considered by many the greatest performance of the role in this century, is given detailed attention in Rosamond Gilder's *John Gielgud's Hamlet* (Oxford University Press, 1937, 234 pp.). Finally, Raymond Mander and Joe Mitchenson provide a pictorial history of the play in *Hamlet Through the Ages: A Pictorial Record from 1709* (London, 1952).

Othello

James Ruoff

❖ CONTENTS

Index to Critics Cited and Their Entry Numbers   79

Short Titles of Collections of Othello *Criticism*   81

The Criticism of Othello   82

    Introduction   82

    Entries for the Criticism of Othello   86

Sources and Date   131

    Introduction   131

    Entries for Sources and Date   132

Textual Criticism   135

    Introduction   135

    Entries for Textual Criticism   136

Editions   138

Staging   140

    Introduction   140

    Entries for Staging   141

Index to Critics Cited
and Their Entry Numbers

Adamowski, T. H. 92
Adams, Maurianne S. S4
Allen, Ned B. 93
Arthos, John 56
Auchincloss, Louis 103
Auden, W. H. 69
Battenhouse, Roy W. 98
Bayley, John 62
Bentley, G. E. E4
Bethell, S. L. 37
Bodkin, Maud 21
Boehm, Rudolf 87
Bradley, A. C. 12
Brooke, C. F. Tucker 15, E2
Burke, Kenneth 33
Bush, Geoffrey 47
Campbell, Lily B. 18
Carlisle, Carol Jones ST 8
Chambers, E. K. 17
Charlton, H. B. 26
Clemen, Wolfgang 34
Coghill, Nevill T6
Coleridge, Samuel Taylor 4
Cronin, Peter 104
Dean, Winton 39
Doebler, Bettie A. S6
Doran, Madeleine 88
Dowden, Edward 9
Draper, John W. 38
Echeruo, M. J. C. 89
Eliot, T. S. 20
Elliott, G. R. 41

Empson, William 35
Evans, K. W. 99
Everett, Barbara 23
Fergusson, Francis 105
Flatter, Richard 31, T1
Fleissner, Robert F. 100
Furness, H. H. E1
Gardner, Helen 48
Gerard, Albert 52
Gilbert, Allan 60
Goldstone, Richard 39
Goll, August 82
Granville-Barker, Harley 27
Greg, W. W. T4
Hagopian, John V. 63
Hallstead, R. N. 94
Hapgood, Robert 83
Hayes, Ann L. 73
Hazlitt, William 7
Heilman, Robert 49
Hinman, Charlton K. T2
Holloway, John 68
Homan, Sidney R. 101
Hubler, Edward 57
Hunter, G. K. 90
Hyman, Stanley Edgar 106
Jackson, J. R. de J. 4
Johnson, Samuel 2
Jones, Eldred D. 80
Jones, Emrys S8
Jorgenson, Paul A. 74
Kernan, Alvin 70, E7

Kernan, Joseph 39
Kirschbaum, Leo 75
Kittredge, George Lyman E8
Knight, G. Wilson 19
Kott, Jan 95
La Mar, Virginia A. E6
Lamb, Charles 5
Lawlor, John 64
Leavis, F. R. 23
Lennox, Charlotte S1
Levin, Harry 76
Low, Anthony 107
Mason, H. A. 108
Mason, Laurence E2
Matthews, G. M. 77
McGee, Arthur 78
Mendonça, B. H. C. de S9
Money, John 42
Moulton, R. G. 13
Muir, Kenneth S2
Myrick, Kenneth 24
Nash, Walter 58
Nowottny, W. M. T. 40
Ornstein, Robert 66
Osborn, Neal J. 33
Overmyer, Janet 110
Oyama, Toshikazu 91
Parker, M. D. H. 44
Pompignan, Jean-Jacques
    Le Franc 3
Ranald, Margaret L. 71
Reid, Stephen 96
Ribner, Irving 65, E8
Richmond, Hugh 84
Ridley, M. R. T5, E5
Rosenberg, Marvin 45, St4
Ross, Lawrence J. 85, St5
Rymer, Thomas 1
Schlegel, A. W. 6
Schucking, Levin L. 16

Schwartz, Elias 109
Sedgewick, G. G. 28
Seltzer, Daniel St 3
Sewell, Arthur 36
Shaffer, Elinor S. 4
Shaw, George Bernard 11
Shaw John 86
Siegel, Paul N. 53, S3
Sisson, C. J. 72
Smith, Gordon Ross 61
Speaight, Robert 46
Spencer, Theodore 25
Spivack, Bernard 59
Sprague, A. C. St1, St9
Sproule, A. F. 50
Spurgeon, Caroline 22
Stanislovski, Constantin St2
Stauffer, Donald A. 29
Stewart, Douglas J. S7
Stewart, J. I. M. 30
Stirling, Brents 51
Stoll, E. E. 14
Stone, George Winchester, Jr. St7
Swinburne, A. C. 10
Trewin, J. C. St6, St9
Viswanathan, S. 102
Wain, John 111
Walker, Alice T3, E3
Walton, J. K. 67
Wangh, Martin 32
Watson, Thomas L. S5
Watts, Robert A. 97
Webster, Margaret 54
West, Robert H. 79
Whittaker, Virgil K. 81
Wilson, Harold S. 55
Wilson, J. Dover E3
Wilson John 8
Wright, Louis B. E6
Zeisler, A. 43

Short Titles of Collections of <u>Othello</u> Criticism

Some entries cited in the bibliography may be found in the following collections. An asterisk (*) before the title indicates that the book is available in paperback. Dates of paperback editions are listed second in each entry of the bibliography.

Dean—*A Casebook on Othello, ed. Leonard Dean. New York: Crowell, 1961.

NV—*Othello: A New Variorum Edition, ed. H. H. Furness [1886], with introduction and supplementary bibliography by Louis Marder. New York Dover, 1963.

Ridler—Shakespeare Criticism 1919–35, ed. Anne Ridler. London: Oxford University Press, 1936; *Shakespeare Criticism 1935–60. London: Oxford Paperbacks, 1970.

Shakespeare Encyclopedia—The Reader's Encyclopedia of Shakespeare, eds. O. J. Campbell and Edward G. Quinn. New York: Crowell, 1966.

Smith—Eighteenth-Century Essays on Shakespeare, ed. D. Nichol Smith. Second Edition. London: Oxford Press, 1963.

Wain—*Othello: A Casebook, ed. John Wain. London: Macmillan, 1971.

The Criticism of <u>Othello</u>

INTRODUCTION

By the time of Coleridge the three problems that would largely occupy critics of *Othello* for the next century and a half were already established: (1) the integrity of the plot, (2) the character of Othello, and (3) the motives of Iago. The first of these critical problems has evolved two aspects: (1) the relative effectiveness of the long first act (and its structural relationship to the rest of the play), and (2) the astonishing brevity between the landing at Cyprus, at the beginning of Act II, and the murder of Desdemona less than twenty-four hours later—during which time the war is ended with the Turks, Montano has time to arrive from Venice to relieve Othello of command, and Iago executes his elaborate conspiracy against the lovers.

Shakespeare's eighteenth-century critics, writing under the aegis of the neo-classic "rules," concerned themselves chiefly but not exclusively with the first of these three problems. The earliest critic of *Othello*, Thomas Rymer, a lawyer with a Calvinistic passion for logic and a strong preference for the neo-classic dramas of Racine over the romantic plays of Shakespeare, found *Othello* to be most vulnerable in its "irregularities" and "absurdities" of plot. In his spectacularly irreverent diatribe, *A Short View of Tragedy* (1693), Rymer excoriated the play for its disregard of the "unities," its "farcical" conflict of sexual jealousy, and its childish "improbabilities." T. S. Eliot's statement, "I have never seen a cogent refutation of Thomas Rymer's objections to *Othello*" ("Hamlet and His Problems," *Selected Essays 1917–32*), is in itself illustrative of a certain perversity of judgment which has haunted *Othello* criticism since Rymer's essay.

Certainly Rymer's stiff-necked but quite systematic attack was not cogently refuted by his contemporaries. Charles Gildon replied with *Some Reflections on Mr. Rymer's Short Views of Tragedy and an Attempt at a Vindication of Shakespeare* (1694), which croaked of the bard's "noble irregularity" in notes as dissonant as its puff-title. John Dennis, in five dialogues entitled *The Impartial Critic* (1693), defended Shakespeare's native drama against classical theories. But these essays (like Dryden's great *Essay of Dramatic Poesy*), following hard upon Rymer's attack, pertain to the story of Shakespeare's reputation in general, and not necessarily to criticism of *Othello*.

The first important evaluation of the play after Rymer was by Samuel Johnson. In his emphasis on the plot, he conceded that Act I was indeed too long, but insisted that the rest of the play was admirably economical and compressed. And, although one of his notes suggests that he found Desdemona's murder as painful as Cordelia's, he did not censure *Othello* for any absence of poetic justice. If, as Boswell tells us in his *Life*, Johnson often (but not always) awakened with a start of terror after reading a Shakespearean tragedy, then the exception among Shakespeare's more sobering plays probably was *Othello*—of the four major tragedies, the one least concerned overtly with malevolent nature or omnipresent natural evil.

The eighteenth-century critics of *Othello* are available in two types of sources: collections of critical essays, and surveys of criticism with modern commentary. The best collection of eighteenth-century essays is that edited by Smith—and, as a supplement, Smith's *Shakespeare Criticism*, 2nd edn. (London: Oxford University Press, 1916). There is also a collection by B. E. Warner, *Famous Introductions to Shakespeare's Plays in the Eighteenth Century*. Two excellent surveys of early criticism are by D. Nichol Smith, *Shakespeare in the Eighteenth Century* (London: Oxford University Press, 1928), and by R. W. Babcock, *The Genesis of Shakespeare Idolatry 1776–1799* (Chapel Hill: University of North Carolina Press, 1931).

With the advent of romanticism and its attendant quickening of psychological interest, the focus of *Othello* criticism shifted from plot to characterization, and especially to Othello's character and Iago's motives. Schlegel's lectures, *Über dramatische Kunst und Literatur*, and Coleridge's first series of lectures on Shakespeare, both delivered in 1808, mark the inception of this new era. Unlike Coleridge, Schlegel was concerned chiefly with the discovery of Shakespeare's creative sensibilities, or "soul" (an approach not initiated in English criticism until Dowden), whereas Coleridge set out to justify every aspect of Shakespeare's art. Hence, Coleridge's description of Iago as a motiveless, motive-hunting malignity is not a negative comment but a tribute to Shakespeare's profound use of symbolism. A desultory critic who scattered his ideas over notes, essays, marginalia, and conversations, Coleridge was nevertheless a powerfully intuitive reader who nourished more systematic if not equally brilliant minds. His criticism of *Othello* charted a course for later critics: If Iago is, indeed, "motiveless," what impels his evil actions? Inevitably, perhaps, Coleridge's motiveless Iago led subsequent critics toward a consideration of external forces—toward the theatrical conventions stressed by Stoll (14) and Spivack (59), or toward the Christian allegories of Battenhouse (98), Bethell (37) and Siegel(53).

Collections of essays by romantic critics of the plays are in *His Infinite Variety*, ed. Paul N. Siegel (Philadelphia, 1964,) and in *Four Centuries of Shakespearean Criticism*, ed. Frank Kermode (New York, 1965). Excerpts from the essays of many romantic critics, and especially of the German, are in NV. Critical surveys include those by Augustus Ralli, *A History of Shakespeare Criticism*, 2 vols., I (Oxford, 1932), and A. M. Eastman, *A Short History of Shakespearean Criticism* (New York, 1968). For American criticism during this period, see A. V. R. Westfall, *American Shakespearean Criticism, 1607–1865* (New York, 1939). There are concise surveys in the Shakespeare Encyclopedia and in M. A. Shaaber, "Shakespeare Criticism: Dryden to Bradley," *A New Companion to Shakespeare Studies*, ed. Kenneth Muir and S. Schoenbaum (Cambridge University Press, 1971), pp. 239–248.

The Victorian period saw the first systematization of Shakespeare studies—the founding of organizations and journals—and the emergence of titans like Edward Dowden and H. H. Furness. That long-neglected story, with a great deal of fascinating behind-the-scenes biographical data, is related by Aron Y. Stravisky in *Shakespeare and the Victorians: Roots of Modern Criticism* (University of Oklahoma Press, 1969). Much Victorian criticism, including the criticism of mid-nineteenth-century German writers, is summarized in NV.

After Edward Dowden (9), the first great critic of *Othello* was A. C. Bradley (12), whose Lectures V and VI in his *Shakespearean Tragedy* (1904) revived all three problems of plot, Othello's character, and Iago's motives. Appropriately called "the last of the romantic critics," Bradley descends in his criticism of *Othello* directly from Coleridge (4), Hazlitt (7), and Swinburne (10). Was Bradley a perceptive critic of the play? Much of the answer depends upon how one defines the proper mission of criticism. Certainly Bradley's lectures on *Othello* are the least original, forceful, or synoptic of any of his on the four major tragedies, and yet his two essays on *Othello* were supremely successful. He recognized that the play was unique among the tragedies for its plot design; he emphasized the relevance of sexual jealousy to Othello's stature as tragic hero; and he underscored the thematic significance of Iago's motives or absence of motives.

Indeed, most twentieth-century critics of the play after A. C. Bradley—the generation of Heilman and Ribner—were schooled for combat by Stoll-versus-Bradley skirmishes, with G. Wilson Knight intervening to provide new critical weapons and vistas of conquest. Nevertheless, Knight's essay on *Othello* (19) was not as immensely influential as was his work on the other three major tragedies. To read Knight's "The *Othello* Music" again, forty years later, is to be struck by its strangely uninspired and uncertain passages—and to be taken aback by his unaccountable preference for *Timon of Athens* over *Othello.*

Knight's failure to do critical justice to the play exemplifies an emergent fact about *Othello* criticism since Bradley—that is, that the greatest critics have contributed little if anything to solving the recurring problems of plot, Othello's character, and Iago's motives. Many boggle over "irregularities" of plot in Act I; freeze on the point of Othello's rapid conversion from love to hatred in III. 3, or lose themselves in archly complex "double time" schemes. Stuck in the past on Bradley, they quibble interminably over the role of "chance," or harking back to Coleridge, split hairs over whether Othello was innately jealous, inclined to be jealous, or just apparently jealous. The theological critics, on the other hand, seem strangely preoccupied with the extra-literary debate over whether Othello is destined for heaven, hell, or purgatory. Few critics have succeeded in conveying a vision of the play as a totally integrated and supremely artistic masterpiece. Moreover, some of the most frivolous criticism of *Othello*, notably the parenthetical comments by Eliot (20)— who may not have been entirely serious in that essay—and the tour de force by F. R. Leavis (23) have precipitated reactions far in excess of what they deserve.

At present, the theological interpretation of *Othello* is clearly dominant. In its ranks are some of the most distinguished critics of our time, and even those who are instinctively secular and devoid of allegorical literalism—Granville-Barker (27), Charlton (26), Heilman (49), and, most recently, Stanley Edgar Hyman (100)—conclude major critical studies of *Othello* by endorsing the real or imagined "Christian assumptions" inherent in the play. Readers weary of submerged Christ figures and inverted Judas symbols can, however, seize on the comforting fact illustrated by the survey of criticism that follows—namely, that no approach purporting to pluck out the mystery of *Othello* has long endured, and that in criticism, as in nature, mutations are always recurring and are therefore inevitable. Hopefully, such changes will reveal an *Othello* less obscure than the play described by G. Wilson Knight as "a lone thing of meaningless beauty in the Shakespearean universe."

There are brief surveys of twentieth-century criticism of *Othello* in the Shakespeare Encyclopedia and by Gardner (48). Emphasis is given to twentieth-century critics by Patrick Murray in *The Shakespearean Scene* (New York, 1969); see also the account by Stanley Wells, "Shakespeare Criticism Since Bradley," in *A New Companion to Shakespeare Studies*, pp. 249–261. Works of individual authors are listed in S. A. Tannenbaum, *Othello: A Concise Bibliography* (New York, 1943), in the annual bibliographies of *PMLA*, *Shakespeare Quarterly* (since 1949), and in "The Year's Contributions to Shakespearean Study," *Shakespeare Survey* (since 1948, with Cumulative Index of Volumes I-X in Volume X).

ENTRIES FOR THE CRITICISM OF *OTHELLO*

The titles of some journals are abbreviated as follows:

CE: College English
Critical Q: Critical Quarterly
ELH: Journal of English Literary History
ES: English Studies
PQ: Philological Quarterly
RES: Review of English Studies
SEL: Studies in English Literature 1500–1900
SJ: Shakespeare Jahrbuch
SP: Studies in Philology
SQ: Shakespeare Quarterly

1. Rymer, Thomas. *A Short View of Tragedy* [London, 1693]. Standard modern edition: *The Critical Works of Thomas Rymer*, ed. Curt Zimansky. Yale University Press, 1956, pp. 132–164. Excerpts reprinted in Dean and Wain.

A disciple of French neo-classicism who correctly viewed Shakespeare as the chief threat to the reforming of native English Romanticism, Rymer selected *Othello* as his target chiefly because of its popularity and because its domestic conflict made it susceptible to treatment as comedy or farce. Rymer attacks the play for gross improbabilities of plot and characterization. Othello, as a jealous husband, lacks the character of a soldier as portrayed in Greek and Roman drama, and Desdemona is dismissed as "silly." Rymer concludes that the play is not a true tragedy but "a bloody farce, without salt or savour." (For Rymer's critical precepts, see Marvin T. Herrick, *The Poetics of Aristotle in England.* Oxford University Press, 1930, pp. 57–62.)

2. Johnson, Samuel. *Johnson on Shakespeare* [1756–65], ed. Walter Raleigh. London: Oxford University Press, 1908. (See also Johnson's criticism of Shakespeare edited by W. K. Wimsatt [New York, 1960], and by Arthur Sherbo [New Haven, 1968]. See also Smith, pp. 9–63.)

Johnson's comprehensive interpretations of the plays are contained in his *Proposals for Printing the Dramatic Works of William Shakespeare* (1756), in his preface to the edition of the complete works (1765), and in his notes to that edition. Although he thought Act I of *Othello* too loosely connected, he found the rest of "a most exact and scrupulous regularity." He read Iago's seduction of Othello as being wholly convincing, and, with a critical eye toward Rymer and Voltaire, praised *Othello* as "the vigorous and vivacious offspring of observation impregnated by genius." With characteristic good sense, he discounted the neoclassic "rules" as irrelevant to Shakespeare's unique artistry.

3. Pompignan, Jean-Jacques Le Franc. *Notice de deux Tragedies Angloises.* Paris, 1784.

This criticism of *Othello* by a distinguished French dramatist has escaped the notice of most literary historians. Pompignan's condemnation of the play is even more vehement than Rymer's or Voltaire's. He finds the characters unrealistic, poorly drawn, and contemptible. The plot, he charges, is absurdly improbable and poorly constructed, and there is no tragic action developed until Act V. Moreover, he sees "the unseemly emphasis" on sexuality and violence as incompatible with the gravity required of genuine tragedy. Like Rymer, Pompignan is classical to the bone and prefers the plays of Corneille and Racine to Shakespeare's romantic dramas. (For a discussion of Pompignan's critical theories, see

Theodore E. D. Braun, "A French Classicist's View of Shakespeare," *Romantic Notes* [Spring 1970], pp. 569–573.)

4. Coleridge, Samuel Taylor. *Coleridge's Shakespearean Criticism* [1808], ed. Thomas M. Raysor, 2 vols. London, 1907. Reprinted by Harvard University Press, 1930, 1960. (See also the edition by Terence Hawkes. New York, 1959.)

Coleridge's comments on *Othello* are scattered throughout his notes for the lectures of 1808–18, his marginalia, and his *Table-Talk*. He defends the dramatic integrity of Act I against the reservations of Johnson (2); insists that Othello is a noble hero not jealous by nature but aroused by moral indignation and offended honor; and, in a famous passage, describes Iago's soliloquies and testimony as "the motive-hunting of a motiveless malignity." This last, very influential, judgment may have been tentative; for he seems to have modified it some years later (see Elinor S. Shaffer [4]). On the racial theme, Coleridge's notes record that "it would be something monstrous to conceive this beautiful Venetian girl falling in love with a veritable Negro," but Raysor states that this passage may have been interpolated by H. N. Coleridge.

4. Jackson, J. R. de J. "Free Will in Coleridge's Shakespeare," *University of Toronto Q.*, XXVIII (1968), 34–56.

A major article showing how Coleridge's change from Hartleyan materialism to a philosophy of free will may have altered his ideas about characters he had previously discussed as unmotivated in *Othello, Macbeth,* and *Lear.*

4. Shaffer, Elinor S. "Iago's Malignity Motivated: Coleridge's Unpublished 'Opus Magnum'," *SQ*, XVIII (1968).

This important article is based on the author's inferences from Coleridge's unpublished notebooks at Victoria College, University of Toronto. Although in his early comments Coleridge described Iago as "motiveless," in these later notes he attributes Iago's conduct to a subordination of morality to intellect, to "thinking of moral feelings and qualities only as prudential ends to means." According to Shaffer, this conception led Coleridge to think of Iago as a villain who had accepted Machiavellian precepts, and this particular kind of cynicism—"the last extreme of self-alienation," according to Coleridge—drained Othello of his identity as an idealist.

5. Lamb, Charles. *The Works of Charles Lamb.* London, 1870, III, pp. 102ff. Excerpt reprinted in NV.

Lamb's criticism of *Othello* appeared originally in Leigh Hunt's *Reflector* in 1810. As with *Lear,* Lamb believed that any dramatization of *Othello* spoiled the play; seeing a black Othello interferes with Desdemona's view of him ("I saw Othello's visage in *my mind*"). Seeing Othello with our own eyes rather than reading about him through Desdemona's is a repulsive experience, for there is "something revolting in the courtship and wedded caresses of Othello and Desdemona." Thus Lamb's comments represent the *reductio ad absurdum* of the "unactable Shakespeare" of the romantic critics. (Nevertheless, their disregard for the theatre ought not be condemned until one has read Rosenberg [St4] and learned how wretchedly Bowdlerized *Othello* was on the stage in the early 1800's.)

6. Schlegel, A. W. *Lectures on Dramatic Art and Literature,* trans. John Black, 2 vols. London, 1815, II, pp. 189ff. Excerpt reprinted in NV.

Schlegel's essay is a general dithyramb, but it exerted great influence on his contemporaries. He describes a savage, passionate Othello illustrative of the "tyranny of the blood over the will." Unlike Desdemona, who is of "angelic purity," Othello is divided between the higher and lower spheres of soul and passion. Schlegel's view may have prompted later critics to see *Othello* as a morality play.

7. Hazlitt, William. *The Characters of Shakespeare's Plays.* London, 1817, pp. 54ff. Excerpt reprinted in NV and Dean.

Partly inspired by the lectures of Schlegel [6] in 1808, this book is the most specific treatment of Shakespeare's characters by an early romantic critic. Hazlitt focuses on Iago, whom he presents as a moral and philosophical abstraction, "a diseased activity" destructive of all human values.

8. Wilson, John. *"Othello." Blackwood's Magazine* (November, 1849; April, 1850; May, 1850). Reprinted in *Transactions of the New Shakespeare Society* (1875-76; 1877-79).

Wilson was the first to propose a time scheme for the play. Noting the brevity of time elapsing from the landing at Cyprus at the beginning of Act II and the murder of Desdemona less than thirty-six hours later, Wilson suggested that the play presents two experiences—actual time versus "long time," the latter being the illusion of time passing created by the language and action. For a précis of Wilson's discussion see *NV*, pp. 358-372.

9. Dowden, Edward. *Shakespeare: A Critical Study of His Mind and Art.* London, 1875. Excerpt reprinted in NV.

This book represents the first full-scale interpretation of the plays and the most influential critical study after Coleridge's Shakespeare lectures. Dividing Shakespeare's work into the four distinct periods of "In the Workshop," "In the World," "Out of the Depths," and "On the Heights," Dowden attributes *Othello* to the "depths" because the play reveals "severity" in its disregard for human motives and rational reasons, and in its denial of any justifications of pain and evil. Nevertheless, in contrast to later critics such as Granville-Barker (27) and Charlton(26), he finds in the play a pervasive "moral vision" which sees the lovers as spiritually victorious, with Desdemona forgiving Othello (who dies upon a kiss of reconciliation), and only the totally evil Iago suffering defeat. The conflict in the play is between Iago, symbolic of a satanic intellect devoid of beauty, and Othello, representative of "barbaric innocence and regal magnificence of soul." Dowden's interpretation held the center of the critical stage until the work by Bradley (12).

10. Swinburne, A. C. *A Study of Shakespeare.* London, 1879.

The essay on *Othello* first appeared in two installments of *The Fortnightly Review* (May, 1875; June, 1876). Unlike much of Swinburne's literary criticism, which inclines to ethereal rhapsody, his analysis of *Othello* is suprisingly coherent. Othello is the "noblest man of man's making," Iago his antithesis, "a demi-devil" but also "an inarticulate poet" (a phrase from Thomas Carlyle employed later by Bradley). Iago is, as Coleridge suggests, motiveless; but he is driven nevertheless by unused resources of satanic power. Swinburne's essay, which seems to have been suggested in part by Hazlitt (7), is a vivid characterization of Iago that influenced Bradley and other critics. It still warrants a careful reading.

11. Shaw, George Bernard. *Shaw on Shakespeare* [1897], ed. Edwin Wilson. Baltimore: Penguin Books, 1969 (pp. 152–156 in the 1962 edition). Reprinted from articles in *Saturday Review* (May 29, 1897; March 12, 1898) and *The Anglo-Saxon Review* (March, 1901). Excerpt in Dean.

Shaw admired the play for its "word music" but condemned the characters and action: "Tested by the brain, it is ridiculous; tested by the ear, it is sublime." Desdemona is a "prima donna," the plot "pure farce." Characteristically, Shaw gives advice to actors on how the play ought to be performed.

12. Bradley, A. C. *Shakespearean Tragedy* [1904]. New York: Macmillan, 1970. Excerpt in Dean.

Chapters V and VI of this immensely influential book examine every detail of action and testimony as if the characters were actual people. Chapter V is discursive, as if Bradley were searching for a key to open the play: he discusses the unique construction of the plot, the absence of comedy, the major conflict (sexual jealousy), and the element of "chance" in determining events. Unlike most critics, Bradley sees the situation in the play as wholly feasible—any husband, according to Bradley, would have been troubled by Iago's intrigue. Othello is supremely heroic and poetic ("the greatest poet of Shakespeare's heroes") but unaccustomed to reflection and inclined to instantaneous action.

In agreement with Coleridge(4), Bradley argues that Othello was not innately jealous. Bradley tends to accept the testimony of other characters but insists that everything Iago says must be interpreted critically as the statements of a habitual liar. Under the influence of Swinburne (10), he discusses Iago as a supreme artist of evil, "cold by temperament" and with great powers of self-control. He rejects the "motiveless" Iago of Coleridge, and presents an Iago motivated by unconscious forces, chiefly by an obsession for power. His "thwarted sense of superiority wants satisfaction." Like his "melancholy" Hamlet, Bradley's unconscious Iago opened the way to psychoanalytic interpretations.

13. Moulton, Richard G. **Shakespeare as a Dramatic Artist: A Popular Illustration of the Principles of Scientific Criticism.* Oxford University Press, 1906.

Eclipsed by Bradley's book, with its more urbane style and superior human interest, Moulton's comprehensive study is still of some value in spite of its awkard terminology and pretentious claims to "scientific objectivity." Pages 225 to 245 constitute a very through analysis of the formal aspects of plot in *Othello*, and Moulton's demonstration of the unity of the plot is still, in some respects, a definitive critical performance.

14. Stoll, E. E. *Othello: An Historical and Comparative Study.* Cambridge University Press, 1915.

This is the first of several important books on Shakespeare by Stoll; others include *Hamlet* (1919), *Art and Artifice* (1934), and *Shakespeare's Young Lovers* (1935). In all of these Stoll attacks critics like Bradley (12), whose psychological interpretations cause them to treat characters as if they were real people instead of imaginary dramatic creations designed to appeal to the taste of an Elizabethan audience. In *Othello* Stoll finds characterization less important than plot and language. In contrast to later critics such as Clemen (34) and Stauffer (29), he stresses the importance of the poetry without attending very closely to specific imagery or word patterns. He is mainly concerned with Elizabethan stage conventions, literary traditions, and techniques of characterization—with recreating the emotional and intellectual expectations of what he believed to be a "typical" Elizabethan audience. In his efforts to attribute to the "Othello of Shakespeare's audience" moral and artistic values and traditions radically different from those in the modern theatre, Stoll anticipated such historical critics as Campbell (18), Draper (38), and, in one sense, Spivack (59).

14. *Art and Artifice in Shakespeare: A Study in Dramatic Contrast and Illusion.* London: Cambridge University Press, 1934.

Chapter II and most of the Appendix of this volume represent the completion of what Stoll began in his first important work, *Othello* (1915). The two studies differ only slightly in methodology and con-

clusions. Certainly this second book contains much more forensic justification of his approach than is actually required. In 1934 Stoll's old
adversary, A. C. Bradley, is replaced by G. Wilson Knight (19), who,
as had Bradley, "ignores the play as a play."

To the distress of the New Critics, Stroll stoutly maintains that
his critical goal is the revelation of "the author's *intention*." Characteristically, he frees the reader from any "psychologizing" of characters:
Othello's conversion to jealousy is "psychologically impossible" but
quite feasible as a tragic *convention*, as a "constructive artifice" pertain-
ing to legend and myth rather than to real people. Similarly, Iago's
"motives" are best understood with reference to the conventional Machiavellian stage villain. Instead of "unity" (that shibboleth of the New
Critics in 1934) Stoll finds that the plot of Othello is "Gothic" and "ex-
uberant," its underlying unity an "illusion never broken." For his almost
dialectical consistency, Stoll represents an important landmark in the
criticism of Othello.

14. "Slander in Drama," *SQ*, IV (1953), 533–550.

Without accepting the psychological validity of the situation, the
Elizabethan audience would have comprehended Iago's slander of Desdemona for two reasons: Othello has been portrayed as "nobly credulous," Iago as an "honest" man with a reputation for wisdom. Characteristically, Stoll views the action in the context of stage conventions rather
than of psychological probability.

15. Brooke, C. F. Tucker. "The Romantic Iago," *Yale Review*, VII
(1918), 3–59.

One of the earliest and most eloquent presentations of Iago as
"misunderstood" rather than villainous. From the perspective of the
Elizabethan audience, Iago would have been no more villainous than
Falstaff but, rather, a confused man who commits wrongs through no fault
of his own.

16. Schücking, Levin L. *Character Problems in Shakespeare's Plays*.
London: Harrap and Co., 1922, pp. 63 ff.

Like Stoll (14), Schücking opposed Bradley's psychological approach and attempted to interpret the plays in the light of Elizabethan

stage conventions. Like Clemen (34) in treating imagery, he also viewed a character in the context of characters in Shakespeare's other plays. In this essay he compares Iago with Thersites in *Troilus and Cressida,* and with Macbeth. He argues that Iago, as a stage villain, requires no "probable" psychological motive except the conventional ones of envy and revenge. Unlike Heilman(49) and other later critics, Schücking insists that the testimony of Iago—like that of Shakespeare's other villains—cannot be read as clues to the hero's true character. In spite of its weaknesses in dealing with language, this is a major work that must be read in its entirety.

17. Chambers, E. K. *Shakespeare: A Survey* [1925]. London: Hill and Wang, 1958; Baltimore: Penguin Books, 1970.

In six pages (218–225 in the 1925 edition), Chambers gives a concise, trenchant analysis following the approach of Dowden (9) by interpreting the play in terms of Shakespeare's emotional and philosophical development. In *Othello,* he finds, "the issue has shifted from the relations of man and man [*Julius Caesar, Hamlet*] to the relations of man and his creator [*Macbeth, Lear*]." Othello is noble but doomed, "a child in spirit"; and Iago is motivated by "the willingness of evil to be convinced of evil." Chambers's view that Iago manipulates souls "like puppets" is vehemently opposed by Kirschbaum (75). Chambers finds the genesis of Iago in Marlowe's Barabas, his later development in Iachimo of *Cymbeline.*

18. Campbell, Lily B. *Shakespeare's Tragic Heroes: Slaves of Passion* [1930]. London: Methuen, 1970, pp. 148–174.

By reference to Elizabethan medieval and psychological treatises, and especially to Varchi's *Blazon of Jealousie,* translated by Robert Tofte (1615), Campbell sets out to establish what is denied by Coleridge (4) and Bradley (12)—that is, that Othello was in fact afflicted by chronic jealousy. She accepts Iago's testimony regarding his own motives; consistent with Elizabethan psychological theory, Iago's frustration changed to envy, then finally to rage and hatred.

19. Knight, G. Wilson. * "The *Othello* Music," in *The Wheel of Fire.* London, 1930. Reprinted by Ridler (I, 347–371) and Wain.

The "music" originates in two worlds, Othello's and Iago's, and discord occurs when Iago usurps Othello's harmony and Othello, in turn, descends to Iago's animal world. Othello's language is described as "over-decorated, highly coloured," and it ultimately "fails of a supreme effect." (Compare the conclusion of Clemen [34], who finds Othello's imagery suggestive of sincerity, innocence, and "integrity.") The dominant motif of the play (picked up subsequently by Bayley [62] and other critics) is alienation and separation, a mood reinforced by Othello's "detached" dialogue. Othello's fatal flaw is simplicity, Iago's motive a devilish cynicism —and "other suggestions are surface deep only." Unlike the other three major tragedies, *Othello* is devoid of "universal truth" and "divorced from wider issues."

19. *Principles of Shakespearean Production.* London: Faber and Faber, 1935, pp. 134–152.

This is a fascinating account of a performance directed by Knight at the Hart House Theatre, Toronto, in December, 1934. Knight explains how the experience of producing *Othello* modified greatly his concept of the play set forth in *The Wheel of Fire.*

20. Eliot, T. S. "Shakespeare and the Stoicism of Seneca," *Selected Essays 1917–32.* New York, 1932. Also in *Elizabethan Essays.* London: Faber and Faber, 1934. Reprinted in Ridley (I, 209–225) and in Wain.

This controversial, influential essay centers on Othello's concluding speech. According to Eliot, "What Othello seems to me to be doing in making this speech is *cheering himself up*"—which is to say, deceiving himself even further by attempting to escape the reality of his crime. Eliot's Othello is ignorant, egotistical, and self-centered, the very antithesis of the humble Christian. (For the most detailed criticism of this essay, see Clifford Leech, *Shakespeare's Tragedies and Other Studies in Seventeenth Century Drama* [New York, 1950], pp. 87–110.)

21. Bodkin, Maud. *Archetypal Patterns in Poetry.* London: Oxford University Press, 1934, Chap. V, pp. 217 ff.

In this seminal study employing the precepts of Jungian psychology, with its emphasis on myths and symbols, Bodkin contrasts Shakespeare's Iago and Goethe's Mephistopheles, and studies the emotional effects of the landing on Cyprus. She is not so much concerned with analyzing characters as with probing effects on the reader—that is, on "experience communicated to *ourselves* when we live in the art of the play." In Appendix II she skillfully defends this approach against objections to "psychological criticism" made by Stoll (14).

22. Spurgeon, Caroline. *Shakespeare's Imagery and What It Tells Us.* London: Cambridge University Press, 1935.

This pioneer study can be consulted as a convenient encyclopedia listing the images, by topic and patterns, in *Othello*. In spite of its sometimes vague conception of imagery and its futile effort to infer specific biographical data from Shakespeare's language, it is still valuable for its exhaustive, statistical lists of images and its emphasis on the contrasts of images used by different characters. Especially enlightening is Spurgeon's analysis of Iago's influence on Othello's language after III.iii.

23. Leavis, F. R. "Diabolic Intellect and the Noble Hero; Or, the Sentimentalist's *Othello*," *Scrutiny*, VI, No. 3 December, 1937. Reprinted in F. R. Leavis, *The Common Pursuit* (London: Chatto and Windus, 1952), pp. 136–159, and in Wain, pp. 123–146.

Although this essay has become a point of departure for much subsequent criticism of *Othello*, it is difficult to see how anyone could take Leavis' impressionistic diatribe very seriously. With some motive more parochial than Eliot's religious bias, Leavis picks up where Eliot left off by describing Othello as the "simplest" of Shakespeare's tragedies, and the play itself as totally devoid of "symbolical ambiguities." Among critics his chief targets are Coleridge (for denying that Othello was jealous), Stoll, and especially Bradley (a "mischievous influence"). Iago, Leavis argues, is only "ancillary" to the action because in Act III.iii, Othello falls with "extraordinary promptness to suggestion." Presumably, even Roderigo could have seduced him. According to Leavis, Othello is of "ferocious stupidity" and cannot be considered "noble" in any sense.

23. Everett, Barbara. "Reflections on the Sentimentalist's *Othello*," *Critical Q*, III (1961), 127–39.

The most lengthy and detailed refutation of Leavis. It challenges the legitimacy of his critical assumptions and methods.

24. Myrick, Kenneth. "The Theme of Damnation in Shakespeare's Tragedies," *SP*, XXXVIII (1941), 221–245.

In this seminal article on religion in *Hamlet, Macbeth,* and *Othello,* Myrick stresses the importance of the themes of guilt, repentance, and damnation to Elizabethans, for whom "enticements of the devil" were "daily experience." Not an allegorical or symbolic study, this article proposes that Shakespeare's three tragedies appeal to "a mood essentially religious and Christian." Myrick's work represents a forerunner to the more symbolic, literal interpretations of Christian ideas set forth by Siegel (53) and other "theological" critics.

25. Spencer, Theodore. **Shakespeare and the Nature of Man.* London and New York: Macmillan, 1942, Chap. 5, pp. 122–135.

Spencer compares Iago with the traditional characters of (1) Vice in the morality plays, (2) Machiavellian villain, and (3) Senecan villain-hero. He concludes that Iago is a unique conception—a character who, in the total discipline of his passions, suggests the Renaissance ideal of virtue and yet, ironically, is entirely bad. Spencer's conception of Iago as "an emotional eunuch" continues the interpretation by Bradley (12). Spencer discusses at length the philosophical significance of the Turks as symbolic of chaos, and Venice as representative of civilization and order. This interpretation is further developed by Kernan (39).

26. Charlton, H. B. *Shakespearean Tragedy.* London: Cambridge University Press, 1948, pp. 113–40.

Much of this essay analyzes Shakespeare's treatment of Cinthio's tale. The time scheme is also treated at length, especially the "double time" concept of Granville-Barker (27). Othello's conversion to Christianity is emphasized: although consciously a Christian, he is unconsciously, emotionally "primitive," and this dualism causes his tragedy. Charlton concludes with a theological interpreation of the play.

27. Granville-Barker, Harley. **Prefaces to Shakespeare,* 4 vols., Vol. IV: *Othello* [1948]. Princeton University Press, 1963.

This is an important essay by a critic who is both an erudite scholar and an experienced actor and theatre director. His criticism represents an informed reaction against such romantic critics as Coleridge, Hazlitt, and Bradley, who discussed Shakespeare's characters as real people rather than artistic creations intended for stage presentation. Granville-Barker studies Cinthio as a clue to Shakespeare's artistry, examines the unity of the plot (in reply to Samuel Johnson), and explains the time scheme after Act I as "double time," the actual time of twenty-four hours or less from the landing in Cyprus, and "dramatic time," the artistic illusion conveyed on the stage. His concept of the time scheme is an elaboration on the ideas first suggested by John Wilson (8). He pauses to analyze pools of action outside the mainstream of the plot—Othello's slapping of Desdemona, for example—in order to show how these relate to greater emotional affects. Following Hazlitt (7) and Swinburne (10), he interprets Iago as a demonic artist whose medium (not unexpectedly, in view of Granville-Barker's own interest) is *acting:* "Love of his art for its own sake turns him egoist." If Iago is the "artist in real life," Othello is "the poet born."

28. Sedgewick, G. G. *Of Irony, Especially in Drama.* Toronto: University of Toronto Press, 1948, pp. 85–116.

Chapter IV, entitled "Irony as Dramatic Preparation: *Othello*," is from Sedgewick's Alexander Lectures at Toronto University. In replying to Rymer (1) and Stoll (14), who agreed for quite different reasons that Othello's rapid seduction by Iago in III.3 is grossly improbable, Sedgewick shows how Othello's fall is anticipated and thoroughly prepared for by dramatic irony in Acts I and II. Iago's "web of trust" creates a dramatic irony so pervasive that Othello's submission to Iago's will becomes, for the audience, a required fulfillment of expectations. Thus, in terms of the "psychology of life," Othello's quick seduction by Iago is incredible; by what Sedgewick terms the "psychology of drama," however, it becomes entirely "probable" and even inevitable in view of Shakespeare's sustained concentration on dramatic irony in Acts I and II. Thus, both Rymer and Stoll err in seeing Othello's seduction as "incredible" because, according to Sedgewick, ". . . it is not a train of argument or a body of convention that makes an event credible, but an attitude of mind induced one way or another in the spectator by a train of actions pointing . . . to that event." Sedgewick is especially detailed in his analysis of dramatic irony in Act I.

29. Stauffer, Donald A. *Shakespeare's World of Images: The Development of His Moral Ideas.* New York: Norton, 1949, pp. 163–220.

This important essay continues, with considerable linguistic sophistication and a combining of different techniques, the works of Dowden (9) and Clemen (34). *Othello* is seen as belonging to a period in Shakespeare's development when the only moral certainty was that man creates his own fate (an idea in opposition to the emphasis on chance first stressed by Bradley). Iago is a social outcast who, in his alienation, inverts all moral values. With Sisson (72), Stauffer categorically denies that the play can be classified as a domestic tragedy.

30. Stewart, J. I. M. *Character and Motive in Shakespeare* [1949]. London: Longman, 1965.

In this major critical work the characters are approached in the manner of Bradley; the dramatic situations are seen to be realistic and profoundly psychological, yet infused with complex symbolism. The chief symbolic conflict is Othello's struggle to achieve spiritual realization versus Iago's efforts to stunt and corrupt his potentially noble soul. Stewart's most original insight is his conception of Time as a character in the play (an idea he imaginatively relates to the time scheme after Act I): Time, shown to be as inimical to love in this play as it is in the Sonnets and elsewhere, is Iago's natural ally. Like Iago, Time is "calumniating" and "envious." Stewart gives a systematic analysis of the criticism by Bradley (12), Stoll (14), and Schücking (16).

31. Flatter, Richard. *The Moor of Venice.* London: Heinemann, 1950.

Like the author's previous book on Shakespeare, *Hamlet's Father,* this one combines conventional treatment of elementary questions with some rather unorthodox and sometimes bizarre critical opinions. Flatter thoroughly examines each character with attention to the major problems raised by critics from Coleridge to G. Wilson Knight, but his admirable specificity is often lost in an exclamatory, impressionistic style of writing. He agrees with Granville-Barker (27) in interpreting Iago as a character who is obsessed with "a craze for play-making," a villain who is not consciously motivated, yet not entirely a symbolic abstraction. Iago is an entirely human and even "natural" villain driven by an insatiable lust for "self-aggrandisement." Othello, though neither credulous nor simple-minded, is nevertheless "a jealous fool." *Othello* criticism since Coleridge is thoughtfully surveyed, especially in the early portion of the book.

32. Wangh, Martin. "*Othello:* The Tragedy of Iago," *Psychoanalytic Quarterly,* XIX (1950), 202–212.

One of the earliest and most influential of the psychoanalytic treatments, this one argues that Iago is motivated by a "delusional jealousy" of Desdemona that is, in turn, inspired by homosexual obsession for Othello. Like most psychoanalytic studies, this assumes that any rational explanation of Iago's motives is patently absurd. Freudian symbols are discovered everywhere: Iago's raging tooth is a phallus; Othello's handkerchief a breast symbol. (This approach was dramatized on the stage as early as 1938 in a production starring Laurence Olivier as Othello and Ralph Richardson as a homosexual Iago.)

33. Burke, Kenneth. "*Othello:* An Essay to Illustrate a Method," *Hudson Review,* IV (1951), 165–203. Reprinted in **Perspectives by Incongruity* [1951], Indiana University Press paperback, 1970.

An important, influential essay that not only interprets *Othello* but "illustrates" Burke's critical approach, which combines the poetics of Aristotle and Longinus, symbolic logic, Freudian psychology, erudite intuition, and esoteric terminology. There is an extensive analysis of *Othello* with attention to Bradley, to Emilia as a character, to Prospero in *The Tempest,* and to Desdemona, whom Burke sees as "property" versus "aesthetic object."

33. Osborn, Neal J. "Kenneth Burke's Dilemma: A Courtship of Clio?" *Hudson Review,* XIX (1966), 267–275.

A sharp criticism of Burke's essay, especially of his emphasis on Desdemona as "property" rather than heroine loved and in love. Osborn finds a dramatic antithesis of ambition versus sensual values a prime motive not only in *Othello* but in *1 Henry IV, Romeo and Juliet, The Tempest,* and *Anthony and Cleopatra.*

34. Clemen, Wolfang. **The Development of Shakespeare's Imagery* [1951]. London: Methuen, 1970.

This book was originally published in German as *Shakespeares Bilder* (Bonn, 1936), and appeared the same year as Spurgeon's (22). Clemen analyzes the imagery of the plays to establish definite periods of

Shakespeare's development as thinker and artist. In contrast to Dowden (9), who is intuitive and philosophical, or to Spurgeon, who classifies images topically, Clemen attempts to measure the intensity of images and to show how they connect within the play and to other plays. Othello's imagery shows, significantly, that he "never discusses general human values," and it reflects a character that is generous, noble, sincere, and compassionate; yet Othello is preoccupied with himself and oblivious to sophisticated moral abstractions.

35. Empson, William. " 'Honest' in Othello," in *The Structure of Complex Words*. London, 1951. Reprinted in Wain, pp. 98–122.

The words "honest" and "honesty" (occurring fifty-two times) provide a key to Iago's motives and characterization. Turning to the inquiry characteristic of Stoll (14)—"How would an Elizabethan audience have understood the play?"—Empson points out that the word "honest" altered its connotations after the Restoration and that Shakespeare may well have anticipated these changes, playing skillfully upon the multiple ambiguities of "honest." Empson's linguistic research suggests that Elizabethans might not have viewed Iago as purely evil, or even as Machiavellian. At first they may have seen him as fascinating and later as wicked—but always as completely human.

36. Sewell, Arthur. *Character and Society in Shakespeare*. Oxford University Press, 1951, pp. 91–121.

Sewell sees the action in terms of Othello's fall from grace, a movement into a lower sphere. That sphere is symbolized by Venice, the social, pragmatic world that he formerly transcended. This is the world of "means" where usefulness is the primary value. At the conclusion of the play Othello appeals for acquittal in terms of this world—he has done the state some service—but his original condition is, like the innocence of man after the fall, irretrievable.

37. Bethell, S. L. "Shakespeare's Imagery: The Diabolic Images in *Othello*," in *Shakespeare Survey 5*, ed. Allardyce Nicoll. Cambridge University Press, 1952, pp. 62–80.

In this important article, Bethell explains his own methodology in the context of three established approaches to imagery: the psychoanalytic, the contemporaneously relevant (in the way of G. Wilson Knight), and the historical—which attempts to interpret imagery in the light of Elizabethan meanings. For Bethell, imagery in Shakespeare functions in three not entirely mutually exclusive ways: to clarify a passage, to illustrate a character, and to elucidate a theme. In Bethell's careful analysis of the diabolic images in *Othello*, he rejects the "image-hunter's fallacy of treating all similar images as equally significant in spite of their context," and attempts to see the complex interconnections of these three general functions of imagery. He illustrates how imagery reveals theme by contrasting the diabolic imagery of *Macbeth* with Holinshed's very neutral language, and *Othello* with Cinthio's *novella*, which is totally devoid of diabolic imagery. In contrasting *Macbeth* and *Othello* for diabolic imagery, he finds that, although Othello's exotic rhetoric may give readers a different impression, *Othello* is more permeated with eschatological diction than is *Macbeth*.

Bethell reads *Othello* on three coalescing "levels": the personal, wherein it is a domestic tragedy not substantially different from Cinthio's tale; the social, wherein it portrays a struggle between Iago as the atheist Machiavel and Othello as the traditional chivalric hero; and, finally, the metaphysical, wherein it dramatizes the ancient conflict of Good versus Evil. This last level is especially manifested by diabolic imagery, most notably that surrounding the demonic Iago, who is "mastered by the sins which caused the angels to fall, Pride and Envy." Othello's sin is that of Adam (as in *Paradise Lost*): "He allows passion to usurp the place of reason." On this level less important characters like Bianca and Emilia "keep up the theme" by their reiteration of diabolic images. Bethell demonstrates how Shakespeare successfully integrates all three levels of the play without resort to allegory. In the last part of the essay he analyzes the diabolic imagery in the final two scenes of the play and concludes that Othello, "self-willed to the last," rushes blindly to his own damnation. Bethell's essay is as much an illustration of a critical method as it is an illuminating interpretation of the play.

38. Draper, John W. *The Othello of Shakespeare's Audience*. Paris: Marcel Didier, 1952.

A collection of revised lectures and several previously published articles, this book systematically analyzes each of the characters in the light of Renaissance history, medicine, politics, and psychology. To each character is assigned one of the medieval humors. In opposition to Lily B. Cambell (18), who described Iago as melancholic, Draper portrays him as choleric; moreover, he is shown to be a basically "honest" man driven to revenge by a rigid Renaissance code of honor. In a lengthy discussion of "Tempo," Draper tries to establish the tone of dialogue by analyzing its spoken rhythms. By the marshalling of historical background, Draper gives great emphasis to Brabantio. The book provides the fullest account of Venetian caste, social habits, and politics, although it cites many sources Shakespeare could not have read.

39. Goldstone, Richard. "Experiments with Audio-Visual Aids in Teaching Shakespeare," *CE*, XIII (1952), 319–322.

An imaginative account of how Verdi's *Othello* can be used effectively in the teaching of the play.

39. Kernan, Joseph. "Verdi's *Otello*, or Shakespeare Explained," *Hudson Review*, VI (1953), 266–277.

A knowledgeable discussion of how a comparison of the play and the opera reflects the genius of both Verdi and Shakespeare.

39. Dean, Winston. "Verdi's *Othello*, a Shakespearean Masterpiece," *Shakespeare Survey 21* (1968), 87–96.

Boito's libretto, Verdi's music, and *Othello* represent a blending of great art forms, and the changes made in the opera realize the fullest potentials of both media. This is a detailed, knowledgeable analysis of both opera and play.

40. Nowottny, Winifred M. T. "Justice and Love in *Othello*," *University of Toronto Q*, XXI (1952), 330–344. Reprinted in Dean.

A close reading of the play to reveal how Shakespeare's concept of justice, pursued also in the other plays, is ironically contrasted to the dominant theme of love. Othello's killing of Desdemona is to him an act of justice for the betrayal of their love. He commits sucide for the same reason. "Othello's death is perfectly consistent with his life. From first to last he is the judge."

41. Elliott, G. R. *Flaming Minister: A Study of Othello as a Tragedy of Love and Hate.* London: Cambridge University Press, 1953.

Like that by Heilman (49), this book represents one of the most patient analyses of the play to date. Considering the play scene-by-scene, Elliott shows that the cardinal theme is Pride, chief among the Seven Deadly Sins, and explains how it changes the virtue of love into sin and hate. Unlike Heilman, Elliott does not treat the play as a poem but as a visualized action on the stage. This approach, reminiscent of that by Granville-Barker (27), is combined with a utilization of Renaissance historical sources similar to that employed by Campbell (18). Othello, not Iago, is seen as the "main force of the tragedy." Hence Elliott's book represents a significant step away from the romantic criticism of Coleridge and Bradley.

42. Money, John. "Othello's 'It Is the Cause . . .': An Analysis." *Shakespeare Survey VI* (1953), pp. 94–105.

The author treats the murder in IV.ii. with sensitive appreciation of the formalized incantatory effects of the scene, pointing out the legal implications of "cause" and its significance in terms of Othello's motives.

43. Zeisler, A. *Othello: Time Enigma and the Color Problem.* Chicago: Alexander J. Isaacs, 1954.

As the title indicates, Zeisler deals with two aspects of the play: time scheme and Othello's race. After the landing at Cyprus, "short time" (two days) is juxtaposed to "long time" (two weeks). In discussing race, he concludes that Shakespeare intended Othello to be black. Full of inaccuracies and vituperative attacks on opposing critics, this brief book (60 pages) contributes very little of value to the two problems it considers.

44. Parker, M. D. H. *The Slave of Life: A Study of Shakespeare and the Idea of Justice.* London: Chatto and Windus, 1955, pp. 149–174.

This essay focuses on Iago to the exclusion of other characters; he is discussed with such other villains as Richard III, Edmund, and Claudius. According to Parker, Iago's motives are implicit in his "Nietzschian egoism: he must play his tawdry game of power because it springs from his fallen nature." The perspective and emphasis are chiefly theological.

45. Rosenberg, Marvin. "In Defense of Iago," *SQ*, VI (1955), 144–158.

Rosenberg repudiates both the "romantic," or misunderstood, "decent" Iago of Brooke (15) and the symbolic, "satanic" villain of Bethell (37) and Heilman (49). Instead he proposes, on the basis of Elizabethan and modern psychological theories, a totally "neurotic" Iago whose repressed "jealousy, envy, pride, fear, humiliation, hate, self-contempt" make him entirely human and understandable. (See St. 4.)

46. Speaight, Robert. *Nature in Shakespearean Tragedy*. London: Hollis and Carter, 1955, pp. 69–88.

In this somewhat whimsical but provocative essay the author pursues the hard question of why Othello was so easily made jealous of Desdemona's virtue. One answer he finds in the character of Othello, who is, though not servile, primitive and naive—basically "simple." Another answer is less certain: Was there something about the consummation of the marriage that fanned the flames of Othello's jealousy? As for Iago, he cannot realize his own motives because he is consumed by evil.

47. Bush, Geoffrey. *Shakespeare and the Natural Condition*. Harvard University Press, 1956, pp. 53 ff.

Othello, Timon of Athens, and *Coriolanus* are related tragedies because they "accept the terms of Bacon's natural philosophy: they are explorations of natural character, of natural causes, and of natural things in themselves." Bush argues against the interpretation of Eliot (20) that Othello's last speech is "a moral failure" and is in agreement with Granville-Barker (27) that *Othello* represents "the bleakest points of Shakespeare's vision." Thus no religious interpretation can be relevant; Othello experiences no tragic revelation nor spiritual reconciliation, and the play is "a tragedy without meaning."

48. Gardner, Helen. "The Noble Moor," *Proceedings of the British Academy*, XLI (1956), 189–201. Reprinted in Ridler (II,348–370) and in Wain.

An attack on the reduction of Othello's stature by Eliot (20),

Empson (35), and others, and an effort to reassert the "noble" Othello of Johnson (2) and J. I. M. Stewart (30). *Othello* is seen to baffle many modern critics, especially the psychological and symbolic ones, because the play cannot be interpreted readily as simplistic realism or facile allegory. In addition, modern critics instinctively repudiate the idea of heroism. Her conclusion here is similar to that set forth in *Shakespeare Survey 21*, page 3: "*Othello* reflects a genuine dilemma for many twentieth-century critics, who find themselves confronted with a work of obviously supreme artistic power and beauty which does not satisfy their characteristic concerns. . . ."

48. "*Othello:* A Retrospect, 1900–67," *Shakespeare Survey 21*, ed. Kenneth Muir (1968), pp. 1–10.

As the title suggests, this is a survey, with critical commentary, of *Othello* criticism since A. C. Bradley. Gardner analyzes the contributions of most of the major critics—Bradley, G. Wilson Knight, Lily B. Campbell, Spivack, *et. al.* If Miss Gardner shows a bias in her commentary, it is in her opposition to criticism emphasizing psychological and/or intricately symbolic approaches. Her essay is an excellent introduction to twentieth-century criticism of the play.

49. Heilman, Robert. *Magic in the Web: Action and Language in Othello.* Lexington: University of Kentucky Press, 1956.

With very close attention to both dramatic action and nuances of language, Heilman shows how the parts of the play combine to form "a dramatic poem about love." He finds in this central theme of love both "magic and web," for love, like the handkerchief, conveys magical powers of transformation. It changes Desdemona from "infatuated girl" to "devoted, enduring wife" and finally to martyred saint. Selfless love is symbolically associated with magic and witchcraft, and this value of love Iago opposes with his wit (reason perverted by service to passion); between these poles of witchcraft versus wit all the main characters "find their orientation," and Othello stands like the hero of a morality play, torn between Love (Desdemona) and Hate (Iago). He chooses the latter because he "never surrendered to the magic that transforms personality. . . . He was never wholly freed from self-love." Moreover, according to Heilman, "He essays to reason when reason is not relevant: he substitutes

a disastrous wit for a saving witchcraft." In summarizing the theme, Heilman states: "Shakespeare's point is that love is beyond reason."

Othello is "noble," but that nobility is ironically the clue to his
tragedy, for his puritanism, self-love, and histrionism—all suggested by
his actions and rhetoric—combine with "a stoicism of the flesh unmatched
by an endurance of spirit." In describing Iago, Heilman is equally concerned with "humanizing" him without detracting from his symbolic
role. In this way Heilman takes issue with Bradley (12), who is so preoccupied with Iago's psychological nature that he neglects his symbolic
function, and with J. I. M. Stewart (30), who gives so much stress to
Iago as symbol that he neglects his essential humanity. In contrast,
Heilman attempts to moderate between these extremes by an approach
he calls "*both-and*": as human being, Iago is "spiritually deprived" and
lusts to steal by "wit" the creative magic he lacks; but he is also, as symbol,
the mythic Enemy ("the universal destroyer of ultimate values") as well
as the Vice of the morality play and the Machiavel of the later drama.
Between these polarities as individual and conventional symbol he is, in
addition, psychopath, megalomaniac, and "mass mind" vulgarian. "There
is," concludes Heilman, "no single way into this extraordinary characterization," and Heilman expresses a receptivity to "any critical metaphor
that will keep the scope of Iago wide enough." This interpretation of
Iago typifies Heilman's pragmatic, pluralistic criticism throughout the
book—an approach he accurately terms as "flexible." Thus, although he
finds Christian metaphors sustained throughout the play, and concurs
rather cautiously in a theological interpretation, he refrains from narrow-
ing the play to a literal allegory. The thrust of his criticism is not ideological but aesthetic; his primary motive is to show how characterization,
action, imagery patterns, and recurrent diction interconnect to form an
integrated, complex work of art.

No brief summary can do justice to Heilman's subtle, inductive
analysis of the play. Only G. R. Elliott (41) is equally exhaustive, and
the two books complement each other to make up the most significant
body of criticism on *Othello* since Bradley.

50. Sproule, Albert F. "A Time Scheme for *Othello*," *SQ*, VII (1956),
217–226.

Elaborating on a suggestion by Fleay (*NV*, pp. 371–372), Sproule
argues for a three-day time scheme, as opposed to the traditional one of

thirty-six hours, for the events on Cyprus. Reorganizing the usual act and scene divisions, he proposes that the first day is Saturday (II–III), the second Sunday (III–III.iv), and the third Monday afternoon (III.iv–conclusion).

51. Stirling, Brents. *Unity in Shakespearean Tragedy: The Interplay of Theme and Character.* New York: Columbia University Press, 1956, pp. 111–138.

Heilman (49) and Stirling, colleagues at the University of Washington, published their books the same year, and both critics stay very close to the text. Stirling, however, narrows the context to a single emphasis to achieve additional depth and, in contrast to Heilman, tends to view the play as an expanding metaphor somewhat in the manner of G. Wilson Knight (19). Stirling locates the ironic center of *Othello* in the idea of reputation, and, perhaps influenced by G. R. Elliott (41), finds the idea polarized as "right self-esteem" versus "wrong pride." Like Heilman, Stirling treats III.iii and most of V in terms of symbolic ritual. For its graceful mastery of complexities and its lucid style, Stirling's essay should continue to be instructive to advanced students of the play.

52. Gérard, Albert. " 'Egregiously an Ass': The Dark Side of the Moor," *Shakespeare Survey 10* (1957), pp. 98–106.

With Leavis (23), Gérard concludes that Othello is neither noble nor heroic but criminally "savage" and even downright stupid. This essays represents a radical effort to reduce Othello's stature as a tragic hero.

52. "Alack, Poor Iago! Intellect and Action in *Othello*," *SJ*, XCIV (1968), 218–232.

This essay develops further some of the ideas set forth in Gérard's previous article. The play is seen to dramatize a hopeless polarization of Othello's mindless idealism versus Iago's cynical materialism. The first is deficient in intellect, the second in morality. *Othello* signifies, therefore, the dominant pessimism of the major tragedies—the idea that life can be lived neither by reason and intellect, symbolized by Iago, nor by instincts and emotions, represented by Othello.

53. Siegel, Paul N. *Shakespearean Tragedy and the Elizabethan Compromise.* New York: New York University Press, 1957, Chap. 8, pp. 119–141.

Siegel interprets the play as a Christian allegory: Cyprus is Eden, Othello is at first Adam and later Judas. Desdemona is symbolically equivalent to belief in Christ and the means of salvation for Emilia and Cassio. Siegel finds many Biblical analogies, echoes, and parallels. He is more fundamentalist than most theological critics when he suggests that Shakespeare's Venice reflects "some features" of a sinful Elizabethan England, or that Othello's Turk of Alleppo in his final speech symbolizes the evil in his own human nature that is destructive of a higher (presumably Christian) order. Siegel defends his view by insisting that although Othello repents, his repentance is "without faith in the mercy of God" and therefore ineffectual. (For a cogent defense of Siegel's theological approach, see the first two chapters of his *Shakespeare in His Time and Ours*, University of Notre Dame Press, 1968.)

54. Webster, Margaret. *Shakespeare Today*, with an introduction by M. R. Ridley. London: Dent, 1957, pp. 231–238.

Miss Webster, a distinguished actress and director of Shakespeare, continues the informative *obiter dicta* begun in *Shakespeare Without Tears (1955). If actors playing Othello "know their business," she insists, there is no need to "suspend belief" in motives, as Stoll suggests is necessary for readers. Most critics (and some actors) cannot appreciate the play because they fail to imagine an Othello who is passionate enough to make his actions credible. Her discussion of Othello concludes with an explanation of why Othello should be presented on the stage as completely black and not, as she puts it, merely as a white man with "a sun tan."

55. Wilson, Harold S. *On the Design of Shakespearean Tragedy. Toronto: University of Toronto Press, 1957, pp. 52–67.

For Wilson, "Christian assumptions" form the basis of *Othello*, as they do also of *Romeo and Juliet* and *Hamlet*. Although in *Othello* sin and suffering is the theme, the hero is not "damned," for he is redeemed by his agony and contrition. Wilson refutes the low estimate of Othello by Eliot(20), and, as might be expected of a critic who finds divinity at work everywhere in the play, he devotes considerable space to rejecting Bradley's idea that chance plays an important role. He defends the play against Rymer's ancient charge that it is full of improbabilities by invoking the importance of dramatic conventions. On this last point he relies rather heavily upon Stoll (14). Wilson's essay is a valuable introduction to some basic critical problems although his own solutions are eclectic and his Christian interpretation largely given *ex cathedra* and without substantiation from the text.

56. Arthos, John. "The Fall of Othello," *SQ*, IX (1958), 93–104.

A comparison of *Othello* and *Macbeth* in an effort to determine the climax and turning point in *Othello*. Arthos argues that the central action is not the murder of Desdemona, which is only an outcome, but the conflict of Othello's love versus his honor. In contrast to a "love and honor" play like Corneille's *Cid*, *Othello* shows "the displacement of love by the *idea* of the superior sanctity of honor," and Othello's concept of honor is false.

57. Hubler, Edward. "The Damnation of *Othello:* Some Limitations on the Christian View of the Play," *SQ*, IX (1958), 295–300.

A brief but important article attacking the theological critics of the play, chiefly Bethell (37) and Siegel (53) for their alleged pedantry, selectivity, and "simplistic view of symbolism." Hubler argues that because Othello is not a man but a character in a play, no speculations about his future after the play—his "damnation," for example—can possibly be valid or even relevant. Although theological critics assume a uniformly "Christian" audience, that audience was not, he insists, as uniform or as orthodox as these critics contend.

58. Nash, Walter. "Paired Words in *Othello:* Shakespeare's Use of a Stylistic Device," *ES*, XXXIX (1958), 62–67.

In this concise article Nash employs the techniques of Empson (35) to show the dramatic effectiveness of such "paired" words as Othello's "flinty and steel couch of war"—an expression ironically aped by Iago. (For reactions to this article, and the author's reply, see *ES*, XXXIX, 212–216.)

59. Spivack, Bernard. *Shakespeare and the Allegory of Evil.* New York: Columbia University Press, 1958. Excerpts of criticism on *Othello* in **Shakespeare: The Tragedies,* ed. Alfred Harbage. Twentieth-Century Views Series. Englewood Cliffs, N.J.: Prentice-Hall, 1964, pp. 85–92.

In this impressively documented study of how several Shakespearean character types grew out of early native dramatic traditions, Spivack attempts to establish Iago's affinities to the Vice of the morality plays. Iago requires no psychological "motivation" in any realistic sense because, as Vice, his motives are already established for the Elizabethan audience. Iago's statement "I hate the Moor" is sufficient as motivation because in the morality tradition Vice always hates Virtue. If Spivack's historical approach has limitations, one might be that he occasionally tends to treat characters as archaeological remains rather than conscious artistic creations: "Iago's hatred," Spivack suggests, "having become isolated from its allegorical predication, survives unattached." Thus Hyman (106), although convinced by Spivack that Iago owes something to the traditional Vice, complains that Spivack makes Iago a comic character and attributes humor to passages which Hyman, as a modern reader, cannot accept as comic. Nevertheless, Spivack's book is perhaps the most successful effort to date at achieving the ultimate critical aim of Stroll (14) and Draper (38)—that is, to see *Othello* through the eyes of Shakespeare's Elizabethan audience. (For alternative theories to Spivack's concept of Iago as Vice, see Spencer [25].)

60. Gilbert, Allan. *Principles and Practice of Criticism: Othello, Merry Wives of Windsor, and Hamlet.* Detroit: Wayne State University, 1959.

Using an approach he describes as "minimum interpretation," Gilbert abjures subtle symbolic analysis and "overcriticism"; yet his analysis of *Othello* proves unorthodox indeed. He finds that neither *Hamlet* nor *Othello* is a tragedy but a mingling of tragedy and comedy. Gilbert discovers more implications of "humor" in *Othello* than any other critic to date.

61. Smith, Gordon Ross. "Iago the Paranoiac," *American Imago,* XVI (1959), 155–167.

Smith substantially agrees with the psychoanalytic view of Iago as the paranoiac proposed by Wangh (32), and suggests that Shakespeare may well have known of paranoiac symptoms and their affinities to homosexuality. This interpretation is extended, briefly, to include *Julius Caesar, Hamlet, Macbeth,* and *Anthony and Cleopatra.*

62. Bayley, John. **The Characters of Love: A Study in the Literature* of Personality*. London: Constable, 1960, pp. 125–202.

In his chapter "Love and Identity," Bayley expands with sophistication and subtlety on the idea by G. Wilson Knight (19) that *Othello* portrays "separated" and "alienated" worlds. All of the characters are shown to exist in isolated states of mutual "incomprehension." Bayley systematically refutes Coleridge (4), Bradley (13), Eliot (20), and Leavis (23); he analyzes in great detail Shakespeare's psychological and philosophical motives in changing Cinthio's story, and explains what he terms the aesthetic "gap" between Othello's story as fiction and as drama. Bayley's essay is a thoughtful, complex analysis of both the play and some significant concepts in aesthetics.

63. Hagopian, John V. "Psychology and the Coherent Form of Shakespeare's *Othello,*" *Papers of the Michigan Academy of Science, Arts, and Letters,* XLV (1960), 373–380.

Seizing upon the failure of criticism since Coleridge to account for Iago's motives and Othello's sudden jealousy and violence, the author finds that only psychoanalysis can give coherent form to characterization and motives.

64. Lawlor, John. *The Tragic Sense in Shakespeare*. London: Chatto and Windus, 1960, pp. 87–106.

Lawlor attempts to solve several different problems of characterization and action by reconciling dramatic tradition and innovation, myth and realism. For example, Iago is seen as both a reality as Machiavellian villain and as a pure dramatic convention as devil. Moreover, the element of chance in the play, first noted by Bradley, is skillfully interwoven with motives and actions. This is a thoughtful, complex essay dealing with the inner aesthetics of the tragedy.

65. Ribner, Irving. **Patterns in Shakespearean Tragedy* [1960]. London: Methuen, 1970. Pages 91–115 in the 1960 edition.)

In this very literal theological construction, Ribner agrees with Spivack (59) in his interpretation of Iago as owing much to the character of Vice, and with Lily B. Campbell (18) in his conception of Othello as a chronically jealous man whose love is perverted to fear and then to hatred. Yet Ribner's Iago is more devil than Vice, his Othello more symbolic than psychological: "Othello is like the conventional morality play hero between the Satanic Iago and the angelic Desdemona. Both vie for his soul, and in his human imperfection he chooses wrongly." From this perspective, the plot shows a remarkable "neatness and precision of construction." In agreement with Elliott (41) and Parker (44), and in opposition to Bethell (37), Siegel (53), and Sewell (36), who insist that Othello is "damned," Ribner maintains that he achieves "eventual salvation."

66. Ornstein, Robert. *The Moral Vision of Jacobean Tragedy*. Madison, Wis.: University of Wisconsin Press, 1960, pp. 217–219, 227–234.

On pages 217–219, Ornstein discusses Ford's debts to *Othello* in a very inferior play, *Love's Sacrifice*. In Chapter IX he compares *Othello* and *Macbeth*, chiefly with attention to characterization and theme. From his study of other Jacobean plays, Orenstein concludes that *Othello* is unique. If Middleton had written Cinthio's story, for example, he would have done an ironic tragedy of "honor" in the manner of *Women Beware Women*. However brief, Ornstein's comments on *Othello* repay study. For him, Othello experiences no tragic revelation, learns nothing from his deception by Iago: "The overwhelming sadness of his fate is that he could love Desdemona selflessly only when he had lost all sense of self, only when he had nothing left to wager on her faith." As a Jacobean villain, Iago is equally unique. Not simply Machiavellian, "His philosophy rests upon a continuing denial of the reality he daily perceives."

67. Walton, J. K. " 'Strength's Abundance': A view of *Othello*," *RES*, n.s., XI (1960), 8–17.

According to Walton in this original and provocative article, critics have erred in stressing the frailties of the chief characters. The source of tragedy is ironically implicit in the great strengths, not weaknesses, of Othello and Desdemona.

68. Holloway, John. *The Story of the Night: Studies in Shakespeare's Major Tragedies.* London: Routledge and Kegan Paul, 1961, pp. 37–56, 136–155.

The approach is archetypal, mythic, and ritualistic in the vein of Bodkin (21), with Othello seen as a sacrificial victim. The first essay is almost exclusively on Othello; the second attempts to refute the idea that Othello was not innately jealous, set forth by Bradley (12), and that Othello was too easily seduced, maintained by Leavis (23). Although the book sets out to remove "obstacles" for the modern reader, it sometimes creates them by its preoccupation with ancillary critical questions.

69. Auden, W. H. "The Joker in the Pack," in *The Dyer's Hand.* New York: Random House, 1962, pp. 246–272. Reprinted in Wain, pp. 199–223.

Iago is characterized as the archetype of the "practical joker" who defies the crucial social distinction between moral seriousness and play—a distinction on which society largely depends for its coherence. Motivated by a compulsive desire for self-destruction, Iago is an anarchistic masochist; Othello is a social climber; Desdemona is "a silly schoolgirl." In this clever, iconclastic essay the play is viewed as racist and the concept of "double time" is peremptorily rejected.

70. Kernan, Alvin. * "Introduction," *Othello,* ed. A. Kernan. The Signet Shakespeare: New American Library, 1963.

This is a lively and well-written essay for students reacting against A. C. Bradley and searching for what Kernan describes as the "gross mechanics"—the larger ironic patterns of character contrasts and symbolic interactions of characters and events. Kernan interprets the play for its allegorical implications without recourse to theology, stressing the irony of appearance versus reality in all the characters. Reminiscent of the romantic critics, he sees Iago as an "anti-life spirit which seeks the destruction of everything outside the self."

71. Ranald, Margaret L. "The Indiscretions of Desdemona," *SQ*, XIV (1963).

Using an approach similar to the historical one of Lily B. Campbell (18), Miss Ranald shows that Desdemona's behavior is totally at odds with that prescribed by Renaissance courtesy books on female "decorum," and that her defiance of those precepts renders her especially vulnerable to Iago's insinuations. For a similar conclusion based on quite different premises, see Janet Overmyer (110).

72. Sisson, C. J. *Shakespeare's Tragic Justice*. London: Methuen, 1963 pp. 28–51.

Refuting the theological allegorists, Sission denies that there is any "divine justice" in the play and proposes that the real theme is that of reputation, an idea he skillfully relates to Iago's motives and Othello's jealousy. He treats the play as revenge tragedy, but one of "wild justice" by both Othello and Iago. By citing historical and literary background, he attempts to demonstrate that Shakespeare intended the play to be a condemnation of private justice. This chatty, leisurely essay also contains lengthy digressions on the origins of Othello's name, the racial aspects of the play, and an imaginary conversation among Shakespeare, Burbage, and Lowin on the casting assignments for the first performance of *Othello*.

73. Hayes, Ann L. "Othello," in *Lovers Meeting: Discussions of Five Plays by Shakespeare*. Carnegie Institute of Technology Series in English, No. 8 (Pittsburgh, 1964), pp. 53–67.

This essay is appropriate for very elementary students. Although it covers most of the critical problems of the play, especially those concerning character, it does so in a discursive, distracting style heavy with rhetorical questions. Hayes tends to accept all of Iago's expressed motives as valid, and her analysis of Othello's character is rather traditional: He is noble at first, then declines under Iago's evil spell. Hayes sees the characters as complex, the plot as basically "simple."

74. Jorgenson, Paul A. " 'Perplexed in the Extreme': The Role of Thought in *Othello*," in *Shakespeare 400* (1964), 265–275.

An ingenious essay that explores Renaissance concepts of false and valid thinking (as a process). The tragedy dramatizes how a false-thinking villain destroys a hero who cannot think properly because he cannot tolerate uncertainties. Thus the essay opens a new dimension of Othello's character.

75. Kirschbaum, Leo. "The Modern Othello," *ELH*, XI (1964), 283–296. Reprinted in *Character and Characterization in Shakespeare*. Detroit: Wayne State University Press, 1962. Reprinted in Dean.

In this interpretation of Othello's character, Kirschbaum, in his characteristically declamatory style, refutes the views of E. K. Chambers (for his "simple" Othello), Kittredge (for his "heroic" Othello), and Stoll (for his "psychologically inconsistent" Othello). Instead, he posits an Othello whose total personal responsibility gives dignity to his terrible fate, an Othello who is so much the romantic idealist in his view of himself and others that his "overtrust speedily shifts to undertrust on the first provocation." Hence Othello never really loved Desdemona, only his own romantic image of her. Bent only on establishing Othello's responsibility for his actions, Kirschbaum would not go as far as Leavis (23) in reducing his essential nobility of character.

76. Levin, Harry. *"Othello and the Motive-Hunters,"* in *Centennial Review*, VIII (1964), 1–6.

A sharp and eloquent attack on the *Othello* of Coleridge's "motiveless" Iago, Eliot's shallow Othello, and Rymer's "silly" Desdemona, this essay argues that *Othello* was written with compassion for all except Iago; the hero's fall is not inevitable but profoundly pitiful, showing how the dignity of man is vulnerable to deception and malice. Bradley's "chance" is credited as a legitimate element: Othello's fall results from his "credulity" and "bad luck."

77. Matthews, G. M. *"Othello and the Dignity of Man,"* in *Shakespeare in a Changing World* (1964), 123–145.

An important contribution to the gathering literature of *Othello* and race, this essay argues that the play is not about how Othello reverts to barbarism but how "a white barbarian . . . tries to make a civilized man into his own image."

78. McGee, Arthur. "Othello's Motive for Murder," *SQ*, IV (1964), 45–54.

A close reading shows that Othello, deeply afflicted with sexual jealousy, was driven to murder by the conviction that Desdemona had been unfaithful during the courtship period in Venice. McGee argues that the time scheme theory proposed by Granville-Barker (27) and others is applicable only to Act I.

79. West, Robert H. "The Christianness of *Othello*," *SQ*, XV (1964), 333–343.

West concisely summarizes some principal objections to the methods and conclusions of theological critics, especially those of Battenhouse (98) and Siegel (53), who make "peremptory application of Christian dogmatics." West's criticism includes some points not found in the similar essay by Hubler (57).

80. Jones, Eldred D. *Othello's Countrymen: The African in English Renaissance Drama.* London: Oxford University Press, 1965.

On the basis of historical and legendary accounts since Herodotus, together with evidence from about forty-five plays and from many non-dramatic literary works, the author concludes that in Shakespeare's time Moors were considered villainous, although Iago (and Aaron in *Titus Andronicus*), and not Othello, conforms closely to the stereotype. Jones also describes makeup and costumes of Elizabethan stage Moors. This is a valuable, comprehensive treatment of a long-neglected subject, and it should be consulted by anyone interested in the racial aspects of the play.

81. Whittaker, Virgil K. *The Mirror Up to Nature: The Technique of Shakespeare's Tragedies.* San Marino: Huntington Library, 1965, pp. 241–275.

In spite of its date, this essay reflects little awareness of the important criticism done on *Othello* during the past twenty years. Act I is considered too lengthy "to get the play started," so that Othello's temptation and rapid fall must be crowded into one scene (III.iii). Infelicities of plot structure and an absence of concern for nature or for mature philosophizing by the hero combine to make *Othello* an inferior product preliminary to such greater efforts as *Macbeth*. With Coleridge and Bradley, Whittaker agrees that Othello is not jealous by nature; Othello's fatal flaw, or "heresy," is his uxorious deification of Desdemona. The essay concludes with a theological interpretation that is not convincingly substantiated by the text.

82. Goll, August. "Iago," in *Criminal Types in Shakespeare*, trans. from the Danish by Mrs. Charles Weekes. London: Haskell House, 1966, pp. 206–265.

Although this lengthy essay employs neither a psychological nor a sociological approach, it describes Iago as being devoid of "normal motives" because he is a psychopath obsessed with a "lust for destruction." A close reading of II.3, in which Iago and Cassio discuss Desdemona, reveals Iago to be "an antipathetic cynic" of a profoundly sensual nature. He is, in effect, a compulsive rapist who seeks a perverse gratification by humiliating women (witness his contemptuous, brutal treatment of Emilia). Whereas Robert Heilman discusses Iago's criminality as being chiefly larcenous, Goll views Iago as a homicidal type whose penchant for violence stems from depraved sexuality: "He is the enemy of civilization itself, and is, therefore, the very personification of crime, its apotheosis; the orgin and source of each individual crime, the willing and conscious criminal mind itself." Ironically, it is Emilia, Iago's sole link with "civilization," who destroys him with her testimony.

83. Hapgood, Robert. "The Trials of *Othello*," *Pacific Coast Studies in Shakespeare*, ed. Waldo F. McNeir and T. N. Greenfield. Portland, Ore.: University of Oregon Press, 1966, pp. 134–137.

Hapgood explores trials in which Othello figures: that of Othello by the Duke of Venice; of Cassio after the brawl; of Desdemona before her death; and of Othello at the conclusion of the play. With regard to the first of these trials, Hapgood takes issue with Robert Heilman (49); contrary to Heilman's thesis that the theme of justice is ironically portrayed as a deterioration in fairness, Othello's examination of Cassio is much fairer than the Duke's trial of Othello. For Hapgood the theme of justice is the essential key to Othello's true character, and although he agrees that G. R. Elliott (41) has disclosed a significant aspect of that character with his emphasis on Othello's pride, Hapgood would modify Elliott's interpretation by adding to pride "an excessive assurance of his innate rectitude," a flaw which the theme of justice clearly reveals. Hence Othello's judgment of Desdemona at the end of the play, although representing the "grossest violations of elementary, practical justice," is nevertheless committed by a noble hero sincerely devoted, ironically, to the loftiest ideals of justice. And in the final "trial" of the play, Othello's judgment of himself in this world and the next, he "tips the scales now to one side and then to the other," delicately balanced between extremes. Important as the theme of justice is, therefore, final judgment in tragedy takes second place to what A. C. Bradley (12) calls "attraction and repulsion, pity, wonder, fear, horror, perhaps hatred. . . ."

84. Richmond, Hugh. "Love and Justice: *Othello*'s Shakespearean context," *Pacific Coast Studies in Shakespeare*, ed. Waldo F. McNeir and T. N. Greenfield. Portland, Ore.: University of Oregon Press, 1966, pp. 148–172.

Richmond explores Othello's affinities to other Shakespearean and non-Shakespearean heroes: Oedipus, Faustus, Romeo, and Angelo (in *Measure for Measure*). Like Oedipus, Othello "precipitates his doom in asserting his own high resolution to be master of his fate"; like Faustus, he experiences a "descent from confident dominion over his environment to a vivid sense of his own damnation." Hence Richmond's Othello is a fully noble yet flawed hero who is not damned for murder but for "usurping judgment of himself with fatal harshness." In this particular he resembles the self-demanding moral perfectionist Angelo. Ignorant of original sin, these heroes—Oedipus, Faustus, Angelo, and Othello—"find their own fallibility at first inconceivable, and then unpardonable." Othello's high ideals and harsh judgment of himself result in a "noble schizophrenia" that enables Iago to become his repressed, diabolic alter-ego.

Like Shakespeare's Juliet, Desdemona is more mature and responsible than her lover; like Juliet, too, she represents "life and sexuality" in contrast to her lover's "extravagant sentimentality" and "suicidal tendencies." Yet, just as Cordelia's reckless devotion to integrity precipitated Lear's disaster, Desdemona's "bold generosity of spirit" in aiding Cassio causes Othello's suspicions. Her death establishes her, for Othello, "on an ideally unattainable pinnacle of perfection" and fixes their tenuous relationship in an immutable "aesthetic form."

Influenced by Denis de Rougemont's conception of heroic love as essentially destructive and death-prone (*Love in the Western World; Passion and Society*), Richmond takes account of the "nexus of difficulties" and abrasive misalliances portrayed by Shakespeare, not only in *Othello* but in *Henry VI*, Part I (Margaret and Suffolk), in *King John* (Lewis the Dauphin and Blanch), in *A Midsummer Night's Dream*, and in *Romeo and Juliet, Hamlet,* and *Measure for Measure*. In these plays, as in *Othello*, love as a grand passion is shown to be a sublimated deathwish.

85. Ross, Lawrence J. "Shakespeare's 'Dull Clown' and Symbolic Music." *SQ*, XVII (1966), 107–128.

Ross finds in the clown's entry in III.i. a suggestion of Platonic and Pythagorean concepts of divine musical harmony. Far from being an excrescence, the clown conveys Shakespeare's ideas of love as harmony, and of Iago's destructive influence on that love.

86. Shaw, John. " 'What Is the Matter?' in *Othello*," *SQ*, XVII (1966), 157–161.

Noting that the question occurs in *Othello* twenty times, Shaw examines the locution for its ironic implications, concluding that the word "matter" has complex legal implications comparable, in general, to the question "What is the truth about things?" Shaw combines the techniques of Empson (35) and Heilman (49).

87. Boehm, Rudolf. "Die Verleumdungsszene bei Shakespeare," *SJ* (1967), 221–236.

About a third of Shakespeare's plays contain "calumny scenes," most of them involving conflicts arising out of murder or sexual infidelity; among these *Othello* is unique for its psychological complexity and exclusive concern with this theme. The first calumny scene (II.1), in which Iago tells Roderigo of Desdemona's concupiscence and inevitable infidelity, is actually a false start, yet it enlists Roderigo's support and leads directly to Cassio's loss of reputation. Boehm finds that tracing calumny scenes leads to illumination of the structure and the meaning of the play as a whole.

88. Doran, Madeleine. "Good Name in *Othello*," *SEL*, VII (1967), 195–217.

A man's "good name," according to medieval law, is an aspect of hereditary property which can be stolen, and restoration of "good name," once impaired, is difficult. Traditionally the enemy of "good name" is slander, Iago's role in the play. Hence Othello's final speech is not, as Eliot suggests, an effort to "cheer himself up," but to restore his "good name."

88. "Iago's 'If': An Essay on the Syntax of *Othello*," in *The Drama of the Renaissance*, ed. E. M. Blistein. Providence, R.I.: Brown University 1970, pp. 69–99.

A searching linguistic analysis in the manner of Empson (35) which purports to explain the ironic implications of III.iii.35–38: "*Oth.*: 'What dost thou say?' / *Iago:* 'Nothing lord, or *if*—I know not what.'" Two syntactical patterns are found to be expressive of irony: those conveying possibility, and those indicative of complex certainty.

89. Echeruo, Michael J. C. "The Context of Othello's Tragedy," *Southern Review*, II (1967), 299–318.

The "context" is seen as racial. Historical, textual, and dramatic evidence is brought to bear to show that Othello was, indeed, black, and that certain Elizabethan concepts about blacks, evident in a long literary tradition, influenced Shakespeare's delineation of Othello. (Compare the book on this subject by Eldred D. Jones [80].)

90. Hunter, G. K. "*Othello* and Colour Prejudice," in *Proceedings of the British Academy*, LIII (1967), 139–163.

Hunter mingles fact and speculation, anthropology and selected historical data in an attempt to show that in *Othello* Shakespeare exploited traditional prejudices against Moors in order to instill in his audience a compassion for an innocent man wronged by those same prejudices.

91. Oyama, Toshikazu. "The Tragic Fate of Othello's World of Consciousness," *Anglica*, VI, No. 3 (September 1967), 1–24.

Othello's tragic fate results from his own limited consciousness in a world of ambiguous appearances and multiple perspectives; unlike Hamlet, Othello cannot raise the question "To be, or not to be." For Othello, appearance is simply what it seems, and he remains fatally self-assured and unquestioning. Hence, "Iago's realistic portrayal of the cuckold's life, 'who dotes, yet doubts, suspects, yet fondly loves' is a threatening terror to Othello, because it represents a mode of 'conscience' Othello is completely alien to." Even Othello's closing words are ironically consistent with his rigidity, for they merely represent the extreme reversion of a single-minded, hopelessly idealistic hero.

92. Adamowski, T. H. "The Aesthetic Attitude and Narcissism in *Othello*," in *Literature and Psychology*, XVIII, Nos. 2–3 (1968), 73–81.

As a narcissist, Othello combines histrionic conduct and self-centered attitudes with deep insecurity and lack of genuine self-regard. He is more concerned with what others think than with personal integrity. He is easily seduced by Iago because, as a narcissist, he has little genuine self-esteem, rejects the possibility of human love or value, and acts rashly in times of crisis. To the very end of the play he struggles in confusion to retain an idealized image of himself as the "cynosure in a noble spectacle." (Compare the similar analysis by Stephen Reid [93].)

93. Allen, Ned B. "The Two Parts of *Othello*." *Shakespeare Survey 21* (1968), pp. 13–29.

A fascinating, but highly speculative, study proposing that Shakespeare wrote two plays which he stitched together—first III, IV, and V, later I and II—and that the plot "inconsistencies" and the disconnected Act I result from the fact that Shakespeare "spliced togeather two parts not originally written to go together."

94. Hallstead, R. N. "Idolatrous Love: A New Approach to *Othello*," *SQ*, XIX (1968), 107–124.

In an interpretation similar to that by Kirschbaum (75), Hallstead gives total responsibility for the tragedy to Othello, who, as a romantic idealist, at first deified Desdemona and then, discovering her sexuality, became profoundly disillusioned. Unlike Kirschbaum, however, he interprets the play as a Christian allegory—and yet, in contrast to most theological critics, deals almost sympathetically with Iago. The "pearl" Othello threw away, he asserts, was Christian faith. (This last interpretation is challenged by John E. Seamen [in "Othello's Pearl," *SQ, ibid.,* pp. 81–85], who argues that the pearl is Desdemona, not faith.)

95. Kott, Jan. "The Two Paradoxes of Othello," *Evergreen Review,* X (1968), 15–21. Also published in *Polish Perspectives,* VIII (Warsaw, 1965), 30–35.

Not nearly so provocative nor as thoughtful as Kott's essay on *Lear,* this explores the paradox of Iago's concept of an evil world which brings on his own destruction, and the paradox of Desdemona's love for Othello, which destroys her because the more she loves him the more suspicious he becomes of her chastity.

96. Reid, Stephen. "Othello's Jealousy," *American Imago,* XXV (Fall 1968), 274–293.

Othello's delusional jealousy is not based primarily on homosexual impulses but on an adolescent superego badly bruised by feelings of parental rejection. By avoiding women before meeting Desdemona, he has never experienced normal sexual competition; instead, he has expressed his latent hostility by rejecting women and by dominating men as a great soldier. (His expressed pride in being a solider is, according to Reid, characteristic of the "latency period" of six to twelve years of age.) Othello's patriotism and professional pride function as surrogates for the adolescent father image; his tales of adventure are typical adolescent fantasies. Like T. H. Adamowski (92), Reid emphasizes Othello's narcissism but makes more extensive application of the Oedipal hypothesis. When Othello suspects Desdemona of infidelity, the interjected father reacts with all of the infantile rage of the rejected son.

97. Watts, Robert A. "The Comic Scenes in *Othello,*" *SQ,* XIX (1968), 349–354.

In this brief but important article Watts explains how each comic episode, and especially the appearances of the clown (on two occasions), provides a commentary on the serious action. Each such episode constitutes a microcosm of the play as a whole, an ironic chorus to the tragic theme. Watts' close reading of the clown scenes throws some new light on this neglected topic.

98. Battenhouse, Roy W. *Shakespearean Tragedy: Its Art and Its Christian Premises*. Indiana University Press, 1969.

In two chapters, "Othello as Judas" and "Iago's Pelagianism," Battenhouse summarizes the theological approach he adopted in several earlier articles. From Battenhouse's perspective of "inverted analogy" and "scriptural analogue," Iago is seen as Satan, Desdemona as "Christ-like" but not actually Christ, and Othello as at first "a pseudo-Christ figure" and later "among the reprobate." Opposing both what he sees as the "romantic" school of Coleridge (4) and the "Hegelian cast" of Bradley (12), Battenhouse represents one of the most Scholastic and literal of the theological allegorists.

99. Evans, K. W. "The Radical Factor in *Othello*." *Shakespeare Studies*, V (1969), 124–140.

In opposition to Heilman, who treats race as ancillary, Evans insists that "no analysis of the play can be adequate if it ignores the factor of race." The racial stereotype—described definitively by Eldred Jones (80)—has great relevance, claims Evans, to Othello's characterization: "Prominent among supposed Moorish qualities were marked sexual capacity and promiscuity, a savagely jealous regard by male Africans for chastity in their wives, and an astonishing credulity, often accompanied by a belief in magic. Moors were said to have ungovernable tempers and to be pitilessly cruel."

The racial factor is behind Othello's deep insecurity and Iago's sense of "social inferiority." Hence Othello's peculiar vulnerability: "He has always seen European society from the outside, as it professes to be, and it is to this outlandish idealism that Iago opposes his equally exaggerated scepticism." Nevertheless, Shakespeare does not adhere to the racial sterotype in his portrayal of Othello; instead, he expands and humanizes the role by making the "root cause" of his fall inability to accept the "physical reality of love," and this complex psychological motive represents a deliberate departure from the traditional view of Moors. At the conclusion of the play Othello rises to new heights of awareness and nobility.

100. Fleissner, Robert F. "The Magnetic Moor: An Anti-Racist View," *Journal of Human Relations*, XVII, No. 4 (1969), 546-565.

After establishing the theory that Shakespeare must have been familiar with magnetic attraction because of Gilbert's treatise *De Magnete*, Jonson's play *The Magnetic Lady*, and frequent Elizabethan references to compasses, lodestones, and so forth, Fleissner entertains the possibility that the relationship of Othello and Desdemona may represent magnetic attraction of opposites, or, in his phrase, "magnetic coition." Shakespeare, however, could not have looked askance on such a union of polarities, for his own "Catholicism" and his affair with the Dark Lady (presumably black) must have instructed him in tolerance of minorities. The Dark Lady, in particular, "surely could have enhanced his understanding of her race and of the relationship of charity and trust that should prevail between blacks and whites." Fleissner's quixotic article is followed by a lengthy rejoinder by one "D.W.," who attacks Professor Fleissner's work as exemplary of a certain penchant for "irrelevance" among "literary analysts." Fleissner's contrite "reply" follows "D.W.'s" curt annulment of this brief and hectic marriage of literature and sociology. Thus Fleissner's article is noteworthy as being among the strangest contributions yet made to the continuing debate about the racial aspects of *Othello*.

101. Homan, Sidney R. "Iago's Aesthetics: *Othello* and Shakespeare's Portrait of an Artist," *Shakespeare Studies*, V (1969), 141–148.

Iago symbolizes the perverse artist that Puritans and others criticized in the Renaissance, for Iago supplants "a happy reality with an obscene fabrication." As a spurious artist, Iago "lacks any spiritual dimension and thereby offends nature." He violates the cardinal critical dictum that art must be *dulce et utile* and is the opposite of Othello, for whom nature, not art, is the primary source of strength. Homan discusses Iago in the context of Shakespeare's other villainous "artists," Richard III and Don John, and concludes with Bernard Spivack (59) that the Vice of the morality plays inspired Shakespeare's conception of these characters.

102. Viswanathan, S. "Illeism with a Difference in Certain Middle Plays of Shakespeare," *SQ*, XX (Autumn 1969), 407–415.

The title refers to the rhetorical device whereby a character alludes to himself in the third person (e.g., "His madness is poor Hamlet's enemy"). Illeism is found to be especially extensive in *Julius Caesar, Troilus and Cressida, Hamlet,* and *Othello.* In this subtle linguistic analysis Viswanathan explains how illeism expresses the hero's awareness of a multiple identity, of a division between the public and private selves and of a dichotomy between his self-conception and true nature. The discussion is especially interesting in its treatment of Othello's character.

103. Auchincloss, Louis. *Motiveless Malignity.* London: Gollancz, 1970.

Only the first essay, "*Othello*—the Perfect Plot," pages 1–13, is concerned with the play. The book as a whole discusses the significance of lack of motivation in several of Shakespeare's principal characters. According to Auchincloss this absence of motivation can be attributed to Shakespeare's "sense of the perverse and irrational in human nature, a sense that . . . deepened with his experience." The essay on *Othello* is slack and impressionistic, largely a recapitulation of questions raised by Bradley (12). Othello's "alien" role in Venetian culture is, finally, the major cause of his tragic fall.

104. Cronin, Peter. "Language and Character in *Othello*—Part Two," *London Review* (Winter 1970), pp. 3–14.

Cronin studies Othello's dialogue as a highly stylized, "Miltonic" language that conveys the speaker's peculiar remoteness from others. The language suggests Shakespeare's deliberate effort to convey Othello's self-aggrandisement, dignity, egotism, and self-possession. These effects are realized by having him speak English as if it were a foreign language.

105. Fergusson, Francis. *Shakespeare: The Pattern in His Carpet.* New York: Delacorte, 1970, pp. 219–228.

An interpretation depicting Othello as a moral absolutist comparable to Shakespeare's Timon and Angelo, and, like them, inhabiting "a faithless human scene" that destroys his noble idealism. Like Lövborg in Ibsen's *Hedda Gabler,* Othello is "the one vital character in sight, whom everyone loves or envies, and who is inevitably destroyed by those who try to get some of his magic to nourish themselves." Occasionally ingenious but uneven, this essay lacks the sustained brilliance of Fergusson's other efforts.

106. Hyman, Stanley Edgar. *Iago: Some Approaches to the Illusion of His Motivation.* New York: Atheneum, 1970.

Discounting the possibility that Iago, a purely dramatic creation, could have any actual motivations, Hyman systematically considers five interpretations of Iago since Samuel Johnson: as stage villain (genre criticism); as Satan (theological); as a character contrasted to Prospero (with attention to the essay by Burke (33)); as homosexual (psychoanalytic); and as Machiavellian villain (history of ideas). Hyman concludes that Heilman (49) is the best critic of *Othello* because of his "pluralist criticism," and that the most valid interpretation of the play is the "theological."

107. Low, Anthony. "Othello and Cassio: 'Unfortunate in the Infirmity,' " *Archiv für das Studium der Neuren Sprachen und Literaturen,* CXXI (April 1970), 428–433.

Cassio is shown to be not only Othello's foil but a character indicative of the Moor's nobility and fatal flaw. It is this essential nobility in both Cassio and Othello that is the "infirmity" on which Iago preys. The contrast between Cassio and Othello suggests the comic and tragic aspects of the play; Cassio's often humorous deterioration from sober, responsible soldier to drunken reveller ironically parallels Othello's tragic fall from kindly, loving husband to jealous murderer.

108. Mason, H. A. *Shakespeare's Tragedies of Love.* London: Chatto and Windus, 1970, pp. 59–162.

Mason's criticism of *Othello* consists of four essays: "Overdoing It"; "The Structure of the First Two Acts"; "The Devil's Own"; and "Intelligence about Life." The key hypothesis sustained throughout these essays is that *Othello*, far from being a well-made play, shows evidence of "hasty composition and clumsiness of craftsmanship," a weakness of plot that Mason believes has been obscured because critics such as W. H. Auden

(69) have given excessive emphasis to characterization, especially to that of Iago ("Overdoing It"). The inadequacies of plot, according to Mason's second essay, are especially manifest in the first two acts, which are not only repetitive but patently inadequate in developing the characters of Othello, Desdemona, and Cassio. Othello's "nobility" is not unequivocally established at the start, nor are Othello's motives in promoting and trusting Cassio. Desdemona's role is even less realized: "Her love is as strange and challenging to common sense as Othello's grandeur."

In the third essay, "The Devil's Own," Mason finds the relationship of Othello and Iago similar to that between Macbeth and the witches. In both plays the hero's seduction represents an activating of vices dormant but already fully developed. As in the second essay, wherein Mason had agreed with F. R. Leavis (23) that Othello never trusted Desdemona from the start, Mason here further reduces Othello's "nobility" by approving Leavis's suggestion that Iago contributed nothing essential to Othello's fall: "When we look over the dialogue we see that Iago is not really leading Othello, but Othello Iago. In particular we see that Othello is using Iago to give himself permission to go even lower in his suspicions, to encourage what is so rapidly expanding inside him." The analogy here between Othello and Macbeth is apparent.

Since Mason sees Othello degenerating from a man to a fool to a beast, and finally to a devil, he agrees with T. S. Eliot (20) that in Othello's final speech he is merely "cheering himself up." Mason objects even more strenuously than Eliot to the last scene of the play: "A play cannot end on a trick and command our deep approval. (*Hamlet* has a similarly unsatisfactory catastrophe.) The play ought to have a dramatic rather than a theatrical close. The story needed rounding out with a return to Venice and a sentence of banishment. Othello was rightly killed in Cinthio's tale by the kinsmen of Desdemona."

Further evidences of Shakespeare's "hasty composition" are explored in the fourth essay, "Intelligence about Life," which stresses Desdemona's lack of intelligence and "culpable self-confidence" in contrast to Emilia's "superior force of mind and clairvoyance." Whether Shakespeare planned it that way or not, Emilia emerges from Mason's analysis as a choric character infinitely superior to the heroine. Mason concludes by reiterating his hypothesis that *Othello* is one of Shakespeare's "incomplete" tragedies: "Much could have been done for the play by a more deeply-felt Desdemona, but what the play needed even more was to establish Othello before demolishing him. . . . The balance of the play requires maximum substantiation of Othello as a figure of nobility."

109. Schwartz, Elias. "Stylistic 'Impurity' and the Meaning of *Othello*," *SEL*, X, No. 2 (Spring 1970), 297–313.

The play is seen to function on two integrated levels—the natural, or human, and the theological. On the natural level Othello is seen to be naive, self-assured, and egotistical, and Iago a pathological liar and hypocrite. Incapable of love, Iago struggles to destroy it as a potential for others. On the theological level Othello represents Everyman, and Iago symbolizes a part of that universal humanity. Hence Iago works to dominate the mind and heart of Othello, and as Desdemona continues to offer Othello salvation, the "demi-devil" Iago steadily maneuvers him toward "damnation." Thus the plot of *Othello* is not an "impure" mixture but a highly unified construction in two dimensions. According to Schwartz, Shakespeare's view of love in *Othello* is profoundly pessimistic; love contains within itself the seeds of its almost inevitable destruction.

110. Overmyer, Janet. "Shakespeare's Desdemona: A Twentieth Century View." *University Review*, XXXVII, No. 4 (June 1971), 304–305.

Desdemona's youth and inexperience are shown to contribute to the tragic outcome. Lacking in Brabantio an adequate father figure, and in Roderigo (typifying the "curled darlings" of Venice) a sufficent suitor of her own age group, Desdemona seeks an authority figure in the older Othello, but her naivete renders her hopelessly incapable of dealing artfully with his first pangs of jealousy, and thus she inadvertently helps Iago's cause by her very innocence. Hence the central irony of her role is that she is too innocent, too lacking in sophistication and womanly wiles, to convince Othello of her honesty. Her peculiar modernity resides in the fact that she is "one with the sweet young girls who marry older men seeking the heightened protection, love, and excitement their experience can provide. . . ." Unfortunately, she lacks the "womanly craft" necessary to alleviate Othello's sexual anxieties.

111. Wain, John. * "Introduction," *Othello: A Casebook*. London: Macmillan, 1971, pp. 1–33.

Wain resembles Bayley (62) in emphasizing the mutual "misunderstanding" and total lack of "comprehension" among the characters. Desdemona cannot comprehend her situation because she has been protected from life, first by Brabantio and later by Othello. Othello cannot understand because he is an outsider, Iago cannot because he is ignorant of emotions, and Roderigo cannot because he is a fool. Wain explores the symbolic meaning of the Turks, of Venice, and of other aspects of background; he discusses the role of race sensibly, and provides a perceptive and witty survey of some principal critics. Wain's essay is an informative and interesting introduction, particularly for beginning students.

Sources and Date

INTRODUCTION

Shakespeare read the story of *Othello* in the seventh novella of Giovanni Battista Giraldi Cinthio's *Hecatommithi*, published in Venice in 1566 and translated into French by Gabriel Chappuys in 1584. There is no record of an English translation until 1753, and scholars have disagreed about whether Shakespeare read the tale in French or in the original Italian (see Furness, *Var.*). It is now generally agreed that he read the story in Italian, as he did Boccaccio for the wager plot in *Cymbeline* and *Il Pecorone* for the main story of *The Merchant of Venice*. (For this subject, see G. K. Hunter, "Shakespeare's Reading" in *A New Companion to Shakespeare Studies*, ed. Kenneth Muir and S. Schoenbaum [Cambridge, 1971], p. 62.) M. R. Ridley maintains, however, that Shakespeare must have read the story in a lost English translation of Cinthio because there are no significant verbal parallels between Shakespeare's play and Cinthio's novella.

Many of the stories in *Hecatommithi* derive from actual events; the story of Othello may have been based on a murder in Venice in about 1508. In Cinthio's tale Othello is called the Moor, Iago the ensign, and Cassio the captain.

In addition to referring to Cinthio, Shakespeare consulted a number of peripheral sources. For Othello's speech defending himself against Brabantio's charge of witchcraft (I.3.128–170) he drew upon Pliny's *Natural History*, translated by Philemon Holland in 1601; and for information about Venice, upon *The Commonwealth and Government of Venice* (1543), originally in Latin and translated into English from Italian by Lewis Lewkenor in 1599.

For a discussion of the events that may have inspired Cinthio's story, see Rawdon Brown's account of a Venetian named Christoforo Moro in the NV, which also gives both the full Italian version by Cinthio and an English translation (pages 376–389). There is also a discussion of Cinthio and a translation of his story in Joseph Satin, *Shakespeare and His Sources* (Boston: Houghton, Mifflin, 1966). For additional information, consult Kenneth Muir, *Shakespeare's Sources*, I (London: Methuen, 1957).

The earliest attempt to date *Othello* was by Thomas Warburton, who chose the date 1611 because he saw an allusion in III.4.55 to the creation of baronets by James I: "The hearts of old gave hands: But our new heraldry is hands, not hearts." Few have considered Warburton's interpretation of this line sufficient evidence for dating the play.

A terminal date is provided by the earliest recorded performance at Whitehall on November 1, 1604, preserved in the Revels Accounts printed by Peter Cunningham in 1842. There may also be an early reference to *Othello* in the line "more savage than a barbarous Moor" in *The Honest Whore*, Part I, by Dekker and Middleton, a play known to have been written sometime before March, 1604. Moreover, the so-called "bad quarto" of *Hamlet*, a memorially reconstructed text that can be dated 1603, contains several echoes from *Othello*, and this may indicate, as Ribner suggests (E8, p. viii), that the actors reproducing *Hamlet* had played in *Othello* as well. In any event, scholars have assigned *Othello* to a time very close to the writing of *Hamlet*. Furness suggested 1604 as a probable date, as does E. K. Chambers in *William Shakespeare: A Study of Facts and Problems*, 2 vols. (Cambridge, 1930). Kittredge suggested "late 1601 or 1602." More recently, Peter Alexander, in his revision of the chronology (*Introduction to Shakespeare*, Cambridge, 1964), has assigned the play to 1599, shortly after *Julius Caesar* and *Hamlet*.

ENTRIES FOR SOURCES AND DATE

S1. Lennox, Charlotte. *Shakespeare Illustrated; Or, the Novels and Histories on Which the Plays Are Founded.* London, 1753.

Jonson thought highly of this first female Shakespearean scholar. Her collection is the first compilation of the sources, including Cinthio's tale. Although she sometimes argued that Shakespeare spoiled his plots by not adhering closely enough to his sources, her comments on *Othello* are still worth reading.

S2. Muir, Kenneth. "Shakespeare and Lewkenor," *RES*, n.s., VII (1956), 182–183.

An attempt to establish the influence of Cardinal Gaspar Contarino's *Commonwealth and Government of Venice*, translated by Lewis Lewkenor. Muir's evidence has been accepted by several recent editors of the play.

S3. Siegel, Paul N. "A New Source for *Othello*?" *PMLA*, LXXV (1960), 480.

An appropriately tentative suggestion that Geoffrey Fenton's *Tragicall Discourses*, which contains a story of an "Albanoys Captain" not in Cinthio's tale, may have influenced Shakespeare's play.

S4. Adams, Maurianne S. " 'Ocular Proof' in *Othello* and Its Source," *PMLA*, LXXXIX (1964), 234–241.

An important contribution to the subject of *Othello* and Cinthio, it combines two ideas: justice, and the motif of seeing (perception). It shows how Shakespeare assimilated this ironic idea from Cinthio but omitted Cinthio's moral bias.

S5. Watson, Thomas L. "The Detractor–Backbiter: Iago and the Tradition," *Texas Studies in Literature and Language*, V (1964), 546–554.

Using the historical approach of Campbell (18) and Spivack (59), Watson assembles evidence from medieval and Elizabethan literature to show Iago's lineage as a character type. This is a brief but authoritative supplement to the researches of Draper (38), Spivack, and others who have traced Iago's literary ancestry.

S6. Doebler, Bettie A. "Othello's Angels," *ELH*, XXXIV (1967, 156–172.

Shows how the last scene represents a conscious following of the medieval tradition of *ars moriendi*. An important contribution to the literary backgrounds of the play.

S7. Stewart, Douglas J. *"Othello:* Roman Comedy as Nightmare," *Emory University Q*, XXII (1967), 252–276.

Stewart attempts to prove that certain characters and plot situations traditional to Roman new comedy influenced *Othello*. Hence Othello is compared with the Roman "Miles gloriosus," Iago with the deceitful servant, and so on.

S8. Jones, Emrys. *"Othello,* 'Lepanto,' and the Cyprus Wars." *Shakespeare Survey 21* (1968), 47–52.

Jones discusses the possible influence (which he does not claim is direct) of James I's poem "Lepanto." According to Jones, more important than the poem was current interest in "the Cyprus Wars" (1570–71) and in Lepanto as a historical event.

S9. Mendonça, Barbara Heliodora C. de. *"Othello:* A Tragedy Built on Comic Structure," *Shakespeare Survey 21* (1968), 31–38.

The author agrees substantially with the general approach of Charlton(26), but develops the idea that *Othello* was constructed, in plot and characterization, on the Italian *commedia dell 'arte*. Iago's role was influenced by the Harlequin or "Brighella" of that comic from—an interesting but very speculative hypothesis.

Textual Criticism

INTRODUCTION

Othello was entered in the Stationers' Register on October 6, 1621, for Thomas Walkely and printed by Nicholas Okes in 1622 (Q1). The second publication (F1) was in the 1623 First Folio. Other editions appeared in 1630 (Q2) and 1655 (Q3).

It is generally agreed that Q2 is merely a copy of Q1 and Q3 a reprint of Q2. Hence the main problems of authority focus on the relationship of Q1 and F1, the two substantive texts. F1 contains 160 lines not in Q1, and the elisions from Q1 appear to have been deliberate cuts made in preparation for stage performance; moreover, the stage directions in Q1 are much fuller and more graphic than in F1. The F1 text, although longer than Q1, expurgates all oaths such as " 'Wounds," " 'S' blood," and so on, perhaps in conformity to the 1606 act prohibiting profanity on the stage. Furness long ago established Q1 as having been based on a playhouse copy (*NV*, pp. 342 ff.), but it has become increasingly apparent that F1 is also affiliated with a prompt book.

The consensus is that Q1 was set up from a careless transcript of a manuscript which had been revised for performances by the King's Men, and that F1 was printed from Shakespeare's manuscript ("foul papers") or from a theatrical prompt book, with some corrections made on the basis of a collation with Q1. Certainly F1 contains many compositor's errors, as if the printer found difficulty deciphering a manuscript; and Q1, although drastically revised, may well have provided a "cleaner" copy from which to work. In any event, editors since Malone and Johnson have favored the longer version, but have accorded great authority to Q1. At present there seems to be no alternative to adopting F1 as a basic text and depending heavily on Q1 to correct errors in the copy text.

ENTRIES FOR TEXTUAL CRITICISM

T1. Flatter, Richard. *Shakespeare's Producing Hand* (New York: Norton, 1948).

Flatter closely examines the metrical differences of Q1 and F1 in an effort to show that Q1 was edited by a "pedantic grammarian" with little knowledge of poetry or the theatre.

————. "Some Instances of Line-Division in the First Folio," *SJ*, XCII (1956). 184–196.

In both *Othello* and *Antony and Cleopatra*, a "broken-off verse" is often followed by some silent action on the stage. These instances of "silent action" suggest that Shakespeare was an ingenious director of his own plays.

T2. Hinman, C. K. "The 'Copy' for the Second Quarto of *Othello*," *Joseph Quincy Adams Memorial Studies* (Washington, D.C.: Folger Shakespeare Library, 1948).

Hinman demonstrates that Q2 is a copy of Q1, and that Q2 and Q3 have no independent authority.

T3. Walker, Alice. "The 1622 Quarto and the First Folio Text of *Othello*," *Shakespeare Survey* 5 (1952), 16–24. (See also The New Cambridge Edition, ed. Walker and J. Dover Wilson, pp. 121–135.)

Walker's widely accepted hypothesis is that F1 was not based on Shakespeare's manuscript, as hitherto supposed, but on a correction of Q1, a "licentious copy." The printers of F1 consulted "an authoritative manuscript" which they collated against Q1.

T4. Greg, W. W. *The Shakespeare First Folio* (Oxford, 1955), pp. 362–370.

This is a concise analysis of Q1 and F1 variants in the light of theories by E. K. Chambers (*Elizabethan Drama*, I) and Walker (above). Greg concludes, tentatively, that in about 1620 a transcript was made of

Shakespeare's manuscript by a scribe "of rather careless habits," and that this transcription was used to set up Q1. The editors of F1 cautiously and selectively consulted Q1 to correct errors in their main reference, a prompt book.

T5. Ridley, M. R. *Othello*, the Arden Shakespeare (Cambridge, Mass., 1958), pp. xvi-xliv; 199 ff.

Ridley defends Q1 against Walker's choice of F1 as a basic text. In Q1, according to Ridley, in spite of its omissions and errors, we have "as near an approximation as we are likely to get to the play as Shakespeare wrote it."

T6. Coghill, Nevill. *Shakespeare's Professional Skills* (Cambridge Univ., 1964), pp. 164–202.

In opposition to Greg, Walker, and Ridley, this theory proposes that Q1 was based on an early version by Shakespeare, who revised it after several performances, and that this last version was the basis for F1.

Editions

The editions of *Othello* cited below meet the unique requirements of many types of readers—high school students, undergraduates, graduate students, experienced scholars, and the general public. Entries are arranged according to dates of publication.

E1. **Othello: A New Variorum Edition*, ed. H. H. Furness (Philadelphia, 1886).

A fully annotated edition with F1 as the basic text. Eighteenth- and nineteenth-century critics are well represented, especially the German. This is an essential starting point for scholars.

E2. **Othello*, ed. C. F. Tucker Brooke and Laurence Mason, The Yale Shakespeare Edition (New Haven, 1918; reprinted 1948),

There is an excellent discussion of sources and stage history, with concise notes at the bottom of each page. Extensive commentary on scenes and passages is collected at the back.

E3. **Othello*, ed. Alice Walker and J. Dover Wilson (Cambridge University, 1957).

The New Cambridge Edition, this is the most scholarly critical edition after the Furness Variorum. It includes analyses of characters, date and sources, stage history, and textual criticism. Using F1 as the basic text, it is conservatively eclectic.

E4. **The Tragedy of Othello*, ed. G. E. Bentley, the Pelican Shakespeare (New York, 1958).

The introduction is excellent and occasionally profound. The notes at the bottom of the page are fewer than in Kernan's edition (see below) but quite adequate for graduate students.

E5. **Othello*, ed. M. R. Ridley, the Arden Edition (Cambridge, Mass., 1958).

Together with the New Cambridge Edition, this is the most scholarly modern continuation of Furness' Variorum for its discussions of source, dating, textual problems, and the "double time scheme" treated at length by Furness. Ridley adheres closely to Q1 in opposition to Walker's insistence on the primacy of F1. There is a complete translation and extensive analysis of Cinthio's *novella*.

E6. **Othello*, ed. Louis B. Wright and Virginia A. La Mar (New York, 1961).

This is an elementary but useful text, especially for high school students and general readers. Notes are on pages adjacent to the text, with some illustrations.

E7. **The Tragedy of Othello, the Moor of Venice*, ed. Alvin Kernan, the Signet Classic Shakespeare (New York, 1963).

Annotations at the bottom of the page are thorough. There is a full translation of Cinthio's tale by J. E. Taylor (1855), and four critical essays after the text: Thomas Rymer's essay, Coleridge's lecture, an excerpt from Robert Heilman's *Magic in the Web*, and a long essay on the structure of Shakespeare's tragedies by Maynard Mack. The annotated bibliography is helpful.

E8. **Othello, the Moor of Venice*, ed. George Lyman Kittredge, revised by Irving Ribner (Boston: Ginn and Co., 1966).

A revision of Kittredge's *Othello* in *The Complete Works* (1936), this edition has the advantage of the original notes. Ribner's introduction, though brief, summarizes admirably the essential data about text, sources, characterization, and plot.

Staging

INTRODUCTION

Data on stage performances and theatrical companies can be systematically traced by reference to four definitive works: E. K. Chambers, *The Elizabethan Stage*, 4 vols. (Oxford, 1923); G. E. Bentley, *The Jacobean and Caroline Stage*, 7 vols. (1941–1967), for the period 1603–1660; Emmett Avery, Arthur Scouten, *et al.*, *The London Stage, 1660–1800* (Carbondale, 1960), to be completed in 10 to 12 volumes; and for the period to 1900 the separate volumes of Allardyce Nicoll, *A History of the English Drama, 1660–1900*, 6 vols., Revised Edition (Cambridge, 1952–1959). A convenient checklist of performances for the period to 1700 is Alfred Harbage, *Annals of the English Drama*, revised by S. Schoenbaum (Philadelphia, 1964).

Both The New Cambridge Edition of *Othello* and the Shakespeare Encyclopedia provide concise summaries of stage history. For a more detailed, exhaustive study, see G. C. D. Odell, *Shakespeare from Betterton to Irving*, 2 vols. (New York, 1920), and C. B. Hogan, *Shakespeare in the Theatre*, 2 vols. (Oxford, 1952–1957). For an equally full documentation of stage performances, with emphasis on the modern period, see J. C. Trewin, *Shakespeare on the English Stage 1900–64* (New York, 1964). Information on more recent performances is available in separate issues of *Shakespeare Survey*, published continuously since 1948.

A recent development, strengthened by such studies as Granville-Barker's *Prefaces* and Margaret Webster's *Shakespeare Without Tears*, is to see Shakespeare from the perspective of actors on the stage rather than that of scholars in the study. An excellent account of acting methods and stage techniques is by A. C. Sprague and J. C. Trewin, *Shakespeare's Plays Today: Some Customs and Conventions of the Stage* (New York, 1970). The outstanding authority on the staging of Shakespeare's plays is A. C. Sprague. His *Shakespeare and the Actors: The Stage Business in His*

Plays, 1600–1905 (Cambridge, Mass., 1944) contains a long and brilliant chapter devoted exclusively to the staging of *Othello*, and his *Shakespearean Players and Performances* (Cambridge, Mass., 1953), pp. 78–86, closely analyzes Edmund Kean's Othello (an essay reprinted in *A Casebook on Othello*, ed. Leonard Dean [New York, 1961], pp. 199–205). Another great account of how actors have portrayed the characters in *Othello* from the time of Burbage down to Anthony Quayle and Donald Wolfit is by Marvin Rosenberg, *The Masks of Othello: The Search for the Identity of Othello, Iago, and Desdemona by Three Centuries of Actors and Critics* (Berkeley and Los Angeles, 1961). For a more elementary treatment from the same perspective, see Carol J. Carlisle, *Shakespeare from the Greenroom: Actors' Criticisms of Four Major Tragedies* (Chapel Hill 1969), and Roger Wood and Mary Clarke, *Shakespeare at the Old Vic* (New York, 1957).

Since the turn of the century Shakespeare has increasingly become an international phenomenon. A good brief introduction to performances in Germany, Scandinavia, France, Italy, Central America, Russia, and the Orient is the chapter "All the World's A Stage" in Louis Marder's *His Exits and His Entrances: The Story of Shakespeare's Reputation* (London, 1962). A detailed account of Shakespearean performances—and especially of *Othello*—in Africa is yet to be done. The long-standing popularity of *Othello* in Russia is set forth by N. A. Gorchakov in *The Theatre in Soviet Russia* (New York, 1957), and by Fabian Bowers in *Broadway, U.S.S.R.* (New York, 1959).

It is impossible to cite here all of the bibliographies on Shakespearean production in Europe and the Orient. There is an excellent selected bibliography covering France, Spain, Italy, Germany, Scandinavia, Russia, Hungary, and Serbia in Oswald LeWinter's *Shakespeare in Europe* (New York, 1963), pp. 375–377. For performances of *Othello* in other non-English-speaking countries, consult *The Shakespeare Encyclopedia* under the name of the country, with attention to the brief bibliographies attached at the end of each article.

ENTRIES FOR STAGING

St1. Sprague, A. C. *Shakespeare and the Actors: The Stage Business in His Plays, 1660–1905.* Cambridge, Mass., 1944.

Chapter IV, pages 185–223, provides one of the most comprehensive accounts in print of the staging of *Othello* in the eighteenth and nineteenth centuries. Sprague conducts his analysis act-by-act, explaining how different actors since 1660 have presented various scenes. Characteristic of his approach is his treatment of the so-called "collaring scene" in II.3: "Nineteenth Century Othellos seem always to have taken their Iagos by the throat. Kean made this a great moment in his performance, as did Forrest. Once when Macready was appearing in Liverpool and used the same business, a gentleman in the upper boxes is said to have jumped up and exclaimed, loud enough for all around to hear, 'Choke the devil, choke him!' " There is an extensive bibliography.

St1. Sprague, A. C. *Shakespearean Players and Performances.* London: Adam and Charles Black, 1953.

Two chapters pertain to stage performances: Chapter V, "Edmund Kean as Othello," pages 71–86, and "Edwin Booth as Iago," pages 121–135. These accounts are based on newspapers, diaries, memoirs, and autobiographical collections like Macready's reminiscences and Farington's diary. These chapters on two great actors are the best-written and most thoroughly documented of their kind.

St2. Stanislovski, Constantin. *Stanislovski Produces Othello,* trans. from the Russian by Helen Nowak. London: Geoffrey Bles, 1948.

Never completed nor intended for publication, these notes were written in Nice in 1929–1930 for the Moscow Art Theatre, which was then preparing its famous production of *Othello.* Stanislovski's directions for production include stage settings, costumes, blocking out of actors, rearrangement of acts and scenes, and detailed interpretations of characters. The last are especially interesting for their flamboyant embellishments, as when Stanislovski describes at length Roderigo's futile and humiliating pursuit of Desdemona before her marriage, or Othello's military career before his arrival in Venice. Stanislovski's conception of Othello as the "noble savage" is equally whimsical and hypothetical: "There are many naive and ludicrous habits of the savage in him, and Desdemona would try to eradicate them. She would teach him how to approach a woman and kiss her hand, and this big man, embarrassed and panting, wiping the perspiration from his forehead, would make every effort to master the things he is taught."

Stanislovski divides Act III, Scene 3 into three separate scenes. He transfers part of IV.1 to Act III and combines all of Act V with IV. However romantic and sometimes feverish, his interpretations of *Othello* are phenomenally thorough, thoughtful, and provocative. His bold and masterful innovations should still have value for directors of the play.

St3. Seltzer, Daniel. "Elizabethan Acting in *Othello*," *SQ*, X (1959), 201–210.

Seltzer collects some peripheral evidence—Nashe's Prologue to *Summer's Last Will and Testament*, stage directions, and so on—in an effort to establish how *Othello* was performed by the King's Men in Shakespeare's time. An attempt is made to determine which speeches were intended as soliloquies. (For two related studies, see Geoffrey Tillotson, "*Othello* and *The Alchemist* at Oxford,"*TLS* [July 20, 1933], and Marvin Rosenberg, "Elizabethan Actors: Men or Marionettes?" in *PMLA*, LXIX [1954].)

St4. Rosenberg, Marvin. *The Masks of Othello: The Search for the Identity of Othello, Iago, and Desdemona by Three Centuries of Actors and Critics*. Berkeley and Los Angeles: University of California Press, 1961.

As the full title suggests, Rosenberg compares the interpretations of actors with those of literary critics. Half of the work is devoted chiefly to actors and acting, a valuable survey based on the actors' own testimonies combined with newspaper reviews, memoirs, and critical essays. Rosenberg's discussion of eighteenth- and nineteenth-century actors and performances is especially rich in details. In his study of the eighteenth century, Rosenberg deals at length with Barton Booth, James Quinn, David Garrick, and Spranger Barry; in the nineteenth century with Edmund Kean, Macready, Fechter, Irving, James Booth, Forrest, and Salvini. In his discussion of the twentieth century ("not a good century for Othellos," according to Rosenberg), he reports on personal interviews with Paul Robeson, Earl Hyman, Anthony Quayle, Abraham Sofaer, Wilfrid Walter, and Donald Wolfit. Another valuable feature of Rosenberg's work is its attention to the neglected subject of how the text of *Othello* has been censored for stage performance. In an amusing concluding essay, "A Kind Word for Bowdler," Rosenberg demonstrates that

Bowdler's much-maligned *Family Edition* (1818) actually gave Victorians "a nearly entire" Shakespeare in contrast to the gutted versions of most other editions.

The substance of Rosenberg's contribution is in the first half of the book on actors and performances. The second half does not, understandably, succeed in the very difficult task of "reconciling" acting interpretations with literary criticism; instead, it contrasts the opinions of very few literary critics with Rosenberg's own view of the play. In two key essays, both entitled "In Defense of the Play," he condemns what he sees as two "extremes" of twentieth-century criticism, the "symbolic" represented by G. Wilson Knight and the "skeptical" by E. E. Stoll. The first is guilty of making "extra-theatrical abstractions," the second of turning the play into a historical curiosity. Rosenberg prefers "a human drama" that can be understood and enjoyed in the theatre.

St5. Ross, Lawrence J. "The Use of a 'Fit-Up' Booth in *Othello*," *SQ*, XII (1961), 359–370.

Othello, as well as several other plays performed at the Globe, used a "discovery" booth which served as the symbolic focal point for the action. In this "fit-up" booth Desdemona was murdered.

St6. Trewin, J. C. *Shakespeare on the English Stage 1900–64*. London: Barrie and Rockliff, 1964.

Trewin outlines the theories, changes, and innovations in productions since 1900. There are discussions of *Othello* performances by Forbes-Robertson (1902), Tree (1912), Grasso (1910), Asche (1907), Tearle (1921), Sofaer (1935), Olivier and Richardson (1938), Hawkins and Quayle (1947), Gielgud and Bannen, and others. An Appendix lists all productions at West End, London (1900–64), The Old Vic (1914–64), and Stratford-Upon-Avon (1879–1964). There is a full bibliography.

St7. Stone, George Winchester, Jr. "Garrick and *Othello*," *PQ*, XLV (1966), 304–320.

A thoughful, well-documented explanation of how David Garrick's portrayals of Iago and Othello were affected by mid-eighteenth-century ideas and events.

St8. Carlisle, Carol Jones. *Shakespeare from the Greenhouse: Actors'
Criticisms of Four Major Tragedies.* Chapel Hill: University of
North Carolina Press, 1969.

More than a survey of criticism, this book contains commentary
based on information by Sprague (St1) and Rosenberg (St4), together
with some new data gathered from letters, diaries, and periodicals. The
racial aspects of the play are intelligently and extensively discussed on
pp. 189ff.

St9. Sprague, A. C. and J. C. Trewin. *Shakespeare's Plays Today: Some
Customs and Conventions of the Stage.* London: Sidgwick and
Jackson, 1970.

Stage business in producing *Othello* since Edwin Booth is discussed,
with attention to the assassination scene, the clown, the so-called "collaring
scene," the herald, and the bowdlerization of stage texts. There is a critical
analysis of Tony Richardson's performance at Stratford in 1959. The pages
on *Othello* are quite general and selective but nevertheless informative.

⚙ King Lear

Edward Quinn

❀ CONTENTS

Index to Critics Cited and Their Entry Numbers *149*

Short Titles of Collections of King Lear *Criticism* *151*

The Criticism of King Lear *152*

    Introduction *152*

    Entries for the Criticism of King Lear *157*

Sources and Date *204*

Textual Criticism *206*

    Introduction *206*

    Entries for Textual Criticism *206*

Editions *208*

Staging *209*

Index to Critics Cited
and Their Entry Numbers

Bald, R. C. 36

Barker, Harley Granville 22

Bickersteth, Geoffrey 33

Block, Alexander 69

Blunden, Edmund 23

Bradley, A. C. 17

Bransom, J. S. H. 25

Brooke, Nicholas 59

Bush, Geoffrey 49

Calarco, N. Joseph 73

Campbell, Oscar James 37

Chambers, R. W. 30

Clemen, Wolfgang 27

Coleridge, Samuel Taylor 10

Craig, Hardin 20

Creighton, Charles 19

Danby, John F. 39

Dowden, Edward 13

Duthie, G. I. T2, E3

Elton, W. R. 63

Empson, William 44

Everett, Barbara 55

Fraser, Russell 58

Freud, Sigmund 21

Frost, William 51

Frye, Northrop 70

Furness, H. H. E1

Gardner, Helen 71

Greg, W. W. 29

Harbage, Alfred 34

Hazlitt, William 11

Heilman, Robert 38

Holloway, John 57

Hudson, H. N. 12

James, D. G. 45

Johnson, Samuel 6

Jorgensen, Paul 64

Keast, W. R. 40

Kernan, Alvin 65

Kernodle, George R. 32

Kirkman, J. 14

Knight, G. Wilson 24

Knights, L. C. 53

Kott, Jan 60

Lamb, Charles 9

Lennox, Charlotte 4

Levin, Harry 54

Lothian, J. M. 41

Mack, Maynard 66

Maclean, Norman 48

Markels, Julian 61

Mason, H. A. 67

Maxwell, J. C. 42

McNeir, Waldo 72

Moulton, R. G. 16

Muir, Edwin 35

Muir, Kenneth E2

Murphy, Arthur 5

Murray, John M. 26

Myrick, Kenneth 62

Nowottny, Winifred 50

Orwell, George 43

Rackin, Phyllis 74

Ribner, Irving 52

Richardson, William   7
Schlegel, A. W.   8
Sewell, Arthur   46
Skulsky, Harold   68
Spencer, Theodore   31
Spurgeon, Caroline   27
Stampfer, Judah   56
Swinburne, A. C.   15
Tate, Nahum   1

Theobald, Lewis   2
Tolstoy, Leo   18
Walker, Alice   T1
Warton, Joseph   3
Weitz, Morris   75
Welsford, Enid   28
Williams, G. W.   47
Wilson, J. D.   E3

Short Titles of Collections of <u>King Lear</u> Criticism

NV—*King Lear:* New Variorum Edition, ed. H. H. Furness. Philadelphia: Lippincott, 1880.

Bonheim—*The King Lear Perplex*, ed. Helmut Bonheim (Belmont, Calif.: Wadsworth, 1960).

Kermode—*King Lear: A Selection of Critical Essays*, ed. Frank Kermode (London: Macmillan, 1969).

The Criticism of <u>King Lear</u>

INTRODUCTION

The line from *King Lear* that best summarizes the history of the play's criticism is Kent's: "Nothing almost sees miracles but misery." For the past two centuries commentators have responded to this play in a manner that suggests an intimate relationship between the miserable and the miraculous, between the facts of suffering and death and the human capacity, if not to transcend those facts, at least to make an effort in the direction of transcendence. Moreover, "miracle" seems not too strong a term to describe this play's power to extract from men their deepest beliefs in order to account for its experience.

From one standpoint the latter phenomenon is a mixed blessing. For this is a body of criticism markedly deficient in objective, disinterested analysis. This is as true of contemporary interpretations as it is of nineteenth-century criticism. Whether written by an impressionist like Swinburne, an historical scholar like R. W. Chambers, or a textual critic like G. I. Duthie, *Lear* criticism tends to be more emotive than descriptive, more an act of collaboration on the part of the critic than an account of what goes on in the play. This may be the result of the fact that we are looking for answers where there are only questions. It may be that *King Lear* is of an order of drama that demands imaginative commitment far in excess of the ordinary suspension of disbelief. That commitment having been made, the critic finds himself being asked to be more than simply very intelligent. He finds himself being asked to give witness; to expose himself, like Lear; to feel what others feel. This may not be critical discourse as it is normally understood. In its defense it can be said that since *Lear* has extended our sense of the range of tragic drama, it is entirely appropriate that it should extend equally our sense of what criticism is.

The earliest criticism of *Lear* is Nahum Tate's 1681 adaptation. His alterations represent a reading of the play equally as much as does, say, Bradley's analysis. The difference between the act of criticism and that of adaptation is crucial but it should not be assumed that the latter was carried out either arrogantly or thoughtlessly. It is incorrect to imagine that Tate and the eighteenth-century critics thought of his ending as unquestionably superior to Shakespeare's. What they did claim was that the original ending was unendurable because it violated the law of poetical justice. The belief in poetical justice, however, was no unthinking, unimaginative adherence to the rules of authority. Nor was it—as Dr. Johnson makes clear—an expression of the naive belief that in life virtue always triumphs. Rather, it gave form and body to a more important principle: Art should affirm the reality that reason—sometimes in contradiction to experience—demonstrated to be true.

However diverse the formulations of that truth, they all could be reduced to the concept that there is a rational, moral order in the universe. The death of Cordelia represented not a direct threat to that belief but at least an unassimilable factor in it. Few men have been more sensitive to life as a painful pilgrimage than Dr. Johnson. In fact it might be argued that, unlike some of us, he had no need to look to literature for the *frisson du néant;* he experienced it all too intensely as an aspect of life. In any case, the latter part of the eighteenth century looked at *Lear* either from a psychological perspective (Warton, Lennox, Murphy) or from a moral one (Richardson). The discovery of its larger dimensions awaited the Romantics.

To Schlegel (8) belongs the distinction of first perceiving the play's true stature. In his criticism the perspective shifts from the ethical and psychological to the philosophical. This view enables him to defend the unhappy ending as the play's logical culmination. Stopping short of explicitly defining the philosophical impact, he does suggest that the play's pagan setting is designed to offer us a vision of life without the props of religious faith. This philosophical perspective pervades the view of the English Romantics—Lamb (9), Keats, and Hazlitt (11). In their response they attempt to illuminate the play's towering emotions. Lear is seen not as the pathetic old man of earlier critics but as the great Romantic agonist whose struggles issue in the birth of a terrible beauty. The play is seen, finally, as an enlargement and celebration of the human spirit in which man wrests from his own anguish the perception of "innate sparks of divinity" (Keats' phrase).

The Romantics' contribution to our understanding of *Lear* is enormous, but the largeness of their claims once threatened to universalize the play out of existence. Lamb's stricture about its unactability is a celebrated example of this tendency. Romantic rhetoric provided the most appropriate language for the discovery of the play's scope, but it did so at the cost of bypassing its distinctive problems and characteristics. It offered an emotive correlative for the overall effect, but very little insight as to how that effect is achieved.

Nevertheless, the Romantics provided the mainstream of critical response. Considerably less productive were the nineteenth-century efforts to resolve a debate begun in the eighteenth century by Warton (3) and Lennox (4). The problem arose from the attempt to determine whether Lear is mad from the beginning of the play (Lennox) or becomes mad in the course of the action. Throughout the nineteenth century the question was hotly debated, principally by professional alienists who lined up on one side or the other of the question. In the hands of the alienists *Lear* became a case history, and the crucial distinctions between a dramatic character and a human being were ignored. Post-Freudian observers saw him primarily as the victim of repressed incestuous drives (see Bransom, 25). More imaginative was Freud himself (21), who saw Cordelia as the embodiment of the death wish.

In the latter half of the nineteenth century, Dowden (13) returned to Schlegel in order to develop the position that the pagan setting implicitly allows us to question the nature of the gods. He argues that the chief characters provide a number of different answers to that question, none of which is conclusive. Dowen's hesitancy is brushed aside by Swinburne (15), who argues that the answer is clear and unequivocal: Lear is an indictment of those gods—be they mightly Olympians or pale Galileans —who "kill us for their sport." Confronted with Swinburne, Bradley (17) concedes that the play concentrates on human suffering. However, he says, it provides a vision of suffering as essentially redemptive. Suffering has enabled Lear to see what Cordelia represents. He dies thinking that she lives, and in one sense he is right, for what she represents is indestructible. This idea, as Bradley admits, leads us ultimately beyond tragedy and perilously close to religion. Along with Dowden, he is content to leave us on this frontier of religious mystery.

Bradley's interpretation is the culmination of the Romantic concern with the play's universal aspect, its timeless dimensions. To this the twentieth century has added a sense of its particularity. On the one hand, historical criticism has enabled us to see *King Lear* as an Elizabethan play, fully expressive of the values and attitudes of that period. On the other, *Lear* has emerged as the great Shakespearean drama for our time, the play that speaks most directly to our collective awareness of apocalyptic possibilities. Particularly noteworthy in this connection is the play's sudden and surprising appeal to young people (in many college classes in recent years *Lear* has eclipsed *Hamlet* in popularity among students).

But these special views have been most effective when allied to the larger issues of the play essentially as defined in the nineteenth century. The approach of the historical critics has led generally to the assumption that the religious frontier at which Bradley hesitated is essentially a Christian one, since the play is the product of a Christian era from the hands of a Christian writer (whether or not "he dyed a Papist" he almost certainly lived as a Christian of some denomination). Thus, history-oriented critics such as Chambers (30), Campbell (37), Danby (39), Maxwell (42), Ribner (52), and Myrick (62) see the play in varying degrees as an affirmation of orthodox Christian doctrine as understood in the Renaissance. Their position has been seriously challenged by Elton (63) who provides a formidable historical argument of an essentially Schlegelian view: The play represents a dark vision of life devoid of Christian sanctions, neither questioning nor affirming those sanctions except by implication.

Non-historical Christian interpretations are represented by Bicker-steth (33), Knights (53), and, somewhat more equivocally, Harbage (34) and Bush (49). Bickersteth argues for the presence of Christian archetypes; Knights sees the play's Christian ethos in its elevation of love *(caritas)* as a principle of ultimate signifiance. Bush sees the religious dimension, in the manner of Bradley, as an unrealized possibility but one that is experienced as possibility; Harbage makes an interesting attempt to link the Romantic view of the play—particularly Keats' phrase "vale of soul-making"—with a form of Teilhardian Christianity. (The reference to Teilhard should make it clear that at this point the impact of contemporary theology begins to blur the distinctions between the Romantic humanist view of the play and the traditional Christian view.)

Here the question of doctrinal adherence merges with the more general argument between those who see the play as the expression of an affirmative vision and those who feel it issues in despair. Among the latter category would have to be included Dr. Johnson and other eighteenth-century critics who found the original ending unendurable. In the former category are included not only the Christian interpretations but the views of such critics as Welsford (28), Spencer (31), Heilman (38), and James (45), who see the play affirming specific moral or intellectual values: for Welsford "folly" (unworldliness); for Spencer, an ordered universe; for Heilman faith, intuition, and love; for James "a certain power in human nature to overcome the world."

In the opposing camp are critics such as Everett (55), Stampfer (56), and Kott (60) (and influential directors such as Peter Brook and Herbert Blau), who see *Lear* as preeminently our play—that is, as embodying a vision of life represented in our time by the philosophy of existentialism and the theatre of the absurd. Everett, Stampfer, and Brooke see the play in existentialist terms as the spectacle of human courage and freedom affirming itself in an "imbecile universe." Kott takes an even more extreme position, seeing the play as an absurdist denial of any values either human or supernatural. His version leaves us with nothing but "the earth empty and bleeding." Kott's essay owes much to "*King Lear* and the Comedy of the Grotesque," one of two important but contradictory essays on the play by G. Wilson Knight (24). Knight's essay on the comic element is ultimately negative in its implications, while his other essay, "The *Lear* Universe," celebrates the play as a victory of love. In incorporating two extremes, Knight comes close to a synthesis.

Between the polarities of pessimism and optimism lie the subtly developed positions of Holloway (57), Skulsky (68), Mack (66), Frye (69), and Gardner (70). Holloway's anthropological perspective sees *Lear* within a context of ritual sacrifice. Skulsky looks at the play against a background of intellectual history. Mack ranges from primitive myth to the modern theatre, arguing for an underlying coherence beneath the play's protean forms. Frye offers us a view of the generic structure and an idea of the critical act as the completion of the play. Helen Gardner returns us to Bradley and Dowden to confront the mystery at the heart of Lear in the image of a "secular *Pieta*."

The emergence of a third category has made it clear that the criticism of the play has created its own dialectic and that recent critics are aware of the need for a synthesis of the play's conflicting interpretations. Probably the most satisfactory attempt in this direction to date has been that of Arthur Sewell (46). His approach, based upon the study of the relation between character and vision, provides a perspective that sees the play growing out of "man's perennial hunger for metaphysical being." Sewell attempts to combine scepticism and faith, ethics and metaphysics, in an overarching concept of "society." The explanation of the term requires greater amplification than he gives it. Nevertheless, he has demonstrated that some such conception lies beyond the antinomies that the play appears to express with equal emphasis.

"Nothing almost sees miracles but misery" suggests still another connection with the play's criticism in that it implies more than it says, forcing on our consciousness possibilities and expectations which propel us forward to a crucial final moment. There, if we do not find the hoped-for resurrection, we may at least discover what it means to take upon us the mystery of things. Upon such efforts the gods themselves throw incense.

ENTRIES FOR THE CRITICISM OF KING LEAR

1. Tate, Nahum. *The History of King Lear.* London, 1681. Excerpted in NV, Bonheim, and Kermode. Reprinted in *Shakespeare Adaptations,* ed. Montague Summers. New York: Haskell House, 1966.

Tate's comments on the play appear in the Dedication to his famous adaptation of *Lear.* Despite his considerable alterations, Tate is full of qualified praise for the original. He comments on Shakespeare's creative facility in representing "Lear's real and Edgar's pretended madness," and cites with approval the unusual but uniquely appropriate character of the language and imagery of the play. The play as a whole he finds a "heap of jewels, unstrung and unpolisht yet so dazzling in their disorder that I soon perceived I had seized a treasure." As for his alteration he feels he has unified the play by having Edgar and Cordelia fall in love. Of the happy ending Tate admits to some hesitation about its fitness. Yet the play's success on the stage has convinced him that he followed the right course.

The generosity of Tate's remarks is belied by the liberties he took with *Lear.* Nevertheless, his alterations appear to have been rooted in a sincere response to the experience of the play. In any case, as both Harbage (34) and Mack (66) have pointed out, Tate's alterations have the virtue of being alterations. They at least are not represented as being faithful to the original, unlike many subsequent productions and interpretations that presumed to offer Shakespeare's play.

2. Theobald, Lewis. *The Censor* [April 25, 1715 and May 2, 1715]. London, 1717. 3 vols.

Theobald's remarks—the earliest full-length discussion of the play—are contained in two essays originally published in the periodical *The*

Censor. He prefaces his analysis with a general statement in orthodox neo-classical language on the corrective function of tragedy: "to purge us of those passions that hurry us into misfortunes and correct those vices that make us incur the Wrath of Heaven." In his analysis of *Lear* he proposes to focus on the character of Lear and the "spirit and elegance" of the play's language. He will not dwell on the play's irregularities, its violation of the "rules of Aristotle." By way of introduction, he offers a summary of the Lear story as given in the chronicles. Shakespeare's treatment of the story is designed to point up two moral lessons, one directed against "Rash and Unwary Bounty," the other against "Ingratitude of Children." The former evokes compassion, the latter detestation. Shakespeare skill-fully manipulates the action so that the emotions reinforce each other: the greater our compassion for Lear's suffering, the greater our hatred of the daughters' ingratitude. (Hazlitt was to make the same observation one hundred years later.) The only serious flaw in the play is the catastrophic conclusion. Tate's alteration is a definite improvement in this respect. The essay concludes with praise for the consistency and credibility with which Lear's character is represented.

The reputation of Theobald as a competent textual scholar with a narrow, unimaginative view of literature is belied by his essays on *Lear*. On the contrary, he here emerges as an original and imaginative critic. He is perfectly capable of dismissing the "rules" as irrelevant and of dis-playing considerable subtlety in analyzing the relationship between the structure and the emotional impact of the play. Finally, his interest in the character of Lear anticipates much of the criticism of the latter half of the eighteenth century.

3. Warton, Joseph. *The Adventurer*, Essays 113, 116, and 122 [1753–1755]. London, 1797. Excerpted in NV and Bonheim.

Warton's comments appear in three numbers of *The Adventurer*, an eighteenth-century periodical. In the first of these (No. 113, Dec. 4, 1753), he celebrates Shakespeare's success in establishing the credibility of Lear's madness by "a broken hint, a short exclamation, a word or a look." This use of understatement, in contrast to the set speeches a Dryden or Corneille might employ, is an indication of Shakespeare's keen psychologi-cal insight.

In his treatment of the play (No. 116, Dec. 15, 1753), Warton an-alyzes the heath scenes, noting how the thunder heightens the sense of

Lear's suffering. The suffering in turn reveals "the secret workings . . . of Lear's mind." His last essay on the play (No. 122, Jan. 5, 1754) focuses on Lear's abdication as the particular event that precipitates his madness. He concludes by citing the chief flaws of the play. Among these he lists the double plot, which destroys the play's unity; the blinding of Gloucester and the Dover Cliff scene, the former too terrible and the latter too improbable for representation on the stage; and the cruelty of Goneril and Regan, "too savage and unnatural" to be credible. In the eighteenth and nineteenth centuries, however, his analysis was best known for its assertion that the cause of Lear's madness was the ingratitude of his daughters. Thus Warton and Charlotte Lennox (4) were responsible for the major positions later adopted on the question of Lear's madness. Apart from that dreary controversy, however, Warton's psychological approach anticipates much of the finest nineteenth-century criticism of the play.

4. Lennox, Charlotte. *Shakespeare Illustrated*, Vol. III. London, 1754. Excerpted in Bonheim.

Charlotte Lennox's comments on the play are notable chiefly for her remark that Lear's response to Cordelia in the opening scene demonstrates that the old man is already mad. This is the earliest expression of a point of view which occupied much of the attention of critics in the nineteenth century. She also deplores Shakespeare's violation of the rules of poetic justice, viewing his alterations of the traditional story as "neither probable, necessary or just." She concludes with an account of the play's sources, including the first citation of the *Arcadia* as the source of the subplot.

For an account of the development of the Lennox position that Lear is mad from the beginning of the play, see Irving Ribner's "Lear's Madness in the Nineteenth Century," *Shakespeare Association Bulletin* XXII (1947), 117–129.

5. Murphy, Arthur. *The Gray's Inn Journal* [1754]. London, 1756. 2 vols.

Murphy's analysis appears in three numbers (65, 66, 87) of *The Gray's Inn Journal* under the pseudonym of Charles Ranger. In No. 65 (Jan. 12, 1754) he takes issue with Warton's assertion that the cause of Lear's madness is his abdication of royal power. For Murphy, the king becomes mad at the precise moment of Tom O'Bedlam's entry on the heath. Lear's statement that Tom must have been brought to his condition by unkind daughters makes it clear that Lear's fixation on his daughters' ingratitude—not the abdication of his power—is the precipitating cause of madness. In No. 66, Murphy publishes a letter from a reader qualifying the assertion that Lear's madness is precipitated by ingratitude. The unidentified writer alleges that ingratitude brings Lear to the point of insanity, but it is the realization that he has abandoned his royal power that drives him over the brink. The theme of the play is concerned as much with the "folly of parents" as with the ingratitude of children. In No. 87 Murphy reasserts his original argument, adding that the subplot is an unnecessary distraction and that Garrick's performance as Lear remains the greatest commentary on the play. He concludes with the observation that the original ending would probably be unendurable if represented on the stage, but adds that he would wish to see it done as an experiment.

Here again the nature and cause of Lear's madness occupy the main concern of the commentator. More interesting are Murphy's comments on the play's ending. He is far from unresponsive to the original ending. Like Johnson, he considers it not necesssarily inferior to Tate. He goes even further than Johnson in acknowledging a desire to see the original ending performed on stage.

6. Johnson, Samuel. "King Lear" [1765] in *Samuel Johnson on Shakespeare*, ed. W. K. Wimsatt. New York: Hill and Wang, 1960. Excerpted in NV, Bonheim, and Kermode.

Johnson applauds the ability of the play to seize the attention of the audience. He defends the credibility of the opening scene and answers Warton's objections (3) concerning "excessive cruelty" and the double plot. The cruelty of the daughters, he argues, Shakespeare found in his sources (Johnson's reference is to "historical fact"). As for the blinding of Gloucester, he acknowledges that this is an act "too horrid for dramatic exhibition." The subplot is justified since it is interwoven into the "chief design" of the play. Not justified, however, is the death of Cordelia: "I was many years ago so shocked by Cordelia's death that I know not whether I ever endured to read again the last scene of the play till I undertook to revise them as an editor." Tate's happy ending, enabling Lear to conform to the principle of poetic justice, does not weaken the play. Witness the continuing popularity of the Tate version on the stage.

It should be noted that Johnson is not denying that Shakespeare's ending is true to life. Nor is he suggesting that the original ending lacks power. His comment about the impact of Cordelia's death upon him makes that clear. What he is suggesting is that art should strive to imitate that invisible justice and order which he and the eighteenth century in general regarded as immutably present in the universe.

7. Richardson, William. *Essays on Shakespeare's Dramatic Characters.* London, 1784. 170 pp.

For Richardson, Lear is an example of "the man of mere sensibility, undirected by reflection." He is impulsive and unstable, dominated by his passions. Yet his capricious, inconstant nature is not without capacities for great feeling and warmth. His madness is the natural result of his suffering, but that suffering is also the means of his final achievement of self-knowledge. His "poor naked wretches" speech is an act of perfect contrition. Here Lear has arrived at reflection in his self-condemnation.

Richardson's criticism is here, as elsewhere, characterized by its strong moralistic tone. His emphasis on Lear's acquisition of knowledge through suffering gives him the distinction of being the first of a long line of critics who saw the final meaning of the play residing in a perception of moral value by the old king.

8. Schlegel, A. W. "Criticism on Shakespeare's Tragedies," Lecture XXV in *Lectures on Dramatic Art and Literature,* trans. John Black. London, 1808. Excerpted in NV, Bonheim, and Kermode.

Schlegel sees the movement of the play as a precipitous descent in which "humanity is stripped of all external and internal advantages and given up as prey to naked helplessness." Lear is reduced to a condition in which all he is capable of is "loving and suffering beyond measure." He defends the subplot by arguing that in reinforcing the theme of the main plot Shakespeare has universalized it, leaving us with the impression of a "great commotion in the moral world." He deplores Tate's happy ending, arguing that the logic of the play demands Shakespeare's ending. There is no redemptive scheme in the play. Its deliberately pagan setting is designed to suspend the religious question and thereby to enable us to perceive life as it is, given a purely secular perspective: a "dark pilgrimage."

Schlegel, like Lamb, is one of the most important nineteenth-century critics of the play. His defense of the subplot is still quoted by critics. He is also the first critic (excluding Addison, who offered only casual remarks) to argue that the play's ending is not a flaw but the natural expression of its underlying vision. Beyond that, he is the first to suggest the play's philosophical—as opposed to ethical—character.

9. Lamb, Charles. *On the Tragedies of Shakespeare* [1811]. Excerpted in NV, Bonheim, and Kermode.

Lamb's essay offers probably the most celebrated critical statement ever made about the play: "The *Lear* of Shakespeare cannot be acted." The theatre can only represent the physical dimension of this play, not its vast spiritual and intellectual range. The stage offers us a Lear we can see, the play offers us a Lear we can be. We partake of his "mighty irregular power." The profundity of his experience is mocked by the spuriousness of Tate's happy ending: "as if the living martyrdom that Lear has gone through . . . did not make a fair dismissal from the stage of life the only decorous thing for him."

Lamb's criticism had two significant contradictory effects upon the history of *King Lear*. Negatively, it served as the *locus classicus* for the belief that "the *Lear* of Shakespeare" was unplayable. Positively, it was the earliest expression of the sublimity of the play and of the heroic stature of its leading character. Not until Granville–Barker (22) could Lamb's apparent contradiction be resolved. Finally, as Harbage (34) points out, in the phrase "living martyrdom" Lamb reveals a sacrificial dimension of the play which comes to be regarded as highly significant in subsequent criticism.

10. Coleridge, Samuel Taylor. "Notes on *Lear*," [1812–1819] in Coleridge's *Shakespearean Criticism*, ed. T. M. Raysor. 2 vols. New York: Everyman's Library, 1960. Excerpted in NV, Bonheim, and Kermode.

Coleridge's comments consist of a series of notes on various aspects of the play. He views Gloucester's insensitive remarks about Edmund's illegitimacy in the opening scene as indicative of the insults to which the latter has been subjected all of his life, insults which provide the motive for his villainy. He regards the subsequent action of the division of the kingdom as highly improbable, finds a "faulty admixture of pride and sullenness" in Cordelia's "nothing," compares the heath scene to a Michelangelo canvas, argues that in the blinding of Gloucester "the tragic has been urged beyond the *ne plus ultra* of the dramatic," observes that the Fool's wit increases rather than diminishes our sense of pain in witnessing Lear's suffering, and compares the movement of the play to "the hurricane and the whirlpool, absorbing while it advances."

Aside from these illuminating but fragmentary insights, Coleridge offers no sustained criticism of the play. It remains a peculiar irony that Shakespeare's greatest commentator should be comparatively unresponsive to his greatest play.

11. Hazlitt, William. *Characters of Shakespeare's Plays* [1817]. London: Oxford University Press, 1929. Excerpted in NV and Bonheim.

For Hazlitt, *Lear* is Shakespeare's greatest play, for it represents his most sincere and profound expression in drama. His subject—filial piety—arises from the very depths of all we regard as natural, and the madness that ensues from the disruption of that natural bond reveals the author's profound "knowledge of the connecting links of the passions and their effect upon the mind. . . ." He quotes at length the scenes of Lear's quarrel with Goneril and Regan, and of the reunion of Lear and Cordelia, scenes that incorporate "the wildness of poetry and all the heart-felt truth of nature." He concludes by citing with approval Lamb's comments on the play.

Hazlitt appends a number of general observations derived from his reading of the play. Among these is his version of catharsis: Our sense of pain in witnessing tragedy is overwhelmed by the "swelling tide" of natural affection and desire for the good that is raised at the same time.

Hazlitt's essay is chiefly notable for its early citation of *Lear* as the greatest of Shakespeare's works and for its emphasis on the play's sincerity and depth, picturing Shakespeare "caught in the web of his own imagination." Interestingly enough, that same formulation has been used by some critics who see the play as a failure [see 26, 67].

12. Hudson, H. N. "The Tragedy of Lear," in *Lectures on Shakespeare*. New York, 1848. 2 vols.

Hudson is primarily concerned with the play's revelation of character. He notes that the play's primitive setting provides a perfect backdrop for the fierce, larger-than-life emotions that are to be displayed against it. The character of Lear is Shakespeare's greatest creation in the "art of historical perspective." Lear always speaks from the vantage of retrospect—drawing on the past in a desperate attempt to forestall his impending loss of control. The most noteworthy feature of Cordelia is the powerful sense of presence she creates even when she is not on stage. This testifies to the reality of her spiritual significance as the embodiment of filial piety. The Fool is the key to the play's mystery. He should be seen as a model of selfless love, dying in despair at his failure to prevent the loss of Lear's sanity.

Hudson's analysis has most of the virtues and some of the flaws of nineteenth-century criticism. Overly sentimental and excessively rhetorical, he is nevertheless remarkably illuminating about the feelings which the play and its characters provoke. With Hudson, criticism is an act of sympathetic imagination with the characters of the play. He displays that quality admirably.

13. Dowden, Edward. *Shakespeare: A Critical Study of His Mind and Art* [1875]. New York: G. P. Putnam, 1962. Excerpted in NV and Bonheim.

Dowden sees the play as "the greatest single achievement in poetry of the Teutonic, or Northern, genius." He compares its features—its combination of the sublime and the grotesque—to that of a Gothic cathedral. Identifying the ethical dimension of the play with Stoicism, he argues that the play moves beyond ethics to a vision of life that is not reducible to "a code of precepts or a body of doctrine." However, while not offering any answers to ultimate questions, the play does affirm human virtue divorced from any supernatural agency. What Lear acquires is the sense of Cordelia's value. The pagan setting of the play allows Shakespeare "to put the question boldly 'What are the gods?'" A dazzling variety of answers is offered but all are inconclusive; only impenetrable reality remains. The play leaves us in the presence of mystery.

Dowden's essay defines an important position between the pessimism of Swinburne and the optimism of some twentieth-century critics, a position that has come to be accepted with varying degrees of qualification by a number of mid-twentieth-century critics (cf. 46 and 66). It is all the more effective for the brevity with which it is expressed.

14. Kirkman, J. *Animal Nature Versus Human Nature in King Lear.*
London, 1879.

Kirkman takes a detailed look at the animal references in *Lear*. In
the play are 133 allusions to 64 different names of animals. The majority
of these references are negative in tone, referring to the treachery and
cruelty of the animals mentioned. The Fool's references to animals reveal
a consistent observation of their habits. Edgar's allusions sharpen the parallel between the society of men and that of beasts. Lear's are directed toward the discovery of animality lying at the heart of man. The play offers
us a negative view of animal nature in order to intensify our sense of how
much worse human nature is when it is reduced to an animal-like state.
Thus Shakespeare is a Darwin of the moral sphere—seeing man as emerging from animal origins and reverting to them when "the qualities of rev-
erence, fidelity, conscience and righteousness are foregone."

Kirkman's analysis, like Walter Whiter's *Specimens of a Commentary on Shakespeare* (1794) is one of the pioneering studies of Shakespeare's imagery. Bradley's use of the frequency of animal allusions as the
basis of his analysis, and the subsequent work of Spurgeon (27), Heilman
(38), and others testify to the importance of Kirkman's study.

15. Swinburne, A. C. *A Study of Shakespeare.* London, 1880. 309 pp.
Excerpted in Bonheim.

Swinburne characterizes *Lear* as the "most Aeschylean" of Shakespeare's plays, emphasizing however that the world of *Lear* is darker and
more pessimistic than anything in Aeschylus. For the "keynote" of Shakespeare's play is Gloucester's despairing comment, "Like flies to wanton
boys are we to the gods/They kill us for their sport." With this focus the
play produces a terrible vision in which "nature herself . . . is revealed
as unnatural." Nevertheless, there is a triumph of a kind in that the mon-
strosity of the evil characters reinforces by contrast the greatness of the
good ones. One peripheral aspect of the play is its revelation of Shakespeare's concern and compassion for the poor and the downtrodden. For
Swinburne such concern demonstrates that Shakespeare was "a spiritual,
if not a political, democrat and socialist."

Swinburne's criticism transforms Schlegel's philosophical formulation into a theological one. His specific reference to Gloucester's lines as
the "keynote" of the play has been generally discredited, but, for all his

special pleading, he has brought one valuable insight to the play: that the role of "the gods" is a significant one, however interpreted. Much of the subsequent criticism of the play will be concerned to define the nature of that role.

16. Moulton, R. G. *Shakespeare as a Dramatic Artist*. Oxford, 1885.

As his title suggests, Moulton is primarily concerned with the structural features of the play. He calls attention to a distinctive characteristic, the fact that the turning point occurs in the first scene. The rest of the play is the logical working-out of the imbalance that Lear creates in the beginning. Moulton then considers Shakespeare's skillful interweaving of the play's two plots. Both deal with three tragic actions. In the main plot these are the nemesis against Lear, the suffering of Kent and Cordelia, the destruction of Goneril and Regan. These are paralleled in the subplot by the nemesis upon Gloucester, the suffering of Edgar, and the death of Edmund. What Moulton describes as "the centrepiece" of the play occurs when the two plots converge in the heath scene. Here Lear's real and Edgar's feigned madness combine in a "terrible duet" that constitutes the emotional climax of the play. To this is added the voice of the Fool. The function of the Fool is to give verbal form to Lear's "sin of passion" from which the tragedy springs, and to keep it constantly before Lear's and the audience's eyes.

Moulton's analysis represents a departure from the psychological and philosophical problems of the play. It focuses instead on the action, enabling us to see unity underlying diversity and to understand better the play's superb craftsmanship.

17. Bradley, A. C. *Shakespearean Tragedy* [1904]. New York: Meridian Books, 1955; New York: Fawcett, 1966. Excerpted in Bonheim and Kermode.

Bradley begins by exploring the implications of what he considers a fundamental paradox about *King Lear:* the fact that it is "the best but least popular and least playable of Shakespeare's dramas." Here he echoes Lamb in the belief that the scope of the play is too vast to be represented on the stage. Among the dramatic problems he cites the improbabilities of the opening scene and the Dover cliff scene, the grotesqueness of the blinding of Gloucester, the emotional frustration of the play's ending, and the arbitrariness of the double plot. But it is precisely these defects of the play considered as drama that contribute to its wider significance as an imaginative work of art. For in *Lear* psychological and dramatic credibility are less relevant than certain symbolic values apparent in it.

The play explores the ramifications of a disjunction in man (conveyed by the large number of allusions to animals) that soon encompasses all of nature and that finally leads to a questioning of the nature of the gods. In the character of Lear we see the emergence of nobility through suffering. Thus the play is essentially purgative, and might properly be titled *The Redemption of King Lear*. Lear dies believing that Cordelia lives. The fact of her death is relatively unimportant: "what happens to such a being does not matter, all that matters is what she is." What she represents is a value ("soul") that is indestructible. But too heavy an emphasis on that fact would take us beyond the boundaries of tragedy, and probably into the realm of religion. The play stops short of that, leaving us with the awareness that life is part of a larger impenetrable mystery that offers no final answers and to which we can only submit in patience.

Probably the most influential analysis of the play ever written, Bradley's interpretation is significant for the following reasons: (1) It develops and expands the Lamb thesis that the play is not suited for the stage; (2) It establishes the hypothesis—accepted by many subsequent critics as both correct and crucial—that Lear dies of joy under the delusion that Cordelia lives; (3) It emphasizes the fact of suffering (as both ennobling and redemptive) as the major theme of the play; (4) It suggests that the play is ultimately theological in its implications and—while stopping short of the claim itself—sets the stage for the Christian interpretation of subsequent critics.

18. Tolstoy, L. "On Shakespeare and On the Drama," in *Tolstoy on Shakespeare*, trans. V. Tchertkoff and I.F.M. London and New York, 1906. Excerpted in Bonheim.

For Tolstoy, *Lear* is the supreme example of his thesis that Shakespeare is not only not a great genius, but not even "an average author." He proceeds by providing an unsympathetic summary of the plot of the play. In the course of the far-from-objective "summary" he delivers adverse comments on the lack of motivation of the characters, on their inconsistency, and on their failure to achieve any "individuality of language." He finds the arrangement of the plot arbitrary and full of anachronisms. He then offers a detailed comparison of Shakespeare's play with the old *Leir*, and finds the latter "incomparably and in every respect superior to Shakespeare's adaptation."

Tolstoy's astounding judgments of the play are enclosed within his larger denigration of Shakespeare in general. His repudiation of Shakespeare was partly the result of jealousy, partly an attack on the aestheticism of the nineteenth century, partly the result of his tendency to read Shakespeare's plays as if they were realistic novels, and partly bias derived from his view of Shakespeare as an enemy of the common people and a philosophical fatalist. As for his view of *Lear* itself, George Orwell supplies a provocative and interesting explanation in his analysis of the play [see 43].

19. Creighton, Charles. *An Allegory of King Lear*. London, 1913. 156 pp.

Creighton sees this play as an allegory of the English Reformation. Lear is Henry VIII; his division of the kingdom is the redistribution of ecclesiastical lands and authority. Kent is Thomas More (except for the last scene when he is transmuted into Thomas Churchyard). The Fool is Skelton, Goneril is the papacy, Regan is Anglicanism, Cordelia is humanism. The allegory in the subplot is somewhat more abstract: Gloucester is monasticism, Edgar the legitimate offspring of medieval learning, Edmund the new philosophy (specifically Thomas Cromwell). Thus the play deals with "the overthrow of a thousand years of priestly power grown hopelessly corrupt."

No summary can do justice to the author's ingenuity nor to his self-confidence. We can, however, sample the flavor and quality of his writing in this brief quote on the "five or six and thirty" of Lear's knights who followed him to Dover:

> They rode with him to Dover but it does not appear that they ever arrived there. *They must have stopped at Canterbury*. This body of five or six and thirty are the Articles of Edward VI, which were forty-two. Gloucester's castle . . . is the University of Cambridge. Their stopping place on the way to Dover is Cranmer's see of Canterbury. It follows that the night in the storm must have been a long one—some ten years of English history.
>
> As the night the day. . . .

20. Craig, Hardin. "The Ethics of *King Lear*," *Philological Quarterly 4* (1925), 97–109. Excerpted in Bonheim.

Craig begins by stressing the classical–medieval inheritance of Ren-

aissance thought reflected in the ethical character of *Lear*. In the play the
virtue of justice is developed in accordance with the dominant thought of
the time, as handed down from Aristotle and Aquinas. Justice is seen as
the supreme manifestation of the natural law. Injustice is therefore unnatural. The interpenetration of justice and nature was expressed by one contemporary of Shakespeare in terms of six categories, all of which are
prominently featured in *Lear*: religion, filial affection, gratitude, forbearance, loyalty, and honesty. The final aspect of Renaissance thought on the
nature of justice relevant to the play is that the loss of justice in the state
is paralleled by the loss of reason in the mind.

Craig's essay represents the earliest important application of historical criticism to the play. Thus it is concerned to see the play in the
context of Renaissance thought and culture. It is this pioneering aspect of
the study—providing the groundwork for subsequent criticism of this type
[see 36, 58, 68]—that is its chief distinction.

21. Freud, Sigmund. "The Theme of the Three Caskets," *Collected Papers* (London: Hogarth Press, 1925), pp. 244–256. Excerpted in Bonheim.

Freud calls attention to the similarity in content between the casket
scene in *The Merchant of Venice* and the opening scene in *Lear*. In these
scenes both the leaden casket and Cordelia—the least regarded and best
choices—are notable for their silence and simplicity. These qualities, Freud
argues, are symbolic of death. Lear is an aged, dying man who refuses to
renounce the love of women and to accept death. Therefore, he rejects
Cordelia in favor of Goneril and Regan. The apparent unrelatedness of
Cordelia to death is explained by the principle of "replacement of the opposite," whereby the negative experience is represented in opposite terms.
Lear's last entrance, carrying Cordelia's body, is an emblematic reversal of
his own death.

In his analysis Freud is talking less about the play than the myth
upon which the story is based. Regarded as such, the theory has some
value, but the light that it throws upon *Lear* is a murky one at best.

22. Barker, Harley Granville–. *Prefaces to Shakespeare* [1927]. Princeton University Press, 1965.

Granville–Barker is specifically concerned to rescue the play from
the charges of Lamb and Bradley that it is too grand for the stage. He

argues that the chief problem in theatrical presentation has arisen from the attempt to represent such elements as the storm scene realistically rather than to recognize that Lear's speech ("Blow winds, and crack your cheeks . . .") is creating the storm itself. But this kind of representation requires an actor willing to surrender himself to the "metaphysical power" of the role.

Next he moves to a consideration of the construction of the play, the method of the dialogue, and the characters. He criticizes the subplot as "pedestrian" and applauds the "megalithic grandeur" of the opening scenes. He notes the "balanced orchestration" of the dialogue and the wide range of Lear's language, which moves from the commonplace to the transcendent. He is particularly eloquent in describing the overwhelming "fact of death" as the dominant tone of the conclusion, and in characterizing Cordelia's death as an example of "life's capricious cruelty."

Granville–Barker's unique ability to combine the perceptions of the finest literary criticism with the experience of a man of the theatre is nowhere better illustrated than in his analysis of *Lear*. As a result, he has been the prime force behind the many snccessful productions of the play that have occurred since his analysis was written. Chief among these is his own production of the play (in 1940, with John Gielgud in the title role), regarded by many as the finest *Lear* of the century.

23. Blunden, Edmund. "Shakespeare's Significances," in *Shakespeare Association Papers 1928*, reprinted in *The Mind's Eye* (1934). London: Oxford University Press, 1929. 18 pp.

Blunden directs his attention to the play's language, particularly to the logical substratum of Lear's mad ranting. Lear's monomania is all-inclusive. Incorporating everything in his experience to his theme, he catches up "some idea whether suggested to his memory by circumstances or to his mind by the conversation he hears" and shapes it to his purpose. Thus his references to Tom O'Bedlam as "learned Theban" and "good Athenian" are part of a series of intricate reminiscences of the poetry of Horace. Similarly, he draws upon his knowledge of hunting, falconry, and the art of war to impose a curious consistency to his thoughts. This is evident elsewhere, for example, in the Fool's final line ("I'll go to bed at noon"), a multi-level pun, and, more extensively, in the play's seasonal imagery. All of these references display "the richness, and intuitive complexity and choral harmony of Shakespeare's significances."

Blunden's observations provide a subtle, impressionistic anticipation of the more detailed studies of unifying language patterns in the play.

24. Knight, G. Wilson. *The Wheel of Fire* [1930]. Cleveland: World, 1962, 5th ed., revised. New York: Meridian Books, 1957. Excerpted in Kermode.

Knight is the author of two important essays which are, not uncharacteristically, at the same time both brilliant and inconsistent. In "The Lear Universe" he argues that the play charts a purgatorial experience of "creative suffering." Edmund, Lear, and Cordelia correspond to three periods in the development of man: the primitive, the civilized, and the ideal. The play records the movement toward that ideal, an "awakening into love" that is its ultimate goal.

In *"King Lear* and the Comedy of the Grotesque," Knight directs his attention to the comic dimension of *King Lear.* The play's comedy produces a "sublime incongruity" reflected in the grim humor of the Fool, the madness of Lear ("the terrible bordering on the fantastic"), the attempted suicide of Gloucester, and "the hideous joke of destiny," the death of Cordelia. These elements leave us confronting "the very absence of tragic purpose," the possibility that life is absurd and meaningless. Their presence in *Lear* suggests the mingling of the tragic and the comic in a realm beyond human comprehension.

The major problem of Knight's two essays is that he makes no attempt to integrate them. The comic element belongs in any account of the Lear universe, and its very existence there—as no one has shown better than Knight himself—must qualify radically any view of the play as an "awakening into love." What is clearly needed is a third essay, synthesizing the two that have been written. Barring that, of the two essays *"King Lear* and the Comedy of the Grotesque" must be regarded as superior in its originality (although the basic idea is in Dowden) and in imaginative execution.

25. Bransom, J. S. H. *The Tragedy of King Lear.* Oxford: Basil Blackwell, 1934. 228 pp.

Bransom's study begins with the assertion that the correct interpretation of the play "requires the imaginative use of our own experiences." Thus the play speaks to the mature man, who will perceive that its struc-

ture, far from being loose and ragged, is the most closely-woven of Shakespeare's plays. The main focus of the play is psychological—"the rise and
course of the King's insanity." The central facts in the onset of that insanity are the refusal of Cordelia to flatter him, and the refusal of Goneril
to allow him to dominate her. The reason that these twin refusals shatter
Lear's mind is that he harbors a deep-seated, unconscious, incestuous passion for his daughters. Their open rejection of him leads him to the darkness of insanity, an insanity present even at the moment of his death.

Bransom's study looks back to the criticism of the eighteenth century in its concern with Lear's insanity. However, unlike the better critics
of that period, Bransom consistently errs by treating the characters as real
people, supplying numerous, gratuitous hypotheses about their motives,
their activities when not on stage, and their prior life. The result certainly
exhibits "the imaginative use" of the author's experiences, but very little
of the experience of reading or seeing *King Lear*.

26. Murry, John Middleton. *Shakespeare*. London, 1936. Revised ed.,
   1954. Excerpted in Bonheim.

Murry begins his essay by noting an apparent contradiction between
his immediate reaction to the play and the reaction he arrives at upon
reflection. His immediate impression is that the play is incoherent because
its author is too intensely involved in his material. Shakespeare lacks
"imaginative mastery" of his subject, probably because he is here struggling with a vision of life so dark and diseased that he himself only partially understands it. The result is that he is unsure of what he really
wants to say. In short, in *King Lear* Shakespeare seems to be "out of his
depth."

Murry's alternative explanation of the play's failure derives from his
reflection on the considerable craftsmanship evident in it—for example, in
the shaping of the double plot. This suggests that, far from being overly
involved in his material, the author may have been self-consciously striving for "titanic" effects, with the result that he may have been unable to
make an imaginative commitment to his subject. Murry reconciles those
apparently contradictory views by suggesting that Shakespeare used the
play as personal therapy for the exorcism of his private, probably sexual,
devils.

Murry's *Shakespeare* was published in 1936. In the Preface to the
1954 edition of the book he recanted his heresy concerning the incoher-

ence of *Lear*—largely, he asserts, as a result of having read Danby (39):
". . . it was preposterous in me to say that Shakespeare was out of his
depth when the evidence stares me in the face that I was out of mine."
Nevertheless, Murry's analysis of the alleged incoherence of the play does
point up the irregularity of its structure, an aspect which has tended to be
ignored since the eighteenth century. Some of Murry's views have recently been put forth in greater detail by Mason (67).

27. Spurgeon, Caroline. *Shakespeare's Imagery.* Cambridge, 1935, pp.
340–343.
Clemen, W. H. *The Development of Shakespeare's Imagery.* London: Methuen, 1951, pp. 133–153.

As authors of the standard general works on Shakespeare's imagery,
Spurgeon and Clemen have made significant contributions to the study of
Lear. For Spurgeon the dominant image of the play is that of "a human
body in anguished movement." This image is so pervasive and so integrated into the circumstances of the play that we scarcely notice it. It is
conveyed by verbs carrying meanings of striking, stretching, wrenching.
Even the animal imagery in the play is used "to augment the sensation of
horror and bodily pain." To this is added the description of the elements
themselves as the agents that will "smite flat the thick rotundity of the
world," elevating the image to the largest conceivable scale.

For Clemen, *Lear* is the most remarkable example in Shakespeare of
the integration of imagery and dramatic action: Here the imagery plays
"a more meaningful role" than in any other of Shakespeare's plays. This
is largely the result of Lear's character, for whom "imagery is the most
characteristic form of utterance." As he loses contact with objective
reality, his language becomes more evocation and expression than com-
munication. The language of the villainous characters, on the other hand,
is notable for its complete absence of imagery; it is the language of cold,
dry reason. The language of the Fool is rich in imagery. His images are
rooted in everyday reality, to "conterbalance the gigantic dimensions of
Lear's feelings and Ideas." Another effect of Lear's language is to bring
events into a close relationship with the elemental forms of nature and
the world of animals. Thus the linguistic pattern of his madness reveals
that his ranting is "another form of perception." Clemen's analysis provides a significant addition to the findings of Miss Spurgeon and to the
more elaborate and detailed study by Heilman (38).

28. Welsford, Enid. *The Fool: His Social and Literary History*. London: Faber and Faber, 1935, pp. 259–273. Excerpted in Bonheim and Kermode.

Miss Welsford's study of the play is the culmination of a chapter on "The Court-Fool in Elizabethan Drama," itself the central chapter of her account of the origins and history of the Fool. Lear's Fool represents the tradition of the "sage-fool . . . the disinterested truth teller." The question he continually puts before the audience concerns the nature of folly. That question is enacted by Lear himself as, stripped of both power and reason, he re-enacts the medieval *sotie*, "the great reversal when the highest dignitaries appear as fools and the World or even Holy Church herself is revealed in cap and bells." The fools of the play are the good characters, capable of love, for the world has no place for them. Yet it is precisely this folly that the play affirms: "Lear's tragedy is the investing of the King with motley: it is also the crowning and apotheosis of the Fool." However, although this theme has obvious correspondences with Pauline Christianity, the play neither offers nor denies "the metaphysical comfort of the Scriptures."

Miss Welsford's essay offers a new and striking perspective on the play as essentially a paradoxical experience. Her study provided the basis for further work by Empson (44) and Heilman (38).

29. Greg, W. W. "Time, Place and Politics in *King Lear*," *Modern Language Review*, XXXV (1940), 431–436.

Greg reviews the time and location of each scene in the play. His examination reveals certain discrepancies that demonstrate a "double stream of time." This double-time scheme is expressed in the distinction between the immediate duration of events unfolding in each scene and a background sequence of events that does not impinge upon the audience's attention. Thus the invasion of England by the forces of France and Cordelia is apparently planned before the injustices done to Lear. The problem of the invasion is further complicated by the fact that even a fictional invasion of England by France would pose a "patriotic dilemma" for an Elizabethan audience.

Greg conjectures that in the manuscript version of the play there may have been a scene—subsequently cut—which shows that France originally intended to invade England in order to secure Cordelia's share of her inheritance; and that Cordelia, after their arrival in England, had persuaded him to abandon the plan ("Therefore great France/My mourning and importuned tears hath pitied"—4,4,23). Subsequently, Cordelia has employed the army at the news of the injuries done to Lear.

An offshoot of his close textual study of the plays, this article shows the great scholar illuminating a hitheto unremarked aspect of the play, its time scheme. Thus the article provides not only an interesting if unproven hypothesis about one facet of the play, but also a rare example of the interaction of sound scholarship and perceptive criticism.

30. R. W. Chambers. *King Lear*. Glasgow University Publications, LIV (1940). Excerpted in Bonheim.

Chambers begins his analysis with a brief survey of the earlier versions of the *Lear* story. He argues that, contrary to what is commonly thought, most of these accounts end not happily but with the suicide of Cordelia some years after the restoration of Lear. Chambers emphasizes this point in order to refute the argument that Shakespeare deliberately imposed an unhappy ending on the play as the culmination of its pessimistic design. He suggests that the Swinburnian view (15) that the ruling forces are malevolent (if they exist at all) is particularly egregious in its attempt to focus on the "flies to wanton boys" line as central to the play. The fact is that the speech is designed to reveal Gloucester's easy despair and the subsequent rescue by Edgar, not the "keystone" of the play. The ruling principle of the play is the victory of love and the affirmation of providence. Lear's heart, like Gloucester's, bursts "smilingly" in the belief that Cordelia lives. The play is not just purgatorial but paradisal as well, "a vast poem on the victory of true love."

Chambers' analysis is notable as the first avowedly Christian interpretation of the play. Presented with the full force of a strong personality, his position is argued effectively. Nevertheless, his analysis provides less-than-adequate answers to the objections of those who see the play as something other than an affirmation of the principle of love.

31. Spencer, Theodore. *Shakespeare and the Nature of Man* [1942]. New York: Macmillan, 1961, pp. 135–152. Excerpted in Bonheim.

For Spencer, *King Lear* is Shakespeare's profoundest exploration of the "microcosm and the macrocosm," the correspondences that exist among the individual, the state, and the universe. The play presents "the terrible picture" that issues from the upsetting of the principle of hierarchical order that is the fundamental assumption of Renaissance thought. The play operates on two principles: reinforcement, and expansion. The former is reflected in the subplot, the latter in the manner in which individual experience is consistently universalized. All of this is possible because of the assumption that underlies it: the Elizabethan view of the world as a series of structured correspondences between man and nature. Thus the play itself is a "study in relationships," the relationship of child to parent, of man to the state, and of the gods to man. It presents a "terrible picture" of the predominance of animal nature in the individual, the world, and the state. Nevertheless, Lear dies believing that Cordelia lives, that reality is ultimately good. Thus he achieves a kind of order within himself.

Spencer's essay contains much that is valuable. Its chief weakness lies in its failure to confront the consequences of its own conclusion: It Lear's internal order rests upon the delusion that Cordelia lives, then it is that delusion, and not reality, that is finally good. Spencer's desire to see order underlying the play causes him to ignore this possibility.

32. Kernodle, George R. "The Symphonic Form of *King Lear*," in *Elizabethan Studies . . . in Honor of George F. Reynolds*. Boulder, Colorado, 1945, pp. 185–191. Excerpted in Bonheim.

Kernodle analyzes the organization of thematic and structural patterns in the play to reveal its "symphonic" character. This form is based upon the principles of parallelism and correspondence both in character and action. It derives its structure from medieval drama, which in turn is based upon the doctrine of prefiguration, the paralleling of Old Testament figures and events with those in the New Testament. There is a similar twofold structure in *Lear*, the first part of the play marked by the key position of Cornwall and the second part by the replacement of him by Albany. The main themes are reinforced by the use of imagery as verbal prefiguration and echo.

Kernodle's subject deserves a more detailed and sustained treatment than he gives it. Nevertheless, his observations are both sensitive and insightful.

33. Bickersteth, Geoffrey. *The Golden World of King Lear*. London: Geoffrey Camberledge, 1946. Excerpted in Bonheim.

The annual Shakespeare Lecture of the British Academy for 1946, Bickersteth's discussion centers on the play's "revivifying effect upon our minds." He considers the play from three points of view, which he characterizes as "the modern (or romantic), the ancient (or classical) and the renaissance (or neo-classical)." The first focuses on the spectacle of suffering interpenetrated by the comedy of the Fool. These "two forms of beauty, the sublime and the comic" are reconciled in the figure of Cordelia. The classical view focuses on the play as an illustration of the inexorable laws of fate that govern the universe. The neo-classical view is essentially Stoic and sees the play in terms of the need to acquire fortitude and patience in the face of suffering.

The play successfully contains all of these approaches but reflects a deeper "anagogic" meaning as well. On this level the play is a fusion of the Prometheus myth and the Christian myth. But the Christian myth is dominant, for it affirms the most important principle in the play, love. The symbol of that love is Cordelia, who, like Christ, her prototype, "redeems nature from the general curse." Her "resurrection" (that is, Bradley's idea that Lear dies believing that Cordelia lives) causes Lear's heart to break in an ecstasy of joy.

The last section of Bickersteth's lecture is an embarrassing over-indulgence of Christian fervor. However, his analysis of the three approaches to the play is valuable and imaginative. So, too, is his handling of the problem of the transmutation of the "brazen" world of nature into the "golden" world of art.

34. Harbage, Alfred. *As They Liked It.* New York: Macmillan, 1947; "Introduction," *King Lear.* Baltimore: Penguin Books, 1958; *Conceptions of Shakespeare.* Cambridge: Harvard University Press, 1966.

Harbage has discussed the play from a variety of aspects. In *As They Liked It* he deals with the problem of justice in the play, arguing that the death of Cordelia is not a sign of the malevolence or absence of the gods but an effect of the wickedness of man. In *Conceptions of Shakespeare* he devotes a chapter ("The Fierce Dispute") to "the philosophical impact of King Lear" since the seventeenth century, finds the most significant description of the play Keats' "vale of soul-making," and sees Lear as the great exemplar of sacrificial tragedy. His fullest treatment of the play is contained in the Introduction to his edition of the play. Designed for the general reader, it sketches in broad outlines the play's outstanding features. Among these are its mythic parabolic qualities, its Gothic (as opposed to classical) structure, its "inclusively Christian"—

religious but nonsectarian—context, its deep sincerity, and the centrality and spiritual grandeur of the character of Lear. In his analysis of the final scene he concludes that there is "no melioration" in Lear's dying illusion that Cordelia lives. However, the sadness of the audience is subsumed in the recognition that she is not just a casualty but a sacrificial agent, the price we pay "in our continuing struggle to be human."

Harbage's comments summarize a view of the play which constitutes one major stream of critical response since the Romantic period. He falls short of the necessary synthesis by failing to confront some of the harder questions that critics such as Everett (55) and Brooke (59) have asked. But he remains an eloquent and sincere spokesman for a view of the play that sees it affirming the existence of a spiritual dimension both in man and in the universe.

35. Muir, Edwin. *The Politics of King Lear*. Glasgow University Publications, No. 72. Glasgow: Jackson, Son and Co., 1947. Excerpted in Bonheim.

The text of the W. P. Ker Memorial Lecture delivered at the University of Glasgow in 1946, Mr. Muir's analysis sees the play's political theme as a contest between the old order of medieval communal values and the new order of modern individualism. The new order, represented by Goneril, Regan, and Edmund, is a soulless, amoral individualism pitting the idea of nature against that of society. Endorsing this view of nature they become unnatural, animal-like creatures of appetite and power. Poor Tom's description of himself on the heath ("A serving-man proud in heart and mind . . .") is really a portrait of Edmund and of the new generation. Against this view is a vision of society based upon "pity and human fitness." The play ends with the destruction of the old order, and an ominous presentiment of the emergence of the new.

Muir's essay has one obvious flaw; He fails to deal with those members of the "new generation" (Cordelia and Edgar) who clearly do not embody amoral individualism. This is symptomatic of the loose generalizing and moralizing—his real target is modern Fascism—that mar some acute perceptions.

36. Bald, R. C. "Thou Nature Art My Goddess," in *John Quincy Adams Memorial Studies*, ed. J. McManaway, *et al.* Washington: Folger Library, 1948, pp. 337–349.

Bald examines the use of the term *nature* in the play. The traditional sense of the word derives from the medieval concept of natural law as the ordering idea in all relationships. In contrast to this conception, Edmund's "Thou Nature art my goddess" (I, ii, 1) invokes the image of nature as a wild, untamed force. Bald argues that this view of nature had acquired considerable popularity among Renaissance free-thinkers as a justification for libertinism. Thus, to Shakespeare's audience Edmund represents the doctrines of individualism and libertinism. His contemptuous rejection of astrology is further evidence of his identification with this position, which Shakespeare saw as the enemy of order.

Bald's argument provides an excellent example of historical criticism, demonstrating how much is to be gained from a knowledge of the play's original frame of reference. The only quarrel with Bald's essay might be with the implicit conclusion that Shakespeare is concerned in the play to defend the traditional idea of order. A more sophisticated historical analysis of this problem is given by Skulsky (68).

37. Campbell, O. J. "The Salvation of Lear," *ELH,* XV (1948), 93–109. Excerpted in Bonheim.

To Campbell, Lear is "a sublime morality play," a representation of man's quest for eternal, enduring values at the point of death. However, Lear's "salvation" is not simply that of orthodox Christianity but a condition which reflects a mixture of Stoicism and Christianity. Thus, like Everyman in the morality play, Lear's preparation for death leads him to the discovery of true values. However, he differs from the Christian archetype in that he is the "Stoical unwise man," the slave of his own anger, entangled in his own possessions. Also like Everyman, Lear discovers the faithful companion—Cordelia, the principle of love—who accompanies him to the grave. This technique of heightening medieval ideas is typical of the Jacobean period during which the play was written. Thus in Marston, Tourneur and other Jacobean dramatists, the morality play devices are linked to an intense obsession with death. In *Lear,* Shakespeare develops this style to the "point of utter sublimity."

Campbell's analysis may be seen as the application of the Bradleyan thesis (the Redemption of King Lear) by an historical critic. Thus Campbell adds to Bradley the evidence of the general indebtedness of Elizabethan drama to the medieval theatre. Nevertheless, his representation is not entirely free from charges of reductive categorizing and of searching for the play's meaning in the cultural context in which it was written rather than in the play itself.

38. Heilman, Robert. *This Great Stage: Image and Structure in King Lear.* Baton Rouge, La., 1948. 339pp. Excerpted in Bonheim and Kermode.

Heilman's volume—probably the best-known full-length study of *Lear*—offers a detailed study of the play's imagery. He suggests that the most important patterns of imagery in the play are those relating to sight, clothing, animals, nature, age, values, madness and, religion. These various patterns fall into one of two categories, the ontological or the epistemological: "The clothes, nature, animal, age and justice patterns present the complex world that is to be understood; the sight and madness patterns . . . are concerned with the process and method of understanding . . . that complex world." Each of these patterns is expressed in terms of a paradox, and these paradoxes contribute to the "total statement of the play." That statement is necessarily paradoxical. It affirms the existence of order and justice in a world apparently given over to the opposite of those principles. It argues that in order to see through the appearance to the underlying reality we must abandon the empirical, quantifying, rationalist, modern world-view in favor of the "folly" and "madness" of faith, intuition, and love.

The appearance of Heilman's study in 1948 marked the earliest book-length application of the new criticism to a Shakespeare play. As such it was the focus of controversy over the validity of the new critical technique, a fact which tended to obscure its merits and defects as an analysis of *Lear.* In this latter respect *This Great Stage* has proven to be valuable in its elucidation of the complex verbal interrelatedness that contributes to the impact and tone of the play. What the author has not demonstrated is that the metaphors he perceives represent the values he says they do. Here he is extremely vulnerable to he charge of Keast (40) and others that he has insinuated his own ethical and religious values into the play.

39. Danby, John F. *Shakespeare's Doctrine of Nature: A Study of King Lear.* London: Faber & Faber, 1949. 234 pp. Excerpted in Bonheim.

Danby's analysis rests upon the concepts of nature that he finds in the play. One of these is nature as expounded in Hooker's *Laws of Ecclesiastical Polity:* a benign pattern which sustains the universe and represents the ideal toward which men strive. Nature in this sense is embodied in Cordelia. The contrasting concept is Edmund's nature—an amoral force, autonomous, unrelated both to divine plans and to human values. The play deals with the conflict of these two concepts. Lear the symbol of Everyman, caught between these two visions of the world, zig-zags from one to the other, discovering in the process the vast implications of the conflict before arriving at a new perception of what Cordelia is: "the utopian dream of the artist and the good man." The result brings us to the brink of "religious insight" and beyond. The play "is our profoundest expression of an essentially Christian comment on man's world and his society. . . ."

Danby's thesis has clearly established the importance of the concept of nature in the play and, beyond that, of its relationship to the developing thought of Shakespeare's time. The thesis is less secure when it is made to bear certain allegorical freight—for example in arguing for the perfectibility of Cordelia—and when elevated to the level of a religious experience. Nevertheless, it remains a valuable study of the play, containing among other things an important essay on the Fool.

40. Keast, M. R. "Imagery and Meaning in the Interpretation of *King Lear*," Modern Philology, XLVII (1949), 45–64. Reprinted in *Critics and Criticism: Ancient and Modern*, ed. R. S. Crane, Chicago, 1952. Excerpted in Bonheim.

Keast's essay is a lengthy review article of Heilman (38). He begins by disputing Heilman's basic theory that the imagery of a play is best able to convey its final meaning. He argues that Heilman's analysis of the play rests on private moral, political, and historical convictions imported into the play under the guise of close textual analysis. In any case the verbal elements in a play are subordinate to and dependent upon plot and character. By failing to employ Aristotelian criteria, Heilman has made the mistake of assuming that "the principal effect of the play must be some mode of intellectual activity." Keast also disputes Heilman's conclusion that the play concludes on a note of triumpth gained by Lear's new insights. Is not the conclusion he asks, one of general agony occasioned by the irony that, in the death of Cordelia, Lear loses the one thing in the world he has come to value above all else?

Keast's essay is rigorous, thoughtful, and overstated. Many of his points—the insistence on drama as a temporal experience, the charge that Heilman reads his own beliefs and values into the play—are valid. Less valid is his apparent unwilllingness to admit the existence of any nonliteral, philosophical dimension to the play. In any case, the intellectual rigor of his analysis is undermined by his occasionally contemptuous and unnecessarily rude references to the book he is reviewing.

41. Lothian, J. M. *King Lear: A Tragic Reading of Life.* Toronto, 1949. 109 pp. Excerpted in Bonheim.

This slim volume contains chapters on the source of the play, the character of the Fool and of Edgar, the spiritual progress of Lear and his function as the leading character. The author argues that the play deals with "the spiritual history or regeneration of King Lear." It is a celebration of man's capacity to endure suffering. In his final chapter, he disputes those critics who argue that Lear does not dominate the play. On this last point he takes issue with Bradley and others, arguing that Lear's development is its major focus. That development leads to a vision in which there is no religious consolation but rather "an appalling vision of chaos, of the chasm between reality and justice. . . ."

Written for the general reader, this work provides an excellent introduction to the traditional problems of the play, except for its failure to take account of modern criticism. Thus it is a somewhat old-fashioned but articulate presentation of the "pessimistic" view of the play.

42. Maxwell, J. C. "The Technique of Invocation in *King Lear*," *Modern Language Review*, XLV (1950), 142–147. Excerpted in Bonheim.

Maxwell's briefly argued thesis is that "*King Lear* is a Christian play about a pagan world." The wide variety of religious attitudes are designed to reveal both the nature of the main characters and the underlying Christian philosophy "presupposed and expressed" in the play. One aspect of religious attitudes is revealed by the manner in which various characters invoke the supernatural. Lear's invocations early in the play reveal an attitude in which the "gods" or "nature" are his agents. (Edmund has a similar view.) Eventually, Lear abandons this kind of invocation in favor of compassionate address to his fellow sufferers ("Poor naked wretches"). Cordelia's invocations reveal her role as mediatrix between Lear and the gods. Edgar's indicative rather than imperative references to the supernatural are the touchstone of his "affirmation of the divine ordering of the universe."

Maxwell's arguments are intelligently presented but they lack substantiating details both for his specific thesis and for his claim of the play's underlying Christianity.

43. Orwell, George. "Lear, Tolstoy and the Fool," in *Shooting an Elephant*. London: Secker & Warburg, 1950, pp. 32–52. Excerpted in Bonheim and Kermode.

Orwell is interested in the motives of Tolstoy (18) in attacking *Lear*. He suggests that Tolstoy was particularly hostile to this play above any other Shakespearean drama because he saw in it "consciously or unconsciously" parallels to his own life. Like Tolstoy, Lear is the victim of an illusion. Both engaged at the end of their lives in an act of renunciation in order to gain happiness, both gave up their power and their lands, and both suffered as a result. The moral of *Lear* applies to Tolstoy as well: "Give away your lands if you want to, but don't expect to gain happiness by doing so. . . . If you live for others, you must live *for others*, and not as a roundabout way of getting an advantage for yourself." The spokesman of this position is the Fool. Like all of Shakespeare's other plays, *Lear* affirms life despite the facts of misery and death. In the last religious phase of his life Tolstoy denied life. Thus his hatred of Lear was rooted in what he saw as its undermining of the type of Christian asceticism to which he had committed himself. The intolerance of that commitment is reflected in the dishonesty and ill will of his pamphlet on Shakespeare.

Aside from its analysis of Tolstoy's motives, Orwell's essay provides an interesting insight into *King Lear* which might be called the Fool's-eye view of the action. It suggests that Lear's error is fundamentally political: he has failed to perceive the realities of power. But, however interesting this perspective, it is for most readers too narrow to capture the full significance and scope of the play.

44. Empson, W. "Fool in *Lear*," in *The Structure of Complex Words*. London: 1951, pp. 125–157. Excerpted in Bonheim.

Empson's article surveys the use of the word "fool" in the play, finds that it means both "one who is fooled" and "one who does the fooling." Lear's chief folly—Empson echoes Orwell here—is his confused attempt at renunciation. He renounces the things of this world as an indirect way of retaining them. Using "fool" as his key word, Empson analyzes the action of the play in a manner designed to demonstrate that "Lear has

made a fool of himself on the most cosmic and appalling scale possible,"
for he has also revealed the folly of nature and the gods. Despite this
fundamental horror, however, it is possible to see Lear as a "holy fool,"
but probably more accurate to say that the Lear we see at the end is a
scapegoat who "has been through everything," who therefore evokes our
admiration as well as our pity.

Empson's analysis, written in his usual lively, irreverent, devil's-
advocate style, is filled with incidental insights ranging from perceptive
(on the character of the Fool) to deceptive (he tries to have it both ways
in describing the play's conclusion). On balance it is an interesting, provocative *tour de force*.

45. James, D. G. *The Dream of Learning: An Essay on "The Advance-
ment of Learning," "Hamlet" and "King Lear."* Oxford: Clarendon
Press, 1951. 126 pp.

The thesis of James' volume is that poetry has value as a special
mode of cognition in which reason and imagination are united. Bacon is
taken as the representative of those who would deny cognitive value to
poetry; *Hamlet* and *Lear* as examples of the contrary belief. *Hamlet*
focuses on the problems of the "mind arrested in dubiety" (see *Hamlet*,
48). In *Lear* that problem is externalized and objectified. The emphasis
here is the nature of the world, not on the mind's attempt to apprehend
that nature. *Lear* represents "a poetic experiment with life by the creation
of extreme simplicities of good and evil." It is less concerned with dramatic
or psychological consistency than with the embodiment of the abstractions of good and evil. Evil is the powerful dynamic force in the play,
virtue comparatively helpless. Evil destroys itself, but while the good is
destroyed as well, Cordelia and Lear achieve something, "a certain power
in human nature to overcome the world and to make the world fade in our
imaginations and leave not a rack behind." The recognition of the
capacity of men to create enduring human (not religious) values is the
truth that the play reveals to us.

James' volume has been criticized for its unsubstantiated generalizations about Renaissance thought and its tendency to see *Hamlet* and
Lear as the workings out of abstract philosophical and moral problems.
Despite these flaws, this study provides an intelligent, sensitive analysis of
the moral atmosphere of the play as well as a strong case for literature as
an emotive–intellectual experience of unique value.

46. Sewell, Arthur. "Tragedy and the 'Kingdom of Ends'," in *Character and Society in Shakespeare*. Oxford, 1951.

For Sewell, Shakespearean tragedy is rooted in "man's perennial hunger for metaphysical being." Its form is the realization of imaginative vision in terms of character. Character in interrelationship constitutes society.

In *Lear*, he argues, relationships determine character; the two are "wholly bound up with one another." There are two types of relationships: those dictated by the "bond"—one's social obligation—and those that transcend the bond. In the first scene all of the characters (including Cordelia and Kent) respond according to the bond with a mixture of reason and self-interest. Eventually the good characters move beyond self-regarding reason, to compassionate unreason. Out of this emerges a vision of "society" that enlarges our usual sense of the term. Society in the play comes to embrace not only the human community but the entire universe. There is even a suggestion that it embraces the supernatural structure of the pagan world. Thus the play celebrates the fulfillment of man in society. But it stops short of affirming the existence of the Christian God and a divinely ordered universe. At best what it does hold out, tentatively and fleetingly, is "the promise of grace and benediction."

Sewell's essay represents a formidable attempt to synthesize a variety of approaches to the play, traditional character criticism, symbolic criticism, and the view of character as convention. Even more ambitiously, he fuses a metaphysical view of the play with an ethical one. The degree to which he succeeds remains a matter of individual judgment. Suffice it to say that his essay as it now stands constitutes the most important critical statement about *King Lear* to be written in our time.

47. Williams, G. W. "The Poetry of the Storm," *Shakespeare Quarterly*, II (1951), 57–71. Excerpted in Bonheim.

Williams focuses attention on Lear's invocation to the storm that opens Act III, Scene ii ("Blow, winds, and crack your cheeks! rage! blow!"). The nine lines of speech are given a close verbal and metrical analysis. Williams notes how the interpolation of foreign and vernacular phrases provides a sense of larger extension and range. In his linguistic analysis he points out that Lear's call to "Crush nature's moulds, all germains spill at once" is a demand "for the destruction of both form and matter." The source of human evil is parenthood, and thus, by extension, the sexual act. Thus Lear is calling for the end of all existing things. In short, Lear is here invoking chaos in imagery that combines connotations of the Biblical Deluge and the end of the world.

Williams' essay is a rewarding example of the application of close reading to an important passage. It illuminates not only the passage itself but the rest of the play as well.

48. Maclean, Norman. "Episode, Scene, Speech and Word: The Madness of Lear," in *Critics and Criticism*, ed. R. S. Crane. University of Chicago Press, 1952, pp. 595–615.

The episode of MacLean's subtitle is Lear's declension into madness; the specific scene, Act III, Scene IV; the speech, Lear's "Hast thou given all to thy daughters and art thou come to this"; the word, "this." This movement from the general to the particular is valuable critically, he argues, for it imitates the author's progress in actual composition. Act III, Scene I to Act IV, Scene VI constitutes a single tragic episode designed to reveal a vision of the world which would "make a man a man of salt— but for purposes more magnificent than the laying of autumn's dust." This vision is communicated in a complicated series of analogous actions. Thus, in the heath scene (III. IV) we see a set of variations on the theme of madness that eventually become incorporated into Lear's central theme, expressed by his identification of himself with Tom O'Bedlam ("Hast thou given all to thy daughters and art thou come to this?"). In the one word "this" we have summarized the whole experience of the play: "the suffering of man triumphed over by some slight touch of serenity."

Maclean's essay is an admirable example of criticism that focuses attention equally on action and language. His supposition that his method of analysis mirrors the actual process of creation is gratuitous and un-proven. Nevertheless, he has provided a unique insight into the inter-relatedness of thought, emotion, and action in the play.

49. Bush, Geoffrey. *Shakespeare and the Natural Condition*. Cambridge, 1956.

For Bush the play deals with the basic problem of belief. It explores the natural cause of things—the meaning behind the facts of life. It moves from nature to a suggestion of something beyond nature. This change is embodied in the person of Cordelia, whose reentrance into the play carries with it "possibilities . . . of religious continuance." With her death that possibility is never realized, but it exists as possibility. Thus the vision that the play offers is hedged with ironies: Appearance and reality merge in the discovery of the incompleteness of things-in-themselves within the temporal order. We learn that "to share knowingly in time is to arrive at an extremity of natural existence where the readiness is all and where time and what is beyond time come together."

Bush acknowledges debts to James (45) and Sewell (46) for some of his basic assumptions. His treatment of *Lear* differs from James in his equivocal acceptance of a religious character to the play. He differs from Sewell in his final insistence that our acceptance of the "incompleteness of things" is an aspect of our commitment to dramatic illusion and of the correspondence between drama and reality. The result is an important book, marred by a self-conscious style that substitutes intimation and evocation for detailed and rigorous analysis.

50. Nowottny, Winifred. "Lear's Questions," *Shakespeare Survey*, 10 (1957), 90–97; "Some Aspects of the Style of *King Lear*," *Shakespeare Survey*, 13 (1960), 49–57.

The earlier essay examines Lear's questions, from the first (Which of you shall we say doth love us most?") to the last ("Why should a dog, a horse, a rat have life . . . ?"). All of these questions are subsumed under one exclusive question: What is man? In searching for the answer, Lear discovers that "all a man knows he knows through the flesh." Thus the flesh becomes a point of reference for all the problems raised in the play. The answer to the question "What is man?" is that he is the animal who questions himself and as a result discovers his spirituality rooted in physicality. Thus the play is a revelation of the essential dignity and the inherent frailty of human life.

"Some Aspects of the Style of *King Lear*" sees the basic stylistic problem in the fact that the play wishes to express, among other things, the inexpressibility of the characters' experience. This is achieved by a kind of verbal *montage*. The quarrel scene (II, IV), for example, is "mounted" upon Lear's earlier exchanges with Kent and Gloucester in which attitudes are expressed "not in an overtly heightened theatrical language but through the implications, expressive choices, and significant usages available in the common tongue." The expression of the inexpressible achieves its supreme manifestation in the language of the last scene, marked as it is by "a prosodic brilliance that helps to make the play's language transcend that natural language of human feeling which it so convincingly simulates."

Both of these essays are marked by a sensitivity of response and subtlety of expression which bring us closer to the poetic texture, and thus to the total experience, of the play.

51. Frost, William. "Shakespeare's Rituals and the Opening of *King Lear*," *Hudson Review*, X (1958), 577–585. Excerpted in Bonheim.

Frost is concerned to defend the much disputed opening scene of the play on the grounds that it is deliberately conceived in the mode of ceremonial ritual. The ceremonial lends itself to the mythic quality of the play as well as to producing the effect of "nightmarish inevitability" in denying the possibility of alternatives. The formality of the opening scene provides an ironic contrast to the storm and madness scenes, a movement from ritualized order to chaotic disorder, from elaborate formality to naked humanity. A further contrast is to be seen within the scene itself in the "two contests of affection." The second of these—the contest for the affection of Cordelia among her suitors—provides an ironic commentary to the first. Finally, a contrast is seen between the majesty of the opening scene between Lear and Cordelia and their concluding scenes. Here both figures have lost their symbolic, ritual roles, to "come before us fragile, irreplaceable and particular. . . ."

Frost's analysis demonstrates that the opening scene reveals, as Dr. Johnson observed, an aspect of the primitive, folkloristic quality of *Lear*, enabling us to see it not merely as a necessary and improbable exposition but as an integral and important part of the total experience of the play.

52. Ribner, I. "The Gods are Just," *Tulane Drama Review*, II (1958), 34–54. Excerpted in Bonheim.

As his title suggests, Ribner sees the play as an affirmation of "justice in the world . . . ruled by a God who in his ultimate purposes is benevolent." The action deals with the regeneration of Lear, whose premature abdication has untuned the string of that harmonious system of the universe envisioned in Renaissance thought. The decision—a political error—has repercussions on the individual as well as the cosmic level.

As a result of suffering, Lear learns to reject wordly values and to accept Cordelia's love—a reflection of divine love—as the only enduring value.

Gloucester's sin is not merely lechery but a violation of the law of primogeniture. The character of Edgar is designed to fulfill a variety of roles in the play: As Poor Tom he is man reduced to the bestial level; as his father's guide he is human devotion; as the victor over Edmund, he is divine justice. It is in this sense that his "gods are just" speech (V, iii) affirms the justice of heaven.

Ribner establishes with a reasonable degree of conviction the idea that there is a triumph of human values in the play. What he fails to do, however, is to show how the "gods" (or, as he argues, the Christian God) could be vindicated. Time and again he adverts to Renaissance doctrine, but he does not show that doctrine functioning in the play and therefore fails to meet the objection voiced as long ago as Schlegel (8) that the question of the role of the supernatural is deliberately suspended in the play.

53. Knights, L. C. *Some Shakespearean Themes.* London: Chatto and Windus, 1959; "King Lear as Metaphor," in *Further Explorations.* Stanford, 1965.

In *Some Shakespearean Themes,* Knights includes a revised version of his well-known essay that appeared earlier in *The Pelican Guide to English Literature.* He argues that the play is an exploration, and finally an endorsement, of profoundly Christian values, but an endorsement in which nothing is taken for granted. Lear is the victim of a perverse self-will, deceived by appearances, who discovers that "appetite is . . . universal and authority a sham." Beyond that truth, however, is the reality of the Lear–Cordelia relationship, a reality that persists in the face of "the worst that can be known of man or nature." The play is thus an affirmation of love as "the condition of intellectual clarity, the energizing center from which personality may grow unhampered by the need for self assertion or evasive subterfuge."

In *"King Lear* as Metaphor," Knights focuses on the play's "metaphorical" quality—its capacity to take us beyond our immediate concerns and to undercut and alter our preconceptions. In *Lear* this is accomplished by such key terms as "Nature," "nothing" and "justice." Taking justice as an example, he argues that in the play various attempts to define the quality of justice prove inadequate. Justice is finally experienced less as an abstract condition than as the fulfillment of an individual life. The term has been transformed, and we in turn undergo a similar transforming process. Thus our experience mirrors the action of the play, a movement toward a "new dimension of imaginative thought."

It is possible to go a long way in agreement with these essays without necessarily accepting as definitive Knights' designation of love as the resolving term of the play, and without seeing justice expressed as individual fulfillment. In any case, the journey with Knights is well worth undertaking.

54. Levin, Harry. "The Heights and the Depths," in *More Talking of Shakespeare*, ed. J. Garrett. London, 1959. pp. 87–103.

Levin focuses on the Dover Cliff scene in order to establish its relevance to the entire play. The scene is a miniature reenactment of *King Lear* as a whole. In creating the illusion of his father's leap, Edgar stages the descent from the heights that characterizes the movement of the play for Lear and Gloucester. Edgar's explanation of Gloucester's salvation as the action of the gods is perceived by the audience as a human act of compassion. There is no divine intervention, no "supernatural solicitings" in *Lear*. Thus the play is a revelation of man in nature achieving in his inevitable descent into death the knowledge that death can be fulfillment, that "Ripeness is all."

As in his explanation of the player's speech in *Hamlet* (see *Hamlet* 59), Levin here demonstrates the relationship of the part to the whole, the manner in which a seemingly irrelevant scene incorporates and develops the major themes of the play. For a further development of Levin's thesis see the essay by Kernan (65).

55. Everett, Barbara. "The New *King Lear*," *Critical Quarterly*, II (1960), 325–339. Reprinted in Kermode.

The "new" *King Lear* is the play as interpreted by Chambers (30), Campbell (37), Danby (39), and others, who see it as profoundly Christian in character. Against this view—which she traces back to Bradley as the first of the "transcendental" interpreters of the play—Miss Everett emphasizes the extraordinary vitality that inheres in the play and in its central character. "Lear's greatness lies not in the moral goodness he chooses but in "the transformation, into something vital and strong, of the suffering that is forced in upon him." Lear possesses "a colossal power of life itself." One aspect of that vitality is Lear's tendency to translate everything into his immediate bodily experience. But this vitality is overwhelmed by its opposite—the fact of nothingness. The play offers a definition of man caught between these polarities; in Pascal's phrase, *"un milieu entre rien et tout."* The play does not, as in the Christian interpretation, oppose the "world" and the "soul" but shows the relationship between the two. Finally, it enables us to understand and to master great suffering through our participation in the "mastery inherent in the creative act."

Miss Everett's essay set off a controversial correspondence in the subsequent issues of *Critical Quarterly.* Unfortunately, the essay's polemical notoriety has obscured its value as an independent analysis of the play. Needing greater amplification rooted in the language and action of *Lear,* her interpretation nevertheless is both original and illuminating. It deserves careful and attentive reading.

56. Stampfer, J. "The Catharsis of *King Lear,*" *Shakespeare Survey,* 13 (1960), 1–10.

Stampfer focuses on the play's major problem, its ending. For Stampfer the death of Cordelia establishes a cosmic irony that qualifies and contradicts the play's human values. On the human level the play justifies the Cordelia principle—the bond of love. Even Edmund's "good deed" before his death affirms this fact. Here the movement of the play is to purgation through suffering. However, the play goes beyond purgation to become a tragedy of penance. In the world of the play, penance is shown to be without purpose. The gratuitious destruction of Cordelia is all too clearly the evidence of that fact. Thus the audience experiences a catharsis by confronting its most fundamental fear, the fear . . . that we inhabit an imbecile universe."

Stampfer here reformulates the problem of the ending by setting up a distinction between the human and the universal, the moral and the metaphysical. Most critics assume a conjunction of the two, or argue that the metaphysical has no place in the play. Stampfer's article, therefore, has the value of offering another alternative.

57. *Holloway, John. *The Story of the Night.* London: Methuen and The University of Nebraska Press, 1961. Reprinted in Kermode.

For Holloway the play explores the Elizabethan belief in the potential descent of the world into chaos. In the characters this descent is represented by the movement from humanity to the lower orders of animal existence. Lear is a Job-like figure, made to suffer past the bounds of "probability or reason." Contrary to what is often suggested, the play is not resolved in the affirmation of the principle of love. Nor of natural order: "If there is such an order, it is an order that can accommodate seemingly limitless evil." What affirmation is in the play lies in "the refusal to hide" from the extraordinary suffering and torment that life potentially contains, and in the acknowledgment that this suffering is sometimes necessary in order to restore men to their rightful relationships with each other.

Implicit in the design of the play is the pattern of ritual sacrifice. Lear, like Shakespeare's other tragic heroes, is a scapegoat figure—isolated, pursued, and finally destroyed. Sustained by this archetypal pattern, the play offers us neither insight nor knowledge but a powerful, fundamental experience, one that is very close to the experience of primitive man participating in ritual.

Holloway's presentation is an excellent example of mythic or archetypal criticism employed with discrimination and tact.

58. Fraser, R. *Shakespeare's Poetics in Relation to "King Lear"*. London: Routledge & Kegan Paul, 1962. 184 pp.

By "Shakespeare's poetics" Fraser understands "the underlying principles that sustain Shakespearean drama." He proposes to reveal the presence of these principles in *King Lear* by means of an "iconological" analysis. He defines iconology as the study of an artifact designed to reveal those aspects of it that are "symbolic of the basic attitude of a nation, or a class, or era." His procedure is to isolate the "central motifs of the play and to demonstrate by means of abundant documentation their relatedness to the traditional thought of the age." The motifs are seven in number: (1) the existence of Providence, (2) the nature of Kind, (3) the character of Fortune, (4) the opposition of Anarchy and Order, of (5) Reason and Will, of (6) Show and Substance, and (7) the possibility of redemption. The play is finally a celebration of a morally ordered, if ultimately unintelligible, universe.

At the beginning of his study Fraser proclaims his determination not to represent Shakespeare as "a Churchyard or Tusser, writ large," that is not to circumscribe the richness and complexity of the play within that historical pigeonhole, the Elizabethan world view. Unfortunately, he has not entirely succeeded. The most valuable aspect of his study remains his representation of the prevailing ethical attitudes of Shakespeare's time. His analysis of *King Lear* elicits neither interest nor conviction.

59. *Brooke, Nicholas. *Shakespeare: King Lear*. London: Edward Arnold, 1963; "The Ending of *King Lear*," in *Shakespeare 1564–1964*. Providence: Brown University Press, 1964, pp. 71–87.

This slim paperbound volume is designed as an introduction to the play for college and university students. It fulfills that function admirably, although the student in search of an outline *crib* will be sadly disappointed. For this is more than the standard introduction; it provides an intelligent and serious study of the play for all readers. Brooke begins his discussion by observing that the play does not lend itself well to a naturalistic or realistic interpretation; it is essentially a poetic drama. Both terms are critical. The language is essential, but equally important is the sequence of events. Thus he proceeds to an act-by-act analysis of the play, carefully delineating the linguistic landscape. He sees the general movement of the play as a development from despotism to isolation to suffering to reconciliation and, finally, to defeat and death. Thus his conclusion—stated in greater detail in his article "The Ending of King Lear"—is that Dr. Johnson was right: The ending of the play is unbearable, offering no ordering vision, no affirmation other than the assertion that the truth of reality is somehow less important than the assertion of human values, however deluded and purposeless the latter may be.

The majority will doubtless disagree with Brooke's interpretation of the play's conclusion. Many will feel that the triumph of human values is victory enough and that it does not call for the bleakness of tone that Brooke suggests as the play's ending. Nevertheless, all readers—not just students beginning study of the play—will profit from Brooke's discussion.

60. Kott, Jan. "*King Lear* as Endgame," in *Shakespeare Our Contemporary*, trans. Boleslaw Taborski. New York: Anchor Books, 1964. Reprinted in Kermode.

For Kott, *Lear* is not a tragedy but a species of the "grotesque." The latter involves a vision of human experience as trapped by an "absurd mechanism." Whereas tragedy affirms absolute principles and is cathartic, the grotesque denies the existence of absolutes and offers no consolation.

What emerges from the grotesque theatre is a view of man as a clown. The theme of *Lear* is "the decay and fall of the world." The story itself is a parodical rendering of the Book of Job, performed by a group of clowns. The Fool provides the central focus of the play. Lacking faith or illusion of any kind, he is always conscious of his own folly, of the folly of all other men, and of the absurdity of the world. His baroque, "surrealist" language is the perfect expression of the grotesque that pervades the play. Lear ultimately comes to share the Fool's vision and arrives at the unillusioned perception of the frailty of his own life.

Kott is not the first critic to apply the term *grotesque* to Lear. Dowden acknowledged its presence implicitly in characterizing the play as "gothic." G. Wilson Knight took this idea even further in "King Lear and the Comedy of the Grotesque," in establishing macabre incongruity as an integral aspect of the play. Kott, however, sees the grotesque as dominating the play—and this, of course, is gross overstatement. Nevertheless, the element is present in the play and Kott's essay helps us to see it. Furthermore, his overstatement is, if not justified, at least understandable, when we consider that he is (as Peter Brook observes in his Preface to the English edition) "the only writer on Elizabethan matters who assumes without question that every one of his readers will at some point or other have been woken by the police in the middle of the night."

61. Markels, Julian, "Shakespeare's Confluence of Tragedy and Comedy," in *Shakespeare 400*. New York: Holt, Rinehart, 1964, pp. 75–88.

Markels notes the comparison between *Lear* and *Twelfth Night*, arguing for three points of convergence in the plays: the prominence of the Fool, the use of clothes imagery to validate "the familiar social philosophy of degree and custom," and to represent the inadequacy of the contrasting belief in "Fortune." The difference in the two plays is generic. As a comedy, *Twelfth Night* never questions the order of society, while *Lear* is consistently tragic in moving beyond that order to a more "elemental confrontation" with the cruelty of fate. However, both plots arrive at the same conclusion: "man in society must stand fast by custom even in the face of Fortune."

The essay reveals some striking and noteworthy similarities between two of Shakespeare's greatest plays and points up again (see 24) the importance of the comic element in Lear. Where it goes wrong is in its insistence on adding a didactic tag to its observations, implying as a result that both plays are homilies in defense of tradition. This is surely reductive, and unworthy of the essay as a whole.

62. Myrick, Kenneth. "Christian Pessimism in *King Lear*" in *Shakespeare 1564–1964,* ed. E. A. Bloom. Providence: Brown University Press, 1964, pp. 56–70.

Myrick argues that the "dark view of man" in the play is not at all inconsistent with the concept of Christian pessimism in the *contemptu mundi* tradition. In Shakespeare's time not only Calvinists but Catholics like the Jesuit Robert Parsons and Anglicans like Richard Hooker subscribed to a tragic view of life in which the apparent triumph of evil and the fact of suffering and death were inevitable conditions of life. However, this pessimism stopped short of despair, for it rested on the belief in God's active, if inscrutable, participation in the events of the world. In the play this divine intervention is expressed in the comments of Albany and Edgar, who are not speaking merely personal statements but "choral utterances." The best example of divine intervention is the unmotivated defense of Gloucester by Cornwall's servant. To the Elizabethan audience the servant would have been seen as an agent of divine will.

The pervasive presence of Christian pessimism in the Renaissance is not to be doubted, nor is the presence of the *contemptu mundi* theme in the play. Nevertheless, Myrick's essay has not demonstrated that the dark view of man and the world in Lear has a uniquely or specifically Christian application. A much more detailed alternative explanation is provided by Elton (63).

63. Elton, W. *King Lear and the Gods.* San Marino: Huntington Library, 1966. 369 pp. Excerpted in Bonheim and Kermode.

Elton sets out to refute attempts to view the play as an expression of Christian values. He argues that the play carefully establishes certain pagan religious attitudes as these were understood in Shakespeare's time. Thus in Sidney's *Arcadia,* a major source of Shakespeare's play, there are distinguishable four religious views and these, Elton argues, are present in *Lear* as well. The first of these is the concept of the virtuous pagans, represented by Cordelia and Edgar, who adumbrate Christian values. Another is the pagan atheist, represented by Goneril, Regan, and Edmund.

The third is the superstitious pagan of whom Gloucester is the chief example. The fourth category is that represented by Lear himself, the pagan polytheist of naturalist and skeptical tendencies. In the course of the play this faith is destroyed, later (Acts IV and V) renewed as a Stoic–Christian rejection of the world. With the death of Cordelia, however, that faith too is destroyed and Lear dies unconsoled, with a vision of death as the end of all life and without any sustaining faith. Thus the play might be taken both ways by its Jacobean audience—that is, as an implicit affirmation of Christianity by its negative depiction of pagan belief, or as an expression of the crisis of religious belief that many of Shakespeare's contemporaries were undergoing.

Elton's work was completed some years before its publication, and the delay diminished its effectiveness somewhat. The view that Lear is an "optimistically Christian drama" is nowhere near as pervasive as it once was. Nevertheless, its polemical character aside, this is an important and valuable book. It is the most comprehensive, convincing, and well-documented analysis of the play from the perspective of the history of ideas.

64. Jorgensen, Paul. *Lear's Self-Knowledge*. Berkeley: University of California, 1966. 154 pp.

Jorgensen's study is directed to the idea of self-knowledge in the play. Self-knowledge is the content that Lear achieves; self-discovery is the process by which it is achieved. After some judicious remarks on the limits of historical criticism, Jorgensen examines a number of Renaissance teachings on the doctrine of *nosce teipsum*. The most important of these for the purposes of *King Lear* he finds to be "the study of one's passion and the study of one's body." In Lear's case madness is a necessary preliminary to this discovery. He learns first that he is an individual with a need for love, a desire for recognition, and an awareness of his fundamental folly. Beyond that he discovers a truth of the human condition: Man is fundamentally a corporal entity "pathetic and grotesque." The discovery of that fact leads to the realization—underscored by the sexual references —that generation is itself a tragic activity. Particularly interesting is Jorgensen's account of the process itself: It is not a logical, orderly movement but a series of eruptions of "subterranean thought."

Jorgensen's analysis is distinguished both by the sanity of his judgments and the modesty with which he advances them. It might be argued

that Lear's self-knowledge is less important than the knowledge he gains
of the world around him, or even that Lear at the end of the play shows
very little self-knowledge. Nevertheless, Jorgensen's thesis, however qualified, seems altogether valid.

65. Kernan, Alvin. "Formalism and Realism in Elizabethan Drama: The
Miracles in *King Lear,*" *Renaissance Drama*, 9 (1966), 59–66.

Kernan begins by observing the "counterpoint" between the general
moral scheme of a Shakespearean play and the individuality of particular
characters. This counterpoint provides part of the strength of the play.
Shakespeare is aware of this tension and exploits it to its fullest in such
scenes as the Dover Cliff scene (IV, 6) in *Lear*. Echoing Levin (54),
Kernan argues that the scene dramatizes that precipitous descent which
is the general movement of the play: the fall from the heights to the
depths. However, there is a corresponding ascending movement based
upon the values of human kindness and feeling. This is paralleled by the
scene in which Lear is reunited with Cordelia: "These two interludes—
one in the allegorical, the other in the symbolic mode—reconfirm . . .
orthodox, traditional views of the value and meaning of life." However,
Shakespeare is not satisfied with these traditional views. In Act V events
radically qualify, if not contradict, the values here asserted. Out of this
interplay emerges a sense of the full complexity of the play's felt life.
Kernan's essay adds to our understanding of the Dover scene and,
as a result, of the play as a whole. Particularly noteworthy is the parallel
he draws between that scene and the following one in which Lear and
Cordelia are reunited. Less creditable is his vagueness in describing the
relationship of these scenes to the play's conclusion.

66. Mack, Maynard. *King Lear in Our Time*. Berkeley: University of
California Press, 1966. 126 pp. Excerpted in Kermode.

This volume, the text of three lectures given at the University of
California at Berkeley in 1964, begins with an analysis of some features
of the stage history of the play, moves to a consideration of "the traditions
of thought and feeling" that constitute its imaginative sources, and concludes with a consideration "of what in the play speaks most immediately
to us who live four centuries after its author's birth." His account of the
play's theatrical history is enlivened by the thesis that modern productions,

particularly those of Peter Brook (1962) and Herbert Blau (1964), distort
Shakespeare's play in a variety of subtle ways, in a fashion no less drastic
than the alterations of Tate and his sucessors in the eighteenth century.

Mack locates the root of the play in the archetypal myth of the
Abasement of the Proud King, in early Tudor morality plays and in the
pastoral romance, inverted in *Lear* to "antipastoral." The presence of
these factors makes it clear that many of the problems of character and
action in the play are resolved if we see its characteristic mode as that of
the dream or vision. As for the contemporary relevance of *Lear*, he sees
its unique appeal for our time in its image of gratuitous violence and of
"relatedness" as the essence of our humanity. "Existence is tragic in *King
Lear* because existence is inseparable from relation. . . ."

One problem with this volume is that it attempts to cover more
ground than is possible within the scope of 126 pages. Given the provocative and illuminating concluding chapter, one wishes that the author
had chosen to devote less space to stage history and more to the details of
the play. However, even in its present form the volume constitutes a
serious, important and eloquent discussion of the major aspects of the play
"in our time".

67. Mason, H. A. "King Lear: The Central Stream," *Cambridge Quarterly*, 2 (1966–67), 23–48, 148–166, 212–235. Reprinted in *Shakespeare's Tragedies of Love*. New York: Barnes & Noble, 1970.

Mason offers one of the most controversial readings of the play in
recent years. He begins by decrying the misuse of *Lear* as a source of
edification by modern critics, and proposes to examine the play as it is
experienced in performance (without preconceptions) in order to determine its "central stream," the main current of its momentum. After
this iconoclastic preamble, he proceeds to a scene-by-scene analysis of the
play. He finds Cordelia's reply in the opening scene an insincere "scoring
off her sisters." The Fool is a professional jester and not a very good one:
"we are embarrassed by the thought that Shakespeare may have found him
a satisfactory clown." The most significant actions in the third act concern
Gloucester, who is much more deserving of sympathy than Lear. Lear is
posturing in the storm, "play-acting humility." The reunion of Lear and
Cordelia is beautifully done but the fifth act betrays the play's "radical
incoherence." The last act is a "cathedral surrounded by slums"—bad
writing, cheap moralizing, and tedium punctuated by moments of beauty.

Viewed without preconceptions, *Lear* falls considerably short of being Shakespeare's greatest play.

Mason doth protest too much. As his *analysis* progresses, his tone becomes increasingly shrill, leaving the reader with the impression that he is not so much reacting to the play as against orthodox criticism. The more's the pity, since some of his observations are worth making, not the least of which are his strictures against "edifying" criticism.

68. Skulsky, Harold. *"King Lear* and the Meaning of Chaos," *Shakespeare Quarterly*, XVII (1966), 3–19.

Skulsky begins his analysis by relating the play to *Troilus and Cressida*. In *Lear*, Shakespeare "searches the chaos" that is described in Ulysses' speech on degree. However, *Lear* demonstrates that Ulysses' underlying argument—the identification of the good with the principle of order—is an inadequate formulation. Equally inadequate, of course, is the negativism of Edmund that sees man as little more than a clothed cipher. Lear moves from this position to the perception of justice as a human value. At this point the play enters the mode of the miracle. Both Gloucester and Lear are miraculously brought to an "intuition of the good" not as order but as an "irreducible factor in human existence." Thus the play affirms the "autonomy of the moral life." It does not, however, affirm (as Bradley suggests) the value of suffering. Suffering is neither intrinsically good nor bad, simply the morally neutral condition that permits the discovery of irreducible human value.

Skulsky's essay is among the most valuable that has been written on the play within recent years. It combines the best features of historical criticism with an intelligent understanding of the philosophical implications that subsequent generations have derived from the play. Particularly noteworthly is its qualification of Bradley's view of suffering as redemptive in itself. Its chief weakness is perhaps its failure to confront the possibility that the death of Cordelia represents in fact the reduction of irreducible human value.

69. Blok, Alexander. "Shakespeare's *King Lear*" in *Shakespeare in the Soviet Union.* Moscow: Progress Publishers, 1966, pp. 17–24.

Subtitled "An Address to the Actors," Blok's essay is a statement of purpose in regard to a production of the play at the Bolshoi Drama

Theatre in 1920. For Blok the essence of the play is its "dry and bitter" character. Even the good characters exhibit a lack of life-affirming energy. The purpose of the play is "to open our eyes on those bottomless pits which do exist in life and which it is not within our own volition to avoid." This bleak vision is not qualified by any suggestion of a life after death. The play concludes on a profound note of bitterness, but it is a bitterness that purifies, reinforcing the ancient maxim of the value of knowledge gained in suffering.

Blok's essay is an eloquent, although occasionally overstated, expression of a dominant tone in the play.

70. Frye, Northrop. *Fools of Time.* University of Toronto Press, 1967. 121 pp. Reprinted in Kermode.

In this volume Frye brings to Shakespearean tragedy his comprehensive synoptic views of the nature of literature. For Frye, tragedy is a vision of man-in-time inexorably marching toward annihilation and yet capable of making a counter assertion that suggests the possibility, however remote, of heroism and transcendence. His scheme posits three categories of Shakespearean tragedy, although he is careful to point out that these are not rigidly conceived but are largely matters of emphasis and perspective. *Lear* belongs—along with *Othello* and *Timon*—in the third phase: "the tragedy of isolation," the hero, alienated from society, searching for his identity. The play has an "inner and an outer action." The inner action (Gloucester subplot) is a "morally intelligible tragedy" in which retribution is meted out to both Gloucester and Edmund, and order is restored. The outer action (the Lear plot) is a tragedy of isolation. Lear begins by "depriving himself of his own social context." He then begins an identity quest. In the figure of Poor Tom he confronts himself in the natural condition, but nature itself has been so perverted that the vision of man in nature is expressed by the *saeva indignatio* of Lear's fourth-act ranting against hypocrisy and sexuality. The incompatibility of the human and the natural is given its sharpest expression in the death of Cordelia. The play ends "in a vision of absurd anguish." Lear's experience is our experience, leaving us with a "world to remake out of it"—that is, leaving us with the act of criticism.

With Frye we view the play from a much greater distance than is ordinarily appropriate to the act of criticism. As a result we may complain that individual distinctions are blurred and out of focus, that we are tracing generic outlines rather than perceiving a particular play, that Frye is more interested in the play's essence than in its existence. Nevertheless he offers a perspective—an exhilarating and marvelously clear view—that is, for many, broader and more satisfying than that of any other contemporary critic. And even for those who prefer the critical trees to the theoretical forest, Frye supplies an abundance of illuminating insights.

71. Gardner, Helen. *King Lear.* London: University of London, Oxford University Press, 1967. 28 pp.

Miss Gardner's lecture, delivered at the University of London in 1966, begins with a survey of various aspects of the play: the integration of its action, character, and language; the importance of the opening scene; the nonhistorical character of the play's setting; the function of the comic element; and the character of the double plot. These lead her to a consideration of the main characters, and finally to a judgment about the play's conclusion. To this latter problem there are no answers: "The ultimate mystery is here and Shakespeare simply presents it." The image of the old king with his dead child in his arms provides us with a "secular *Pieta*," offering us no consolation "for there is none which the world, the world of the play, can offer."

Miss Gardner's comments are consistently perceptive and enlightening. Even when her observations (as in her comments of the play's conclusion) are not particularly original they frequently achieve considerable force, as in the comparison to the Pieta.

72. McNeir, Waldo. "The Role of Edmund in *King Lear*," *Studies in English Literature*, 8 (1968), 187–216.

McNeir is concerned with the problem of Edmund's hesitation in recalling his order for the death of Lear and Cordelia. He supplies a detailed description of Edgar's actions in the play leading up to the final scene, and suggests that Edmund's attempt at complete repentance must fulfill three conditions: contrition, confession, and a firm purpose of reparation. Edmund undergoes this process in a "slow and labored" fashion, equivocating until the final moment and finally failing to bring about the necessary reparation. Thus the deaths of Lear and Cordelia, far from being a mere sport of the gods, are shown to be inextricably related to the moral failure of Edmund.

McNeir provides a consistent and logical argument. Many will feel, however, that it invests undue signifiicance in the character of Edmund, and consequently diminishes the impact of the fates of Lear and Cordelia.

73. Calarco, N. Joseph. "The Tragic Universe of *King Lear*" in *Tragic Being: Apollo and Dionysus in Western Drama*. University of Minnesota Press, 1966, pp. 81–120.

Calarco's general thesis concerns the Nietzschean Apollonian-Dionysian antithesis and its application to a view of man that is both historical and anhistorical. The latter distinction Calarco derives from Mircea Eliade's *Cosmos and History*, a study of primitive man's conception of time.

Calarco sees the play as a movement from the Apollonian light of reason (Gloucester's explanation of Edmund's bastardy; Lear's plan for the division of the kingdom) to the dark Dionysian night of suffering and madness. As a consequence of this movement Lear's individual sense of self is shattered, and he discovers himself—naked and unaccommodated, confronting chaos and nothingness. This is the ultimate evil residing in the heart of being. It is offset by Lear's final illusion that Cordelia is alive, an "absurd act of faith," an echo of the absurdity of belief described by Tertullian and subsequently reaffirmed by Kierkegaard. However, it is not intended as an affirmation of the Christian faith. Cordelia's death is an historical reality, an irreversible fact; Lear's illusion is a subjective, anhistorical and mythical "valorization" of human existence, a denial of linear time. Shakespeare offers us both perspectives and refuses to accept one in preference to the other. Some readers will doubtless object to Calarco's abstract and schematic analysis of the play. Few, however, will fail to be impressed by his willingness to grapple with the deeper roots of this drama, and by his capacity to evoke the sense of its profound significance.

74. Rackin, Phyllis. "Delusion as Resolution in *King Lear*," *Shakespeare Quarterly*, 21 (1970), 29–34.

This brief article deals with Lear's last speech:

Do you see this? Look on her, look, her lips, Look there, look there!

Balancing the pessimistic and optimistic interpretations of the speech, Rackin argues that Lear's cry is a creative delusion, similar to that created by Edgar in the Dover Cliff scene. Such a delusion is itself a gratuitous act of faith, unmotivated and unwarranted. By presenting his resolution as a delusion, Shakespeare has anticipated his audience's reluctance to accept either the optimistic or the pessimistic conclusion. As a result, Lear's affirmation of faith is all the more triumphant because of the hopelessness of the situation in which it is uttered.

A subtle and imaginative argument, this point deserves extended treatment.

75. Weitz, Morris. "The Coinage of Man: *King Lear* and Camus's *L'Etranger*," MLR 66 (1971), 31–39.

Weitz argues that both *Lear* and *The Stranger* assert identical propositions about the objective value of man in the world, which is that from a metaphysical standpoint, human values are worthless. Both works confirm the fact that we live "in a world without ultimate meaning." In *King Lear*, however, the implications of that fact are explored in a direction entirely different from that of Camus' novel. The play dramatizes for us the importance of the need to affirm human values in an indifferent universe. The imagery of clothing and accommodation is significant here, for it offers examples of items that are objectively superfluous but subjectively essential.

Rationally speaking, we do not need such human values as filial gratitude, but the play asks us to reason not the need. All that separates the human from the animal is a "tenuous, ephemeral proclamation" that enables man "to mint his own values." In *The Stranger*, on the other hand, this affirmation is denied in favor of a total nihilism.

In relation to *King Lear*, Weitz's argument represents a position that appears to be emerging as the dominant contemporary view of the play (see 66, 68, 71). As such, his presentation is articulate and forceful, although not as detailed as it might be. Less successful is his characterization of *The Stranger* as a nihilistic work.

Sources and Date

The chief source of Shakespeare's play is *The True Chronicle History of King Leir,* an anonymous play published in 1605 but written and performed much earlier (before 1594). Behind that play is an old story transmitted through Celtic mythology and recorded in Geoffrey of Monmouth's *Historia Regum Britanniae* (c. 1137). Holinshed adapted it for his *Chronicles,* and his version was known to Shakespeare. Shakespeare knew as well Spenser's treatment of the story in the second book of *The Faerie Queene,* and John Higgins' account in the 1574 edition of *A Mirror for Magistrates.*

The subplot involving Gloucester, Edmund, and Edgar is derived from the story of the blind King of Paphlagonia in Sidney's *Arcadia* (II.x). Tom O'Bedlam's catalogue of fiends is adapted from Samuel Harsnett's *A Declaration of Egregious Popish Impostures* (1603). The play reveals a linguistic indebtedness to Florio's translation of Montaigne's *Essays,* and a thematic relationship to one of those essays in particular: "Apology for Raymond Sebonde." In addition to these literary sources Shakespeare may have known of the experience of Sir Brian Annesley, the victim of an attempt by one of his three daughters to have him declared insane. He was defended by another daughter, Cordell.

The fullest accounts of the play's main source are given in W. Perrett's *The Story of King Lear* (Berlin, 1904) and in Kenneth Muir's *Shakespeare Sources* (London, 1957). The seventh and final volume of Geoffrey Bullough's *Narrative and Dramatic Sources of Shakespeare*—the definitive account and collection of Shakespeare's sources—discusses the major tragedies. The best account of the indebtedness to Montaigne is given in W. B. D. Henderson's articles in *The Shakespeare Association Bulletin,* XIV (1939), 209–225; XV (1940), 40–56. Irving Ribner provides further evidence of the significance of the *Arcadia* sources in "Sidney's

Arcadia and the Structure of *Lear*," in *Studia Neophilologica*, XXIV (1952), 63–68. Muir gives a detailed account of the influence of Harsnett in "Samuel Harsnett and *King Lear*," RES, II (1951), 11–21, and reprints the relevant material in his New Arden Edition of the play. Chambers (30) discusses the sources in order to defend his Christian view of the play, and Mack (66) takes an imaginative and perceptive look at the influences of folk motifs, morality plays, and pastoral romances in shaping the play's design.

Textual Criticism

INTRODUCTION

The play was first printed in 1608. The determination of the "copy" for this quarto version of the play remains one of the most vexing problems in textual scholarship. The text is corrupt, but not corrupt enough to warrant its being classified as a "bad" quarto. For many years it was thought to be based upon a stenographic report of a playhouse performance. This theory has now been generally discredited in favor of the tentatively held view that the text derives from Shakespeare's "foul papers" through some combination of dictation and memorial reconstruction. In any case, the effect of more recent studies has been to upgrade the authority of the quarto version. This is particularly true in light of the fact that the Folio version appears to be based upon copies of the first and second quartos, corrected with reference to the King's Men's promptbook. The authority of the Folio has been undermined further by the discovery by Charlton Hinman (*The Printing and Proof-Reading of the First Folio of Shakespeare*, 2 vols., Oxford, 1963) that a good portion of the text was set by an apprentice compositor working on cast-off copy, a procedure which increases the likelihood of errors.

ENTRIES FOR TEXTUAL CRITICISM

T1. Walker, Alice. *Textual Problems of the First Folio*. Cambridge University Press, 1953.

In her discussion of *King Lear*, Miss Walker advances a new theory about the origins of Q1. She suggests that the text represents a transcript of Shakespeare's foul papers, supplemented with their own recollection of lines. The Folio text was printed from a copy of Q which had been collated with the company prompt book. Miss Walker's conclusion is that the Quarto needs to be given much greater authority than modern editors have been willing to grant it.

T2. Duthie, G. I. *Elizabethan Shorthand and the First Quarto of King Lear.* Oxford: Basil Blackwell, 1949. 82 pp.; G. I. Duthie and P. G. Buchloh, *Shakespeares King Lear: Historie oder Tragödie.* Kiel: Ferdinand Hirt, 1965. 44 pp.

Published in conjunction with Duthie's critical edition of the play, *Elizabethan Shorthand and the First Quarto of King Lear* disputed the then-prevalent hypothesis that the copy for the first quarto was supplied by a stenographic transcript of a playhouse performance. After providing an account of the three available systems of shorthand at the time, Duthie argues that none of them was capable of reproducing a text as full as the *Lear* quarto. Duthrie's argument has been generally accepted by textual scholars. His own theories as to the provenance of both Q1 and F, however, have been subject to change over the years.

Duthie's most recent conclusions are contained in *Shakespeares King Lear: Historie oder Tragödie.* This pamphlet offers two contrasting views of the textual origins of Lear. Buchloh argues that the Quarto text reflects the political–historical character of the play and is derived from an acting version. The Folio version, on the other hand, he regards as the more literary text, designed to reflect the tragic aspects of the play. Duthie argues for the more orthodox view of the text: The Quarto is derived from Shakespeare's foul papers and the Folio text is derived from the prompt-book.

Editions

E1. *King Lear:* A New Variorum Edition, ed. H. H. Furness [1880]. New York: Dover Publications, 1963. 503 pp.

Now available in paperback, this edition (cited in the text as NV) is an indispensable guide to early criticism of the play. It also provides excerpts from the major sources and from Tate's *King Lear*, and an extensively annotated text.

E2. *King Lear:* The Arden Edition, ed. Kenneth Muir. London: Methuen, 1951. 258 pp.

This is an extensive revision of the old Arden Edition edited by W. J. Craig in 1901. It features a 50-page introduction covering problems of text, sources, and dates, as well as a critical analysis of the play. The appendices include extracts from the play's sources: the old *Leir*, Holinshed, Spenser, *A Mirror for Magistrates*, Sidney's *Arcadia*, Florio's translation of Montaigne and Harsnett's *Egregious Declaration of Popish Impostures*. The book is presented with collations and notes on each page; thus it provides an excellent text for the average reader. As a scholarly work, however, it fails to meet the exacting standards of the textual critic (see Fredson Bowers' review of the volume in *Shakespeare Quarterly*, IV (1953), 471–477).

E3. *King Lear:* The New Shakespeare, ed. G. I. Duthie and J. D. Wilson. Cambridge University Press, 1960.

This edition is noteworthy for its extensive treatment of the play's textual problems, particularly the problem of the provenance of the text. The textual editor (Duthie) arrives at conclusions which cause him to rely more heavily on the authority of the Quarto than recent editors have. Less creditable is Duthie's lengthy critical introduction, representing as it does an extreme and oversimplified view of the play as optimistically Christian.

Staging

Accounts of the play's stage history are given in G. C. D. Odell's *Shakespeare from Betterton to Irving* (2 vols., London, 1920); C. F. T. Brooke's *"King Lear* on the Stage" in *Essays on Shakespeare and Other Elizabethans* (New Haven, 1948); and *The Reader's Encyclopedia of Shakespeare*, ed. O. J. Campbell and E. G. Quinn (New York, 1966). Twentieth-century productions are treated in J. C. Trewin's *Shakespeare on the English Stage, 1900–1964* (London, 1964). The first chapter of Mack's *King Lear in Our Time* (66) takes a jaundiced view of theatrical alterations of the text from Tate to Brook. Muriel St. Clare Byrne's *"King Lear* at Stratford-on-Avon, 1959" (*Shakespeare Quarterly*, XI [1960], 189–206) provides a perceptive review of the production that starred Charles Laughton. The rationale of Peter Brook's controversial 1962 production is explained in Charles Marowitz's "Lear Log" (*Tulane Drama Review*, VIII [1963], 103–121), and eloquently attacked in Alfred Harbage's *Conceptions of Shakespeare* (34). Herbert Blau's Beckettian production at the San Francisco Actor's Workshop is described in his *The Impossible Theater* (New York, 1964). Useful surveys of recent productions include Charles Lanstorle's "Four Lears," *Shakespeare Survey*, I (1948), 98–102; and Lorraine Sherley's "King Lear: The Stage, Not the Closet," *Shakespeare 1964*, ed. J. W. Corder (Fort Worth, Tex., 1965). Still, the classical exposition of the play from a theatrical standpoint remains the Granville–Barker analysis (22).

Macbeth

Joseph Grennen

❖ CONTENTS

Index to Critics Cited and Their Entry Numbers   *213*

Short Titles of Collections of Macbeth *Criticism*   *215*

The Criticism of Macbeth   *216*

     Introduction   *216*

     Entries for the Criticism of Macbeth   *219*

Sources and Date   *268*

     Introduction   *268*

     Entries for Sources and Date   *268*

Textual Criticism   *271*

     Introduction   *271*

     Entries for Textual Criticism   *271*

Editions   *273*

Staging   *277*

     Introduction   *277*

     Entries for Staging   *277*

Index to Critics Cited
and Their Entry Numbers

Adams, Joseph Quincy E3
Bartholmeusz, Dennis St1
Blackmore, Simon A. 17
Booth, Wayne 48
Boyer, Clarence 18
Bradbrook, Muriel C. S2
Bradley, A. C. 15
Brandes, George 26
Brooke, Stopford A. 25
Brooks, Cleanth 41
Campbell, Lily B. 29
Chambers, E. K. 24
Charlton, H. B. 44
Coleridge, Samuel Taylor 6
Coles, Blanche 35
Coriat, Isador H. 16
Curry, Walter Clyde 33
De Quincey, Thomas 7
Doran, Madeleine 37
Dowden, Edward 11
Driver, Tom F. 58
Dyson, J. P. 63
Elliott, G. R. 56
Farnham, Willard 47
Fergusson, Francis 49
Flatter, Richard T1
Fletcher, G. 8
Freud, Sigmund 19
Furness, Horace Howard, Jr. E1
Harcourt, John S3
Harrison, G. B. 50
Hazlitt, William 5

Heilman, Robert 67
Holloway, John 60
Hunter, Joseph 9
Jack, Jane S2
Jekels, Ludwig 52
Johnson, Samuel 1
Jorgensen, Paul 69
Kantak, V. Y. 64
Kirschbaum, L. 55
Kittredge, George Lyman 20
Knight, G. Wilson 28
Knights, L. C. 30
Lawlor, John 59
Liddell, Mark Harvey E2
Lucas, F. L. 51
Moulton, R. G. 13
Muir, Kenneth E5
Murry, John Middleton 32
Nosworthy, J. M. T3
Paul, Henry S1
Quiller-Couch, Sir Arthur 21
Rauber, D. F. 68
Reynolds, Sir Joshua 2
Ribner, Irving 57
Rogers, H. L. 66
Rossiter, A. P. 61
Schlegel, Augustus W. 4
Schucking, Levin 23
Shaw, G. B. 14
Sitwell, Edith 43
Spargo, John Webster 42
Speaight, Robert 53

Spencer, Christopher   T2
Spencer, Theodore   38
Spurgeon, Caroline   31
Stauffer, Donald   46
Stirling, Brents   54
Stoll, Elmer Edgar,   27
Swinburne, Algernon Charles   12
Taine, Hippolyte   10
Tillyard, E. M. W.   40

Toppen, W. H.   62
Traversi, D. A.   34
Van Doren, Mark   36
Walker, Roy   45
Walton, J. K.   65
Webster, Margaret   39
Whately, Thomas   3
Wilson, J. Dover   E4
Winstanley, L.   22

Short Titles of Collections of Macbeth Criticism

Furness—*A New Variorum Edition of Shakespeare: Macbeth*, ed. H. H. Furness, Jr. [5th edition, 1903] (New York: Dover, 1963).

Halio—*Approaches to Macbeth*, ed. Jay L. Halio (Belmont, Calif.: Wadsworth, 1966).

Wain—*Macbeth: A Casebook*, ed. John Wain (London: Macmillan, 1968).

The Criticism of **Macbeth**

INTRODUCTION

Macbeth has always been one of Shakespeare's most intriguing plays. To some, it is the greatest morality play ever written; to others, the finest of high tragedies. Critics have never tired of seeking for the key to its meaning, and though the volume of commentary does not approach that which has been generated by *Hamlet*, it is nevertheless impressively large, running into hundreds of articles and books. Some of the discussion has centered on particular problems of textual authenticity, the ordering of scenes, or the emendation of individual lines, but the greatest attention has been focused on the psychology of the hero and the nature of the Witches, or "weird sisters," and the role they play in Macbeth's downfall.

The Eighteenth Century

Interest in character predominated in the eighteenth century, with various results, stemming from the degree to which the critic remained under the sway of neo-classical concern for "rules" and moral bias. Johnson (1), generally so open-minded about Shakespeare, committed one of his more celebrated *gaffes* in remarking about Macbeth's fate that "every reader rejoices at his fall." Whately (3), in this instance, is sounder in his reading of character, seeing Macbeth as essentially a man of tender feelings who is repelled by the idea of murder. The Romantics' interest in the bizarre and the preternatural is probably best displayed in Hazlitt's (5) study of the violent contrasts of style and dramatic quality to be found in the play, though it leads him to excessively curious illustrations of his basic principle, the structural antitheses of the play being mirrored for him even in the androgynous character of the Witches. Coleridge's (6) influence, in the study of this play, has been largely negative, his rejection of the Porter

Scene having occasioned numerous replies in defense of Shakespeare's authorship, though he has been overshadowed by De Quincey's (7) famous analysis of the knocking at the gate as a symbolic termination of the temporary dominance of the diabolical.

Reaction Against Impressionism

The outright reaction against Romantic "impressionism" is seen at its worst in Taine (10), who seeks to be scientific and ends only in a different kind of impressionism, and perhaps at its best in Moulton (13), whose plea for an inductive approach to the plays in some ways anticipates the (early) new critical rejection of accumulated historical irrelevancies. Probably the best-known and most influential Shakespearean critic of the past century is A. C. Bradley (15), whose search for the keys to the inner psychological life of the characters occasionally led him into absurdities, but whose intelligence kept him in control of the larger issues: total design, mood, and philosophical importance. The formal psychological critics— Freud (19) himself is of course the best-known—include Coriat (16), whose analysis of Lady Macbeth as a case of hysteria attracted some not undeserved ridicule; and Jekels (52), whose more recent study of "character splitting" in the play, and its relationship to Shakespeare's own life and the persons he was acquainted with, is an eminently sane statement of a much attacked position. Freud himself saw Macbeth as a classic example of the psychological phenomenon of "the person wrecked by success."

Early Historical Criticism

Early historical criticism of the play can be found in the work of Schücking (23) and Stoll (27). Schücking interprets character in terms of a tension between surviving conventional modes and new realistic modes of representation. Stoll, in his violent attack on Bradley and his sympathizers, goes so far as to reject the notion of psychological consistency altogether, in favor of a total emotional pattern for a play, which might be at odds not only with psychological consistency but even with ordinary narrative logic. This abandonment of explicit statement in favor of a meaning emerging from "pattern" is treated in a uniquely different manner by G. Wilson Knight (28), who concludes that Macbeth achieves the final triumph of an honest relationship with his milieu.

The New Criticism

The "new criticism," as applied to *Macbeth*, may be said to begin with a famous essay of L. C. Knights (30), strongly opposing the Bradleyan position. Knights stresses the controlling theme of the play and the importance of recognizing the special "dramatic function" of individual speeches and images. An important service was rendered to the study of Shakespeare's patterns of imagery by Caroline Spurgeon (31), whose cataloguing of images (in *Macbeth*, it is the image of "borrowed clothes" which predominates) smoothed the way for later critics such as Cleanth Brooks (41). Brooks uses Spurgeon's discoveries in the service of a reading of the play which sees Macbeth as a man so totally committed to logic that he is helpless in the face of the essential ambiguity of things. Traversi (34), too, is concerned with the force of individual words and images, finding reflected in the very language of the play the central theme of a regal grace and harmony violated and later restored.

Recent Studies

Macbeth has been greatly illuminated by recent study of Shakespeare's sources, both in literature and in social and philosophical materials reflecting the world picture he was familiar with. Curry's (33) book, which emphasizes the destinal character of the Witches, has found a good deal of favor, and studies by Theodore Spencer (38), Farnham (47), and Speaight (53) throw light on various aspects of tradition, social concern, and natural philosophy which enter into a consideration of *Macbeth*. There has likewise been ample discussion of the Christian roots of Shakespeare's thought, extreme positions (with respect to *Macbeth*) being taken by Walker (45) and Elliott (56), who propose eminently Christian interpretations of the play, and by H. B. Charlton (44), who steadfastly rejects them in favor of a more naturalistic reading. In addition, there have been a great variety of special interpretations emanating from no school and showing no special influence. Among these are: Tillyard's (40) attempt to define *Macbeth* as a "history play"; Paul's (51) well-documented assessment of it as a play prepared specifically for a command performance before the King; Booth's (48) and Fergusson's (49) analyses in Aristotelian terms; and the Marxist reduction suggested by Walton (65).

Perhaps the best introduction to the play is the text and introductory discussion of Kenneth Muir (E5), from which one might proceed to the more controversial opinions concerning text, date, and performance offered by J. Dover Wilson (E4).

ENTRIES FOR THE CRITICISM OF *MACBETH*

1. Johnson, Samuel. "Notes on *Macbeth*" [1765], in *Johnson on Shakespeare: Essays and Notes Selected and Set Forth with an Introduction*, ed. Walter Raleigh (London, 1908). Excerpts in Furness, Halio, and Wain.

Johnson's finest remarks on Shakespeare are contained, of course, in his *Preface to Shakespeare*, where, among other things, he praises the poet for creating "human sentiments in human language," and for making "nature predominate over accident." On the negative side, he believes Shakespeare to "write without any moral purpose," and to be the victim of a tendency toward gross jests and quibbles: "A quibble was to him [Shakespeare] the fatal Cleopatra for which he lost the world, and was content to lose it." That he disregarded the unities of time and place, however, struck Johnson as a matter of "happy ignorance," and that he followed no strict principles for the distinction of tragedy from comedy was of little consequence, for his plays exhibit "The real state of sublunary nature, which partakes of good and evil, joy and sorrow, mingled with endless variety of proportion and innumerable modes of combination." His faults are mainly to be explained by the fact that he is a child of his age.

This is true of *Macbeth*, in particular, a play in which "the whole action of his tragedy depend[s] upon enchantment," though this was "both by himself and his audience thought awful and affecting." His knowledge of human nature is best seen in the arguments by which Lady Macbeth induces her husband to murder, but there are "no nice discriminations of character" and "the course of the action necessarily determines the conduct of the agents" (*i.e.*, situation determines characterization rather than the reverse—a much disputed point, on which Bradley (15) and Stoll (27) hold extreme positions).

There is a war in Johnson's mind between what instinct convinces him is good and precept tells him to be bad. Although he must be reckoned a great critic for his sensitive recognition of Shakespeare's genius, his weakness as a practical critic shows itself when he applies coldly rational principles to the plays, and fails to distinguish actual human responses to their drama from the cognitive appreciation of moral and ethical ideas. Only thus could he maintain that "Lady Macbeth is merely detested," and (of Macbeth) that "every reader rejoices at his fall."

2. *Reynolds, Sir Joshua. "Discourse VIII" [1778], modern edition by Roger Fry, *Sir Joshua Reynolds: Discourses on Art* (London, 1905); repr. Collier Books, 1961 (p. 132).

Reynolds' eighth Discourse treats of the necessity for avoiding ostentation in art, for achieving variety without sacrificing simplicity. His term for the requisite quality is *repose*, and he finds it well-illustrated in the dialogue between Duncan and Banquo as they approach Macbeth's castle. Their relaxed conversation "gives that repose so necessary to the mind, after the tumultuous bustle of the preceding scenes, and perfectly contrasts the scene of horror that immediately succeeds." In this "softening of tones" Shakespeare resembles Homer.

Reynolds' observation reflects the eighteenth century doctrine of *ut pictura poesis*, and, together with some of Johnson's comments, heralds the nineteenth-century tendency to remark on isolated "beauties" in Shakespeare's plays to the neglect of the total structure. It looks ahead, moreover, to the Romantic theory of dramatic scenes introduced for the sake of emotional "relief."

3. *Whately, Thomas. *Remarks on Some of the Characters of Shakespeare* (London, 1785). Partially reprinted in *Shakespeare Criticism 1623–1840*, ed. D. Nichol Smith (World's Classics, No. 212).

The *Remarks* is interesting as the earliest example of a developed comparison between Macbeth and Richard III, a matter which has been a feature of *Macbeth* criticism ever since. Whately was not primarily a man of letters, but a politician—Under-Secretary of State under Lord North, 1771–72. His treatise centers on a comparison of the two characters considered as "draughts from nature," and estimates the assiduousness with which Shakespeare fleshed out the portraits in successive scenes of the plays. On this principle, Macbeth is far superior to Richard. In the latter's case "through whole speeches and scenes, character [the revelation of traits of character] is often wanting," but in this Shakespeare may be held guilty only of neglecting, not perverting, his talents.

Macbeth is a more highly complicated, more highly finished figure than Richard, and required more variety and delicacy in the "painting." He is a man of tender feelings, not easily inclined to murder, and, compared to Richard, relatively weak in ambition. His character has therefore been accommodated to the "fable" (plot), and thus calls for "extraordinary incitements" to stimulate him to the performance of the crime.

Though free of the notorious interest in the "historical" life of dramatic characters, of which Maurice Morgann's *Essay on the Dramatic Character of Sir John Falstaff* is the first important example, Whately's discussion centers primarily on the psychology of character. He does, however, recognize the superior claim of the "fable" (Aristotle's doctrine of the "primacy of plot"), but remains, for all that, committed to the typical eighteenth-century interest in rules and realism.

4. Schlegel, Augustus W. *A Course of Lectures on Dramatic Art and Literature*, trans. J. Black and A. J. W. Morrison (London, 1815). Excerpt in Furness.

Schlegel's very influential essay on *Macbeth* shows to good advantage such strengths of the Romantic viewpoint as the interest in organic form, and imaginative sympathy with the strange and even the repugnant. He responds to the *quality* of the Witches' "peculiar language," and recognizes the attractiveness of Macbeth's character along with the abhorrence his deeds provoke. In the final scenes, Schlegel declares, we feel compelled "to admire in him the struggle of a brave will with a cowardly conscience." (The argument between "character realists" and those who prefer some sort of conventional understanding of character often focuses on Macbeth's conscience—whether he has one at all, and if so, what sort it is. The most recent sally in the campaign is Toppen's book-length study of Macbeth's conscience (59).) The brevity of the play does not cause Schlegel to complain or to suspect corruption (all recent editors regard some passages as corrupt), but merely to wonder at "how very much can be compressed into so narrow a space."

Schlegel's position, very modern in its trust in Shakespeare's dramatic acumen, is weak in its pretensions to a solution of Macbeth's struggle in such abstract terrms as the opposition of will and conscience. And there is some truth to Bradley's terming "unfortunate" his notion that the Witches were necessary to the play because natural forces would have appeared too weak to provoke a man of Macbeth's character to murder.

5. Hazlitt, William. *Characters of Shakespeare's Plays* (London, 1817). Excerpts in Furness and Halio.

Like Whately, whose *Remarks* he had read, Hazlitt values Shakespeare for the genius and virtuosity with which he presented so many "distinct" and original aspects of general nature. If *Lear* stands first for the "profound intensity of the passion," *Macbeth* is to be praised "for the wildness of the imagination and the rapidity of the action." His scenes penetrate the memory, as if we had actually known the people and objects portrayed. For Hazlitt, too, the action determines the way in which character shall manifest itself. "The overwhelming pressure of preternatural agency urges on the tide of human passion with redoubled force." He sees the play as organized around a principle of contrasts: life and death; action and reaction; violent antitheses of style; juxtapositions of scenes totally opposite in quality; even ambiguous descriptions, such as that of the Witches, who "should be women, but their beards forbid it." The character of Macbeth himself illustrates this principle, for, unlike Richard III, there is a war within him between ambitious desire and human kindness.

Hazlitt's sensitive responses to poetry are always worth reading, yet the real weakness of his conception of character emerges vivdly in his speculations as to what might have become of the characters of Richard and Macbeth in the hands of another poet. As if Shakespeare's figures enjoyed a life apart from his own conception of them!

6. Coleridge, Samuel Taylor. *Shakespearean Criticism* [c. 1818], ed. Thomas Middleton Raysor. 2nd ed., 2 vols. (London, 1960). Everyman Editions (Nos. 162, 183). Excerpts in Wain.

(*Macbeth* is treated by Coleridge at length in two places: Vol. I, pp. 60–73, and Vol. II, pp. 220–222. His lectures were probably delivered in

1818.) Coleridge's remarks are preserved in the form of notes rather than connected discourse, but he makes a number of comments which have had an influence far beyond what their casual manner of utterance might suggest:

(a) The Weird Sisters are "the keynote of the character of the whole play."

(b) Macbeth's propensity to sin—his imaginative and moral suscepti-bility—is thrown into relief by Banquo's open-hearted but distanced *curiosity* about the Sisters.

(c) Lady Macbeth's strength is really "the mock fortitude of a mind deluded by ambition."

(d) The Porter Scene (II, iii) must have been "written for the mob, by some other hand, perhaps with Shakespeare's consent." He later speaks of it as an interpolation made by the actors them-selves.

In addition to these specifics, Coleridge finds an entire absence of comedy in the play. As for character, Macbeth, like any victorious general, is prey to superstition; his wife is a very *feminine* person (most critics of the period stress her masculinity).

The comments on *Macbeth* are far from being Coleridge's strong-est piece of Shakespearean criticism. While his observations on atmosphere and character are generally noted with approval, his strange intransigence on the matter of jokes and quibbles (like Johnson, so unwilling to think Shakespeare capable of them), and consequent rejection of the Porter Scene, has called forth a torrent of replies. (It is now a widely accepted fact that the scene is not only Shakespeare's, but that the "equivocation" motif is important to the thematic unity of the play.)

7. De Quincey, Thomas. "On the Knocking at the Gate in *Macbeth*," in *London Magazine* (October, 1823). Often reprinted; excerpt in Furness, Halio, and Wain.

De Quincey's essay may well be the most famous statement ever uttered about *Macbeth*. It is remarkable, for one thing, for its blending of personal emotional response with speculative criticism. He had, from his youth, says De Quincey, always felt that the knocking gave the murderer "a peculiar awfulness and depth of solemnity," without his being able to account for it. Years later, mature reflection convinced him that *sympathy*, in the exact sense (a "feeling with"—not "approbation for"), cannot rest with the victim, in whom panic crushes all passion and purpose, but only with the murderer, in whom some great storm of passion must be raging. In the dialogues and soliloquies, Shakespeare, with remarkable discrimination, creates two murderers, with whom the audience so identify that they are temporarily "cut off . . . from the ordinary tide and succession of human affairs." It is the knocking at the gate which causes the world of darkness to pass away—which shows that "the human has made its reflux upon the fiendish."

Although De Quincey's explanation amply displays the impressionism we associate with Romantic criticism, it is offset by his concern to find an explanation of the phenomenon in terms of dramatic structural principles. Though frequently applauded as not only ingenious but right, De Quincey's theory has often been rejected by modern critics (see for example Spargo [47]).

8. Fletcher, G. *Studies of Shakespeare* (London, 1847). Excerpt in Furness.

Typical of his age for his interest in impressionistic character description, Fletcher nevertheless lacks, for all his cranky concern for novelty, the inspiration of a De Quincy or a Bradley. Macbeth has, as Fletcher sees him, a "disproportioned but poetically tempered soul"—and, with utter disregard for the principles of dramatic and poetic decorum, he convicts Macbeth of "nervous irritability" because he is given to "so much highly poetical rumination," and sneers at him for his "poetical whining" and for being "an habitual soliloquist." Macbeth is physically courageous but a moral coward, guilty of morbid apprehensiveness but incapable of remorse, selfishly lacking in sympathetic feeling and moral principle, and vacant of religious scruples. Lady Macbeth is in most respects merely a foil to her husband; the drama, which treats of "the gathering, the discharge, and the dispelling of a domestic and political storm . . . takes its peculiar hue from the individual character of the hero."

Though Fletcher has recently found some sympathetic attention, he is really a far more extreme "realist" in character analysis even than

Bradley, and seems to have been much in the mind of Stoll (27), when he made his attack on the Bradleyan position. None of the more serious recent attempts to reconcile Bradley with newer critical approaches has tried to rehabilitate Fletcher.

9. Hunter, Joseph. *New Illustrations of Shakespeare* (London, 1853). Excerpt in Furness.

Hunter's remarks are interesting for the complacency with which, like the seventeenth- and eighteenth-century revisers and adapters such as Dryden and D'Avenant, he recommends excisions and amplifications in the light of a lingering neo-classical sensibility. The play "would be better if it were longer." Some "too luxuriant expressions" might be removed, and what might the play not have become had the poet been persuaded to introduce here and there a "breadth of verdure" in which the mind could "repose." From these faults, however, Shakespeare may be excused, since the text is certainly corrupt, except that he "ought not to have scattered such precious leaves to the wind."

Hunter betrays no indication of a sense of total design, and accounts for the peculiarity of incident and imagery by supposing Shakespeare "to have intended to concentrate in this play many of the more thrilling incidents of physical and metaphysical action."

10. *Taine, Hippolyte. *A History of English Literature*, trans. H. Van Laun (New York, 1871). Vol I [Book II, Chapter 4, Part 8]. Excerpt in *Shakespeare in Europe*, ed. Oswald LeWinter (Cleveland and New York: Meridan Books [M 156], 1963).

Although avowedly reacting against Romantic impressionism with the instruments provided by the "new biology," which had hoped to make scientific description even of the mystery of poetic creation a reality, Taine in fact succeeds only in the appearance of analytical dissection. Each play, each character, each feature of style must be referred to its exact location in the organic structure which is Shakespeare's imagination. Thus, if *Coriolanus* is "the history of a mood," *Macbeth* is "the history of monomania," and the analysis of the play moves us back and forth from the real world of mania-driven individuals to the world of the play, in the interests of demonstrating the genius of Shakespeare in imagining possible responses beyond the capabilities of ordinary people. After the temptation, Macbeth is said to speak in "the language of hallucination," but his brain is "filled with grand and terrible phantoms, which the mind of a common murderer could never have conceived."

Taine is also an interesting forerunner of the "physiological" critic, who supplies clues for bodily reactions which an actor could hardly translate into meaningful gesture in any case, but which simply replace with platitudes the direct imaginative responses which the poetry itself supplies. Thus, we are told *à propos* of the Banquet Scene (III,iii) of Macbeth's "stiffened muscles" and "dilated eyes," his "body trembling like an epileptic," while a "dull sob swells his panting breast." Shakespeare remains for Taine little more than a psychologist with a genius for creating vivid representations of the passions.

11. *Dowden, Edward. *Shakespeare: A Critical Study of his Mind and Art* (London, 1875); repr. 1962, Capricorn Books (No. 68). Excerpt in Halio.

Dowden stresses the reality of the Weird Sisters, their inexhaustible malignity, and the evil on a cosmic scale which they represent. "Such powers auxiliary to vice" do exist, matching in the world of nature the evil within man. "Between the evil within and the evil without subsists a terrible sympathy and reciprocity." Macbeth has an aptitude for goodness as well as for crime, but he is so "excitably imaginative" that he succumbs to the "mastering inspiration" of the Sisters. (Lady Macbeth is "delicately organized" but a woman of firm resolution.) His nervous imagination finally tells against conscience (we know this from the "multitudinous seas" passage), and he pines away in a "vague imaginative remorse," which is of course not true remorse at all. In the end a world-weariness takes over, and we remain in pain until his necessary death is accomplished. We suffer no dejection, but look ahead to the day when Malcolm will be crowned at Scone.

12. Swinburne, Algernon Charles. *A Study of Shakespeare* (London, 1880).

Swinburne's discussion of *Macbeth* is very brief, but significant as representing the *fin de siècle* temperament applied to an analysis of the play. Without any evidence, he begins by dismissing sarcastically the theory of Middleton interpolation, believing the play to have suffered merely from mutilation, "piteously rent and ragged and clipped and garbled in some of its earlier scenes." Withal, Swinburne admits the scene to contain examples of Shakespeare's worst style—"a style stiffened and swollen with clumsy braid and crabbed bombast"—though the play as a whole is Shakespeare's masterpiece for "steep simplicity of epic tragedy."

Like Pater's famous mood music on the *Mona Lisa*, Swinburne's criticism too often takes the form of a reverie, inspired by the play, in which the characters enter into vital relationships with actors, critics, and readers. Thus, he intones: ". . . against the weird sisters, and her who sits above them and apart, more awful than Hecate's very self, no mangling hand has been stretched forth." (This is Swinburne's florid way of saying that the part of the scene involving the witches has not been mutilated.) Although sketchy and extremely precious on *Macbeth*, the book is generally regarded, despite its verbiage and inflated rhetoric, as sound and frequently illuminating.

13. Moulton, R. G. *Shakespeare as a Dramatic Artist: A Popular Illustration of the Principles of Scientific Criticism* (Oxford, 1885).

Moulton's book, a more consistent application of the scientific method to Shakespeare than Taine's, rejects judicial criticism (as being a matter of taste rather than accurate discernment) in favor of scientific analysis which actually explains the details of a literary work, distinguishes species, and establishes inductively the "laws" of art. *Macbeth* becomes an illustration of plot construction, a play in which three forms of action— Nemesis, Oracle, and Irony—move harmoniously together in a total design. This pattern characterizes both Macbeth's rise and his fall, and the careers of both Banquo in the first part of the play and Macduff in the second, thus creating a symmetry of structure over which preside the three Witches, "agents of nemesis working by the means of ironical oracles."

Moulton next considers the interplay of character in the drama, and concludes that character contrast based on the distinction between the external life of action and the inner life of thought is one of the oldest of literary devices. It is clear that Macbeth is preeminently the practical man, a "union of superficial nobility with real moral worthlessness," and that his wife's nature is the antithesis to his, "an embodiment of the inner life and its intellectual culture"—in which *will* predominates. Each event of the play is then passed in review, and the actions of the two characters interpreted in a manner favorable to the contrast alleged.

Moulton's desire to rid criticism of the shackles of artificial rules and of the whimsicalities of journalists may be applauded. In theory, an inductive approach to literary art without preconceptions is a healthy one. In practice, however, Moulton merely substitutes his prejudices for others, a disadvantage aggravated by the fact that the elements of a work of literature simply do not submit to the same sort of objective measurement as do the objects of biological science. His views have generally been rejected in this century.

14. *Shaw, George Bernard. Various pieces of dramatic criticism in *The Saturday Review*, 1885 and 1898, and in private correspondence, 1920–21, collected in *Shaw on Shakespeare*, ed. Edwin Wilson (New York, 1961).

Shaw has not treated *Macbeth* in any systematic way. His comments on the play are by-products of his reviews of performances he had attended both privately and as drama critic for *The Saturday Review*. It is clear, for one thing, that he thought of Macbeth as a well-constructed play, since he mentions it to the disparagement of several adherents of Scribe's theory of the "well-made play," although he more frequently criticized what he regarded as the absurdities of Shakespeare's plot construction, especially in the Romances.

The most notable contribution Shaw has made to *Macbeth* criticism is twofold: He makes several suggestions for the actress playing Lady Macbeth (not to wash her hands too realistically, for example); and, anticipating by several years the academic reaction against the search for "character consistency" in drama, he opposes to character what he calls "word music"—the quality which "will set people's imagination to work." That quality is all there is to Lady Macbeth or to any dramatic character.

Shaw's famous opposition to "bardolatry" has caused him to be set down as one who failed to appreciate Shakespeare's genius, when, in fact, he simply regarded him as a dramatist with little relationship to the important social issues of his time. Or it may be simply that public endorsement of Ibsen over Shakespeare was more expedient in creating a climate receptive to the sort of drama he himself proposed to write. Consistent reading of his more casual comments reveals, somewhat surprisingly, a genuine appreciation and love of Shakespeare.

15. *Bradley, A. C. *Shakespearean Tragedy* (London, 1904). Repr. Meridian Books (M 20). Excerpts in Halio and Wain.

Bradley's lectures on Shakespeare (there are two lectures on *Macbeth*) are avowedly the attempt of an imaginative, intense, and sympathetic mind, with a nineteenth-century perception of inner psychological life, to range over the plays in search of the keys to character and action. Character is dominant, and the figures tend to be treated as if they had a life of their own, the time between scenes and before and after the play being filled by the speculations of the critic. Thus, we are told that Macbeth is exceedingly ambitious ("he must have been so by temper"), and we are asked to consider the question "When was the murder of Duncan first plotted?" His analysis of the imagery of the play—its darkness, the prevalence of the color of blood, the magnitude and violence of the sentiments—tends to be used in support of the rather flaccid principle that a Shakespearean tragedy "has a special tone or atmosphere of its own," rather than to illustrate the organic connection of imagery with theme.

Amidst the general complaint about Bradley's "psychologism," however, his real merits are often overlooked. He is not prone to reduce Shakespeare's meaning to a set of rigidly defined categories. Evil, for instance, as he views it in the play, is not explicable in simple terms, but is a presence which works "not only in its recognized seat but all through and around our mysterious nature." And he anticipates the New Critics in his emphasis on close reading of the text, and on the importance of irony wrought by juxtapositions and ambiguity. Even for those who cannot subscribe to his principles, however, Bradley is a great critic in the Romantic tradition, with a profound insight into Shakespeare's natural grasp of human psychology. The distinguished modern Shakespearean scholar H. B. Charlton has confessed himself "a devout Bradleyite."

16. Coriat, Isador H. *The Hysteria of Lady Macbeth* (New York, 1912).

Not so well-known as Ernest Jones' psychoanalytic study of *Hamlet and Oedipus* (1923), this analysis by a doctor of medicine interprets Lady

Macbeth's somnambulism as the result of a neurosis brought on by sexual repression. Her behavior before the crisis, particularly her ambition, is explained in terms of the classic features of sublimation. Her speeches are rife with instances of suppressed feelings forcing their way past the censor, and of "substitution." Vainly desiring a child, she translates this feeling into the masculine drive by which she goads her husband into the act of regicide. To the extent that she is a pathological case her moral responsibility is limited. So, too, Macbeth, practically hypnotized by the ritual chants of the witches, acts as if their prophecies amounted to post-hypnotic suggestions, which he was the more inclined to fulfill because they reflected his unconscious desires.

The psychoanalysis of literary characters has been vigorously attacked on the very sensible ground that they are not human beings, with completely developed and consistently behaving psyches. This is not to say, however, that the real human beings whom Shakespeare observed, and whose behavior he transformed into stage lives, did not sometimes suffer from the neuroses and psychoses that science has recently been able to describe and classify with such accuracy, but only that he was not under any compulsion to produce dramatic "case histories."

17. Blackmore, Simon A. *A Great Soul in Conflict: A Critical Study of Shakespeare's Master-Work* (Chicago and New York, 1914).

Blackmore's study is an analysis of the means by which in *Macbeth* there is "exposed the all important truth that every mortal is subject to temptation, and must carve out his own destiny for good or for evil, according as he dominates or is dominated by his ruling passion." This theme the author finds mirrored not only in the events of the plot, but in the very structure of the play—in the harmony of design (in this he follows Moulton) by which the three incidents which lead up to his triumph are exactly paralleled in the three that lead him on to ruin.

Much of Blackmore's discussion centers on the meaning of the Weird Sisters; and, with frequent reference to the Bible, to the writings of theologians like St. Thomas, and especially to the *Spiritual Exercises of St. Ignatius*, he puts forth the theory that a contemporary Christian mind would understand *Macbeth* as "the sensible expression of the secret efforts of the Powers of evil . . . to ruin man by means of his ruling passion." Thus, the Weird Sisters are real—embodiments of Temptation—and the play is a Christian statement with roots in the medieval Mystery Cycles, particularly the play of *Man's Fall in Eden*. Unlike Adam, Macbeth is "overwhelmed" by remorse and driven "in delirium from crime to crime," meeting his doom in despair. The play therefore claims our attention for its practical morality and its universal application.

Though Blackmore's work is helpful in its explanation of some of the features of Elizabethan demonology, and is generally convincing in its discussion of the dramatic structure of the play, there is too much of an eighteenth-century moral-philosophical element in it to make it a reliable guide. While there is unquestionably something of the morality-play tradition still operative in *Macbeth*, the parallels adduced with the Mystery Cycles are overstated.

18. Boyer, Clarence V. *The Villain as Hero in Elizabethan Tragedy* (London, 1914).

It is necessary, for Boyer's thesis, that Macbeth first be proved a villain. By an analysis of the early speeches his free will and moral responsibility for the murder are made clear. But he is also revealed as having a conscience, and it is by this means that the dramatist enlists our sympathies, as well as by the grandeur—the greatness of soul—that we respond to emotionally, and that we almost forgo as a result of the Banquo and Macduff murders. The emotions of admiration and pity proper to tragedy are, however, insured for us by the facts of Macbeth's nature—"sensitive, capable of deeper feelings than those of the ordinary man."

On the other hand, says Boyer, "our moral sense demands Macbeth's death" (What Johnson means when he says "there is no one who does not rejoice at his fall"), but the tragic emotions aroused by our vision of his anguish, his courage, and his struggle take the place of the "goodness" which, in suffering, is responsible for the catharsis in a tragedy involving the fall of a good man. Helping to the same end is the constant fear of the unknown which plays upon Macbeth's imagination and elicits such magnificent poetry from him.

Boyer's analysis is, on the whole, one of the most balanced studies of Macbeth's character within the traditional framework, relying less on intellectual speculations about his probable traits of character than upon the way in which an audience responds to his character at given moments in the performance. It is also one of the more successful applications to Shakespeare of Aristotle's observations on the tragic experience, perhaps because it is concerned with the essence of the tragic catharsis rather than with the mechanics of play construction or schematic definitions of "good men" and "bad men."

19. Freud, Sigmund. "Some Character Types Met With in Psychoanalytic Work" [1915]; repr. in *Collected Papers*, IV (London, 1924–25), pp. 318–344.

The "character type" Freud is mainly concerned with here is that of the person "wrecked by success," of which Lady Macbeth, in her madness following upon her husband's murder of Duncan and achievement of the throne, is an example. Freud cites cases from his own clinical work of people incapacitated by the fulfillment of their strongest wishes, so that all enjoyment of it is annihilated. The forces of conscience responsible for this illness are traced by Freud (just as in cases in which illness follows upon frustration) to Oedipal guilt feelings. Paradoxically, the crime follows rather than precedes the sense of guilt. In view of the abbreviated form of the play, and the lack of circumstantial fleshing-out of character with motive, Freud regards the problem of accounting in specific terms for Lady Macbeth's breakdown as insoluble—though one intriguing speculation might be to see it as a reaction to her childlessness, viewed by her as "impotence against the decrees of nature." Still another interpretation would involve the conception of Macbeth and his Lady as "two disunited parts of the mind of a single individuality," who, between them, "exhaust the possibilities of reaction to the crime"—she the epitome of remorse, and he of defiance.

It is unfortunate, in view of Freud's own charming diffidence, that the popular notion prevails that "Freudian" interpretation of literature is reductivist and constricting. Claiming no absolute value as literary criticism for his responses to works of literature, he is willing to concede the mysterious power of art to move us, and asks for one concession: "The dramatist can indeed, during the representation, overwhelm us by his art and paralyze our powers of reflection; but he cannot prevent us from subsequently attempting to grasp the psychological mechanism of that effect." Kenneth Burke and Lionel Trilling have both written influential essays on Freud and literature, which it would be well to consult in this matter. See Jekels (52) for *Psychoanalysis and Literature,* in which their essays appear.

20. Kittredge, George Lyman. *Shakespeare* (Cambridge, Mass., 1916). Excerpt in Siegel.

Kittredge's greatest contribution to the study of *Macbeth* was his edition of the play (with introduction and notes) in 1939, but the discussion of the Porter Scene in his book on Shakespeare is a characteristic piece of iconoclasm that has given strong impetus to recent appeals to Shakespeare's sense of stagecraft as the primary *raison d'être* for some of his puzzling scenes. In refuting Coleridge's contemptuous rejection of the scene as a low-brow interpolation, Kittredge points to its function as "filler" between the murder and Macbeth's reappearance, and to its further purpose as "comic relief."

Kittredge's first point is unassailable, and yet his theory of "comic relief" (not a new idea, of course) raises difficulties for critics who do not share his view of audience psychology. For a more imaginative view of the scene, see Harcourt (S3).

21. Quiller-Couch, Sir Arthur. *Shakespeare's Workmanship* (London, 1918). Excerpt in Lerner.

Condensing, for convenience, Aristotle's strictures on the nature of the tragic hero, Quiller-Couch sees him as essentially a man of renown, and a man with whom an audience can sympathize. On the first score, Holinshed's Macbeth presented no difficulty; on the second, however, Shakespeare faced a massive problem: how to make an audience sympathetic to a self-seeking murderer. Instead of following up the hint in Holinshed of Macbeth's grievance at being passed over for the succession to the throne, Shakespeare absolutely ignored it, and, to underline the depths of his criminality, painted Macbeth's deed in the blackest terms he could. Having done this, he then used every artifice of diction, and every device for revealing character and thought, to postulate the essential greatness of Macbeth. But none of these alone could accomplish the task; the master stroke was the decision to represent the hero as acting under a "fatal hallucination." It is this that gives the Witches their central importance, and yet the proportions of their influence and Macbeth's initiative are wisely left in doubt by Shakespeare.

This very informal and attractively unacademic analysis has the great advantage of being an eminently cogent statement of a commonsense view of Macbeth's character and the nature of his decision. It is the kind of statement which crops up from time to time when esoteric and willfully perverse theories about the character of Macbeth have become annoying —but it is rarely so effectively put.

22. Winstanley, L. *Macbeth, Lear, and Contemporary History* (London, 1922).

Miss Winstanley's book is an example of a type of literary analysis which seeks to find veiled allusions of contemporary persons and events in works of poetry and drama. In its extreme form, as in this case, plays become "topical allegories"; *Macbeth* is thus a symbolic treatment of such historic events as the Gunpowder Plot, the Darnley murder, and the connections of King James with the fifth Earl of Bothwell.

The difficulty is that theories of this sort are practically impossible to refute, since they depend so heavily on one's personal conviction about the force of the resemblance noted. Except for a few cases, most scholars would agree with Chambers that "apart from some passages of obvious satire in comic scenes, there is [not] much of the topical in Shakespeare, whose mind normally moved upon quite another plane of relations to life."

23. Schücking, Levin. *Character Problems in Shakespeare's Plays* (London, 1922).

Schücking's book is designed to reconcile the psychological approach to Shakespeare's characters with a recognition of the dramatic exigencies facing him. The conflict frequently results in puzzling or ambiguous characterization. The method is to examine the historical roots of Shakespeare's art and to emphasize the survival of primitive conventional techniques of characterization which enter into conflict with realistic modes and produce, for example, villains like Richard III, with a totally objective view of their wickedness, or noble characters who are regarded as noble even by their enemies. This explains Macbeth's praise of Duncan and of Banquo, so often wrongly taken as a subtle hint of the war in Macbeth's own soul.

The kind of problem Schücking means to solve can be seen in Lady Macbeth's evaluation of her husband (the "milk of human kindness" speech), which is clearly erroneous. For, on any objective reading of Macbeth's character, he is a coward, a liar, and a weak man. Since she judges him accurately elsewhere, there is no reason for her to ameliorate his character here, and we must assume that it is Shakespeare who "for a moment misjudges his own creation." Thus, in addition to departures from psychological realism, allowances must be made for "misrepresentation or error of characterization." Lady Macbeth's "fainting fit" is used to establish the impossibility of imputing motives to dramatic characters, and the necessity of avoiding extreme subtleties of interpretation.

Schücking's is the first important statement of the need for historical knowledge—the traditions, conventions, and sources which are the determinates of the unrealistic effects in Shakespeare. Like Moulton, he employs a critical "Ockham's razor," or principle of economy (*i.e.*, the simpler the explanation, the better), but he relies far too much on "common sense" and is frequently guilty of the very impressionistic analysis of character that he condemns in others.

24. *Chambers, E. K. *Shakespeare: A Survey* (London, 1925); repr. Hill and Wang, Dramabooks (D 14).

The *Survey* is actually a collection of essays written between 1904 and 1908 as separate introductions to the plays. Chambers is one of the outstanding literary scholars of the turn of the century whose books, *The Medieval Stage* (1903), *The Elizabethan Stage* (1923), and *William Shakespeare* (1930), make him a commanding authority in the field of Renaissance drama. The last of these is well worth consulting for its treatment of textual and source problems in *Macbeth* (Vol. I, 471–476), particularly the extent of possible Middletonian interpolations.

In his *Survey*, however, Chambers characterizes *Macbeth* as a "cosmic tragedy," strongly pessimistic in tone, in which man is seen as "driven from sin to sin to sin's undoing by resistless forces beyond his control."

This is an extreme position, of course, and tends to ignore the many indications in the play of personal responsibility.

25. Brooke, Stopford A. *On the Plays of Shakespeare* (New York, 1927).

The reliance on personal taste and common sense, so successful an approach for Schücking, appears in a more guileless form in Brooke's essay, which consists mainly of bland pontifications unencumbered by scholarly impedimenta. On the principle that a man of taste knows perfectly well what effects Shakespeare is and is not capable of, Brooke declares the play an abridgment, the Porter's soliloquy definitely Shakespeare's creation (so, too, the Hecate scene in its entirety), and the second scene of the play an amalgamation—probably by another hand. As for character portrayal, Macbeth "is the bold soldier of a rude time" (here Brooke uncritically follows Gervinus), to whom speculations about the operations of conscience do not apply; it is sense of honor which is the key to his character. Nor is he a practical man (Moulton's theory), but rather an imaginative one; a poetic imagination is the "salient element in his character," and it leads inevitably to superstition and to cowardly fear. Lady Macbeth, on the contrary, though wise, intelligent, and courageous, is overcome by impulse, and later by a conscience that finally works together with her womanhood to kill her. Given the characters they are said to possess, their behavior, according to Brooke, is reasonable in the light of a common understanding of human nature.

Brooke's interpretation is typical of the personal and highly idiosyncratic criticism of the late nineteenth century, which values Shakespeare for his insight into human nature and for the vivid reality of his characters. Discourses of this sort usually take the form of a running commentary, punctuated by remarks on the facets of character revealed by action and statement. This is connected in turn with a peculiar understanding of dramatic decorum which allows the "poetic" quality of a character's speeches to be taken as a sign of his imaginative nature. (This is a more complicated issue than it might appear, however, and the theory of Macbeth's poetic nature has recently, with varying degrees of cogency, been reaffirmed.)

26. Brandes, George. *William Shakespeare* (New York, 1927). (A transaction, by various hands, of the original Danish edition.)

Brandes' approach to Shakespeare is similar to, and everywhere influenced by, that of Dowden. He sees the plays mainly in biographical terms—as an ordered reflection of a developing life. In broad terms, Shakespeare moved from an optimistic youth (*Henry IV*), through major concern over the potency of external wickedness (*Richard III*) and brooding concern over inner evil (*Measure for Measure; Macbeth*), to a final benign sublimity (*The Tempest*). *Macbeth* is viewed by Brandes as an antithesis to *Hamlet* and *Lear*, and it comes off rather badly. Though simple in design, grand and clear, it is uninteresting from the "human" point of view—a "rich, highly moral melodrama," though this lack of vitality may be due to its "shamefully mutilated form."

Brandes makes interesting and astute observations about particular scenes, but his conclusions are vitiated for the most part by his extraordinarily naive view of the relationship of a poet's art to his life, as well as by a cavalier treatment of dates and analogies calculated to support his prior conception of the course of Shakespeare's life.

27. Stoll, Elmer Edgar. *Shakespeare Studies* (New York, 1927). Excerpts in Halio.

Stoll's book is the reaction of a "historical" critic to the extraordinary emphasis placed on character by Bradley and other nineteenth-century commentators. He rejects the notion of psychological consistency in characters, preferring to interpret particular actions in the light of an Elizabethan understanding of the dramatic machinery Shakespeare was accustomed to use. Such dramatic "tricks" as the proneness to believe deception (Othello), or the feigning of madness (Hamlet) are "means of contrast, of simplification and compression, which to the psychology of the time gave no offense and of which the conventional character was not recognized as it can be now." In *Macbeth*, for example, Banquo's ghost is not to be taken as an hallucination but as a conventional symbol of an "objectively ironical nemesis"; psychological interpretation is beside the mark.

In *Art and Artifice in Shakespeare* (1933) Stoll speaks of the "cleft between character and conduct" in Macbeth—who does not, in fact, act predictably, and this is to be taken as itself a convention. In the latter part of the play, the audience is aware not so much of Macbeth's inner repentance as of the "external nature of the conscience"—a "demonic conscience" itself becoming his nemesis. In *From Shakespeare to Joyce* (1944) he again insists upon Shakespeare's approach to character as having little to do with ordinary psychological pattterns of behavior. The poet ignored the ample suggestions in Holinshed for rationalizing the murder (by making Duncan unfit to rule, for example) and deliberately emphasized the unreason in the act and the failure to exculpate himself. This sharpens the contrast between the man and his deed, makes him more truly tragic, and this, in effect, *is* the *donné*—a convention.

Stoll is actually attempting to substitute the principle of a particular "emotional effect" for each play, "with which psychology or even simple narrative coherence often considerably interferes." His attack on Bradley's excesses was certainly justified, but his own position neglects the interest in individual human beings which generations of readers have found in Shakespeare. Stoll's position is extreme, though his identification of the conventional nature of a great amount of stage business is a healthy corrective to the naive understanding of dramatic characters which leads to discussions of their lives outside the framework of the play.

28. *Knight, G. Wilson. *The Wheel of Fire* [London, 1930], 5th rev. ed. (Cleveland, 1962). Excerpt in Wain.

Chapters VI and VII deal specifically with *Macbeth*. The first, "Brutus and Macbeth," demonstrates the similarity in the pattern of imagery, rhythm, and logical statement in the speeches of Brutus in *Julius Caesar* and of Macbeth. Both plays deal with the way in which an "inner disharmony," a disorder in "the state of man," is reflected in the external world. The comparison supplies a new point of view from which to read *Julius Caesar*—namely, as the tragedy of a man (Brutus) confronted by "a task from which his nature revolts." The second chapter, "Macbeth and the Metaphysic of Evil," is typical of Knight's critical method elsewhere; he believes, as he says, that "the logic of imaginative correspondence is more significant and more exact than the logic of plot." The play's imagery is not gloomy, but black. It bristles with uncertainties, questions, surprises, and rumors. It is filled with references to hideous creatures, filthy abnormality, and nameless terror. Only at the end does this give way to dawn and daytime beauty. These two elements—doubt and horror—"repel respectively the intellect and the heart of man." This is the nature of the evil, and the source of the play's power. The same quality is reflected in both the characters of Macbeth and Lady Macbeth.

Knight comes, after this examination of image patterns, to his unique

and surprising conclusion that Macbeth has finally "won through by excessive crime to an harmonious and honest relation with his surroundings.
He has successfully symbolized the disorder of his lonely guilt-stricken
soul by creating disorder in the world, and thus restores balance and harmonious contact." This is a conclusion with which few critics are in sympathy, although Knight's subtlety, ingenuity, and graciously rhetorical
style command everyone's admiration. Knight studies other "counter
images" to those of evil in his *The Imperial Theme*, and *The Shakespearean Tempest*.

29. *Campbell, Lily B. *Shakespeare's Tragic Heroes: Slaves of Passion*
    (Cambridge, Eng., 1930); repr. Barnes and Noble (New York,
    1952). Excerpts in Halio.

Miss Campbell's book advances the thesis that Shakespeare's tragedies
are concerned with passion as opposed to action—that each of his tragic
heroes is dominated by a different passion or perturbation of the soul, and
that an historical reconstruction of the body of moral philosophy treating
of these passions can serve to define Shakespeare's intentions. Macbeth is
a prey to *fear*, and the play develops out of the antinomy of the emotions
of fear and rash courage. From beginning to end, Macbeth's actions, and
the various apparitions and "horrible imaginings" are fully explicable in
terms of the contemporary psychology of fear. Even at the end, Macbeth's
seeming bravery is merely an instance of rash courage.

There is no doubt of Shakespeare's familiarity, direct or indirect,
with the formal analyses of fear to be found in his day, and yet Miss
Campbell's treatment of this probability is marred by a simplicity and a
mechanical application that do not do full justice to the play. The author
regards Shakespeare's method as the "study" of a passion in different persons, and conceives of him as having "patterned his study upon the edicts
of the philosophers in their anatomies of the passions."

30. Knights, L. C. "How Many Children Had Lady Macbeth?" in *Ex-
    plorations* (London, 1946). Originally published in 1933.

This lecture, delivered when Knights was a comparatively young
man, was meant and accepted as a challenge to Bradleyan criticism of

Shakespeare. Bradley never asked the question, but the title is a sarcastic allusion to queries of the same sort (e.g. "Did Lady Macbeth really faint?") put and answered by Bradley, and typical, as Knights sees it, of his unwarranted supposition of a life for Shakespeare's characters beyond the limits of the text. Knights was one of the first to suggest that images, scenes, even characters themselves, might have a "dramatic function" beyond the revelation of "character," or a formulaic relationship to the classical divisions of the drama, or its alleged effects of arousing fear, pity, purgation, satisfaction in seeing justice done, and so forth.

One of Knights' now famous examples of explication is his comment on Macbeth's talk with Banquo's murderers, which Bradley regarded as an "irrelevance." In Knights' interpretation, the catalogue of dogs is "an image of order" and degree, related to Macbeth's "attempt to re-create an order based on murder," and to a complex of other images and events centering on order. Similarly, the murder of young Macduff goes beyond simple pathos in being the ultimate violation of the order of nature, and the Malcolm–Macduff scene, so often disparaged, is not intended as realistic characterization but as choral commentary. In general, Knights called for an appreciation of the "concrete realization" of attitudes and feelings in Shakespeare's plays, rather than their reduction to abstract terminology. His rejection of Bradley's claim (on the strength of the famous "Tomorrow" speech) that Macbeth never completely loses our sympathy, which gains so much force from the shape of his argument as a whole, has, however, been called into question more than once. It is not too much to say that this is a crux of Shakespearean interpretation.

In his latest book, *Some Shakespearean Themes* (1959), Knights, without relinquishing his earlier stand, develops more fully the idea of nature and natural order as a controlling theme in *Macbeth*, calling it "a play in which moral law has been made present to us not as convention or command but as the law of life itself." Knights has been an eloquent and effective spokesman for one wing of the "new critical" attack, and it seems safe to say that his principle of the priority of "dramatic fitness" over "personal implications" has gained quite general acceptance.

31. *Spurgeon, Caroline. *Shakespeare's Imagery and What it Tells Us* (Cambridge, Eng., 1935). Cambridge University Paperback, 1965.

Miss Spurgeon's achievement is essentially the assemblage and classification of an extraordinary number of the images occurring in Shakespeare's plays, on the principle that images are "the furniture of the mind" and that this reveals the character of the poet. Early chapters center on such general images as those of motion, color, and sound, and then lead to more specific concerns like gardening, hunting, popular pastimes, cooking, and medicine—all culminating in a chapter (ending Part I) in which the character and physique of the poet are described (he was "lithe and nimble of body," "all his senses . . . abnormally acute," roused to anger by "hypocrisy and injustice"). Part II deals with the leading motives of the individual plays, and *Macbeth* is described as being the richest and most varied of all the plays. The dominant imagery is that of loose, ill-fitting garments (expressing the usurpation theme), reverberating sound (the multiplication of consequences), light and darkness (virtue versus evil), and disease ("Scotland is sick" as a result of Macbeth's sin). Miss Spurgeon attributes the arousing of the emotions of fear, pity, and horror in large part to the operation of this imagery, partly conscious and partly subliminal, on the minds of the audience.

This study is of unquestioned value for its identification of leading images in the play, and the suggestion made as to the relation of imagery to theme. It has, however, been suggested that Miss Spurgeon does not carry her analysis far enough and is unaware of the deepest implications of the image patterns she describes, and this is no doubt true. More open to criticism is her supposition that the personality of Shakespeare can be divined through his choice of images, mainly because it confuses the dramatic *persona* with the character of the author.

32. Murry, John Middleton. *Shakespeare* (London, 1936).

In discussing the kind of reality Shakespeare's characters enjoy, Murry points to the tensions frequently existing between the melodramatic plots Shakespeare inherited and his own need to humanize his characters. The result is most often "a discrepancy between the character and the acts." In *Macbeth*, particularly, there is a sense of this discrepancy even on the part of the main characters themselves, and it becomes part of the very dynamics of the play. Having gone through the process of "becoming not-themselves," they must suffer the continuing "effort to hold self and not-self together in one consciousness." The central image of Time and the play—a time which has slipped its grooves—is thus a vehicle for expressing the new kind of being which is theirs. "The time has been," a phrase which twice occurs in the play, is one means the poet uses to "enforce upon our imagination Macbeth's dreadful experience of a change in the nature of time," a change which is ironically foreshadowed in the "Had I but died an hour before this chance" speech (II, iii), and reflected in many other places, notably the soliloquy "She should have died hereafter" (V, v), of which Murry makes a most sensitive explication.

Though a very brief analysis of the play, Murry's essay is highly regarded, particularly for the suggestion of a new approach to character "realism" which it contains—the sensible balance between the tendency to regard Shakespeare's characters as stages in a historical development away from a purely conventional functionalism (Schücking), and as real personages. Murry's sensitiveness to the relationships of verse form and vocabulary to dramatic meaning is also worth noting.

33. Curry, Walter Clyde. *Shakespeare's Philosophical Patterns* (Baton Rouge, La., 1937).

The larger part of Curry's book concerns *Macbeth*. He traces the term "nature's germens" from the Greeks through Augustine and the medieval Scholastics, concluding that the phrase stands for the technical Latin term *rationes seminales,* and that Shakespeare's use of it "is profoundly metaphysical." The Weird Sisters are "dramatic symbols of the demonic metaphysics which penetrates the inmost actions of the drama." They are actually demons in the form of witches, who can manipulate the causes of things. They trap unwary humans by "diabolical persuasion, by hallucination, by infernal illusion, and possession" (Lady Macbeth, that is to say, is really "possessed" by a devil). Curry suggests that Macbeth never entirely loses his free will, but points to a progressive diminution of his freedom, until, at the end, we feel "that some fatality is compelling him to his doom."

Involved as it is with such scholastic distinctions as those between individual man and essential man, and between potency and act, Curry's discussion sometimes seems excessively technical and philosophical. It is, however, a highly regarded and influential book, and felt by many critics to have settled finally the question of the status of the witches and their relationship to Macbeth's will.

34. *Traversi, D. A. *An Approach to Shakespeare* (London, 1938); rev. ed. (1956), Anchor Books (A 74). Excerpt in Halio.

Traversi's book reflects the new critical interest in language, in the word, which (as he puts it) "is the product of a most intimate relation between feeling and thought, nervous sensitivity and conscious emotion," and in the image and the verse setting. Thus Duncan is not a "weak character" but a focus for images of beauty, fertility, and generosity. The words "grace" and "love" are simply the most significant words in a referential system, characterized also by a rhythmical harmony, that epitomizes the relationship of king and subject which Macbeth is to violate. With the onset of temptation, a "sense of discontinuity" and an ambiguity of utterance begin to prevail, as a sign of the violation of order which is taking place, until, finally, Macbeth's "psychological disintegration" and the overriding sanctions which rule in the play are fused in images like those of the "naked babe." After analyzing the imaginative structure of the first four acts, Traversi pauses at the Malcolm–Macduff scene to consider the relationship of *Macbeth* to the development of the Shakespearean tragic hero, and finds that the studied rejection of realism here, supported by the imaginative suggestions in the last act of the restoration of "grace" as a kingly attribute, indicates Shakespeare's move to symbolic levels of thematic representation.

Traversi's work is a moderate, not oversubtle version of the concern for close textual analysis, and as such has generally been regarded as an extremely useful book. Much recent criticism of Shakespeare, in fact, acknowledges a heavy debt to his work.

35. Coles, Blanche. *Shakespeare Studies: Macbeth* (New York, 1938).

This is not a book with a thesis, but a manual to be used as a supplement to a reading of the text. Containing a scene-by-scene paraphrase and commentary, it attempts to supply the reader with such aids as descriptions of the characters "visualized . . . as they must have appeared in their daily lives . . . [as] Shakespeare saw them before transferring them to the stage," and of the "original scenes [as they] must have been present in the poet's mind." The function of individual scenes is analyzed not with respect to the economy of the play as a whole, but in the light of an impressionistic interpretation of character. Thus Act I, Scene vi "is obviously intended by Shakespeare to throw a light on the gentleness of Duncan and perhaps on the responsiveness of Banquo to the mood of a friend."

The book is mainly interesting as a prime example of the lengths to which the least convincing aspects of Bradleyism can be carried, and remains something of an anachronism, appearing as late as it does.

36. *Van Doren, Mark. *Shakespeare* (New York, 1939); repr. Anchor Books, 1953.

Van Doren's book is a series of lectures on the plays, intended for the intelligent nonspecialist reader and avoiding questions of contemporary history, dramatic conventions, and biographical detail in favor of a close reading of the text as a "human document" and a work of art. Recognizing the part played by a coherent system of metaphors in expressing the peculiar vision of the play (and he has excellent comments to make on the images of disorder, darkness, blood, disease, and fear), Van Doren prefers to approach each play with an open mind and seek for an understanding of that "created life" or "unity of being" which only gradually reveals itself. The keynote to *Macbeth* is "strangeness." Apparitions, miracles, transformations, the "current of change pouring through this universe" create a brilliant effect in brief compass. *Macbeth* "hurls a universe against a man. . . ."

The great merit of Van Doren's book is in his sensitivity to poetic effect, and to the qualities which distinguish play from play. He is immersed in the text of the plays, and can command numerous comparisons (Macbeth's reaction to his wife's death with those of Northumberland to Hotspur's and Brutus to Portia's, for example) which immeasurably sharpen our sense of the unique dramatic merits of *Macbeth*.

37. Doran, Madeleine. "The Undiscovered Country," *Philological Quarterly*, XV (1941), 413–427.

This is an early essay by the author of the influential book *Endeavors of Art*. Concentrating on *Hamlet* and *Macbeth*, Miss Doran distinguishes between the various levels of psychological response the "marvelous" can produce in any audience, even a modern one, and examines the question as it relates to the witches in *Macbeth*. There is conventional "symbolism" (quite the same thing as "literal" meaning) and there is a more profound type of symbolism which touches us at levels deeper than the conscious level. The witches certainly had a set of conventional associations, but these did not exclude, even for an Elizabethan audience, the possibility of profounder subliminal response. While they are "immediately familiar" to Shakespeare's audience, and hence "emotionally exciting" (by being related to Satan and sin) they nevertheless retain a sense of being a "fatality in the drift of events more inexorable than the machinations of Satan." There is a danger to be faced even in a purely historical reconstruction of a work of literature.

The essay is valuable as a statement, by one who is herself an accomplished literary historian, of the need to keep an open mind about the different levels of response possible to a literary work.

38. Spencer, Theodore. *Shakespeare and the Nature of Man* (New York, 1942).

In Spencer's conception of Shakespeare's tragic heroes as embodying the Renaissance dichotomy between the traditional (optimistic) view of man as he should be, and the more contemporary (pessimistic) emphasis on man as he was seen to be by experience, *Macbeth* stands out because the hero is evil from the very begining. Furthermore, the microcosm/macrocosm theory of the reverberation of the effects of individual acts throughout the human, the political, and the cosmic levels of reality, is presented in a unique way, since the various levels are in this case more intimately fused. Convinced of the essentially ambiguous character of experience in the tragic plays, Spencer turns to the problem of the Weird Sisters and what they mean for the question of Macbeth's human responsibility versus fatal influence—and, very cogently, rejects it as a pseudo-problem. Shakespeare himself does not answer it, for "the dictation of what seems to be external destiny and the impulses of individual character are seen as parts of the same vision, and, in a technical sense, as parts of the same dramatic whole." The movement toward a final order, characteristic of Shakespearean tragedy, is different in *Macbeth* because the order is achieved in the realm of the state rather than of the individual, as it is in *Lear*.

Spencer's analysis of the play has not occasioned many demurrals.

As a partial perspective on the meaning of *Macbeth* (and the author admits to this limited aim) it is persuasive, although the logical connections with the background material of his early chapters ceem less clear than with *Hamlet*.

39. *Webster, Margaret. *Shakespeare Without Tears* (New York, 1942); repr. Premier Books (D 54).

A producer of Shakespeare's plays, especially if he respects scholarly traditions, is in a peculiarly favorable position to comment on the problems of character interpretation and the staging of such difficult effects as the Witches' conjuring. Miss Webster, as a producer, is particularly interested in the recorded problems of past actors and in audience reactions all the way back to Shakespeare's time. The fact that Burbage was to play Macbeth, while not a final determinant, aids our conception of the author's intentions. The magnificent poetry spoken by Macbeth "is the expression of a man who is almost psychically receptive to every vibration of the atmosphere around him." What is for the mere critic the "atmosphere" of the play is handled by Miss Webster as a third "protagonist . . . the pervasive power of evil suggestion." The very pace at which evil effects spread themselves is a challenge to the producer, and yet "every sign and signal of this progression may be carried out in clear theoretical terms." The author's remarks about the necessity of keeping the Witches concealed as far as possible, to make their sinister utterances seem the voice of a "terrible Presence" greater than themselves, are based upon long experience with audiences who find realistic staging of the conjuring scenes more ludicrous than convincing.

In the absence of any "Preface" to *Macbeth* by Granville-Barker, Miss Webster, who produced a *Macbeth* in 1941 with Maurice Evans and Judith Anderson in the starring roles, can be regarded as a reliable guide to a few of the major problems of production.

40. *Tillyard, E. M. W. *Shakespeare's History Plays* (London, 1944); repr. Collier Books (BS 105V).

In this book, Tillyard studies the Elizabethan conception of history and Shakespeare's use of it in his history plays. After an opening chapter for the most part epitomizing the material of his earlier book, the very influential *The Elizabethan World Picture* (1943), he goes on to discuss the background in historical writing (works like those of Machiavelli, More, and Hall) and then the literary background (*Mirror for Magistrates*, Spenser, the Chronicle play, and other types). Tillyard conceives of Shakespeare as having written a kind of dramatic epic consisting of two tetralogies (1, 2, and 3 *Henry VI* and *Richard III; Richard II*, 1 and 2 *Henry IV*, and *Henry V*) separated by *King John*. Relying mainly on Hall's *Chronicles*, he gave dramatic expression to what was at root a religious scheme of universal history evolving providentially, through various crimes of usurpation and civil war, toward the England of Elizabeth.

Macbeth comes in for discussion because it contains "the culminating version [of the "politically efficient man"], and with it the whole adjustment of politics to life." It is not some individual, but the "body politic" that defeats Macbeth, and though his own tragedy can be read in terms of the individual will bringing about cosmic disorder, the Providence which sets all to right works finally through political means.

Beyond the obvious difficulty, that *Macbeth* does not conform at all closely to the idea of a history play, is the additional problem that *Macbeth*, by celebrating the establishment of the Stuart monarchy, is in effect writing *finis* to the Tudor establishment which the tetralogies are supposed to memorialize. Tillyard's tetralogy theory in general, and his conception of *Macbeth* in particular, have not enjoyed wide acceptance.

41. *Brooks, Cleanth. "The Naked Babe and the Cloak of Manliness," in *The Well Wrought Urn* (New York, 1947). Harvest Books (HB 11).

This justly famous essay is the first application to Shakespeare's plays (with such thoroughgoing rigor, at least) of the "close reading" associated with the New Criticism. Brooks seizes upon two images in *Macbeth*—Pity, as a naked babe striding the blast; and the grooms' daggers "unmannerly breech'd with gore"—which have proved either consistently puzzling or objectionable to critics in the past, and demonstrates that they inhere in a controlling pattern of imagery in the play. The clothed daggers are only one example of an illegitimate garbing running through the play, of which Macbeth's wearing of Duncan's "robes" is the outstanding instance. So, too, seen in perspective, the naked babe—Pity—is not either simply helpless or simply powerful, but, paradoxically, both; this makes it a symbol of the essential ambiguity of things, which Macbeth with his "overbrittle rationalism" cannot grasp.

By pushing Caroline Spurgeon's findings to conclusions she had not anticipated, Brooks' essay points the way to the manner in which classified lists of images, motifs, and so forth can be used by the subtle reader as an index to larger issues of structure and meaning, and it has had, like the other essays in the volume, an extraordinary influence. The extreme subtlety with which he approaches the text, however, easily leads to over-ingenious explications, and has proved the downfall of lesser minds which lack the discrimination of Brooks himself, who remembers at all times that Shakespeare is not Donne, and that the same approach is not equally fruitful for all poets.

42. Spargo, John Webster. "The Knocking at the Gate in *Macbeth*: An Essay in Interpretation," in *Joseph Quincy Adams Memorial Studies*, edited by J. G. McManaway, G. E. Dawson, and E. E. Willoughby (Washington, D.C., 1948), 269–277.

This essay sets out to prove that De Quincey's famous decision (that the knocking relieves the tension and returns the audience to the normalities of life) is wrong; that the knocking is itself a portent of death, and would be so understood by an Elizabethan audience. Spargo identifies three contexts in which death and knocking would have been closely associated: a well-known line from Horace's *Carmina* in which "pale death" is said to knock on the door "with impartial foot"; a widespread European folk belief that knocking and rattling are mortal omens; and the practice, during plague time, of knocking on doors with spade handles for the dead to be brought out. Thus, the knocking at the gate, following the howl of the wolf and the screech of the owl, is the climactic element in this series of portents.

Despite the attractiveness of De Quincey's ingenious explanation of the knocking, Spargo's theory is probably closer to the truth. It does not, however, rule out other effects, such as the irony which results from a momentary recognition of the Porter as being indeed the Porter of hell-gate.

43. Sitwell, Edith. *A Notebook on William Shakespeare* (London, 1948).

Miss Sitwell's comments do not make up a coherent discourse on the plays, but are precisely a series of notebook jottings. Her treatment of *Macbeth*, however, is easily the longest in the book. She is concerned mainly with the texture of the verse, and provides a leisurely and minute analysis of Lady Macbeth's "The raven himself is hoarse" speech, demonstrating with great exactness the contributions made to the meaning of the passage by the musical and rhythmical effects. On the whole, the *sound* of her speeches, "like a black and impenetrable smoke from Hell," helps to reveal her nature, as the sound of Macbeth's words reveals his own hollowness. Associated with this difference on dramatic accent are the three tragic themes she distinguishes, all having to do in one way or another with the isolation of the two main characters.

As a poet's commentary on the poetry of Shakespeare, Miss Sitwell's remarks are of unquestioned value, especially her response to the tone and atmosphere created by the rhetoric of the speeches. Her method of accounting for this response, however, has to be regarded with some caution, as when she speaks of a "fabric of dull and rusty vowels," for it seems unlikely that there are any absolute meanings or emotions to be attached to individual sounds.

44. *Charlton, H. B. *Shakespearean Tragedy* (Cambridge, Eng., 1948).

Charlton's study is an energetic reaction against certain aspects of the New Criticism, particularly the more mechanical sorts of verbal analysis, image-counting, and symbol-hunting, as well as the imputation to Shakespeare of subliminal, nondiscursive meanings that emerge not from the statements of the plays but from clusters and patterns of imagery (typical of G. Wilson Knight and his followers). The author asks for a return to the simple psychological naturalism of Bradley, in whose terms "Macbeth is just a mortal making in his own experience one of the most momentous discoveries in human history. He is discovering what in its nature evil is." Charlton rejects as irrelevant any appeal to obscure metaphysics and even to theology. In fact, he denies even to such a phrase as "mine eternal jewel" the possibility of being limited to the meaning of "soul" in the Christian sense, calling Shakespeare's practice an "adaptation

of religious phraseology to a purely secular significance or relationship."
Plutarch figures prominently in Charlton's analysis, as a source for Shakespeare's meaning, but not "any particular school of spiritual pathology"
(by which he apparently means Christian moral philosophy).

Charlton's brilliant arguments are most instructive as an insight into
the motivations of characters, but his naturalistic approach to Shakespeare's
meaning has found little favor with historical critics, who remain convinced, for the most part, of the Christian roots of Shakespeare's thought.

45. Walker, Roy. *The Time Is Free: A Study of Macbeth* (London,
   1949).

The Time Is Free is a detailed, scene-by-scene analysis of *Macbeth*
by a critic who is convinced of the essentially theological orientation of the
play. Shakespeare represents "realistically" through the medium of poetic
vision and tragic myth the operation of "what theologians name divine
grace . . . and Satanic temptation." Dividing the play into nine parts,
Walker devotes to each a chapter in which he first discusses textual
problems and then comments on the action, characterization, and meaning
(which is most frequently a *symbolic* meaning deriving from the sometimes overt but more often recondite allusions to Holy Scripture). Thus
the knocking at the gate is said to evoke a suggestion of the Gospel of
Luke, where it is said "Knock, and it shall be opened unto you"; the result
is that Macbeth undergoes a momentary vision of salvation, raises his own
hand to knock, sees its bloody stains, and "for a terrible moment . . .
faces the truth about himself." Similarly, the mention of Duncan's burial at
Colme-kill imports into the play a body of feeling associated with St.
Columba's preaching of Christianity to Scotland; and the "Come seeling
night / Scarf up the tender eye of pitiful day" soliloquy brings to mind
the Biblical admonition about "If thine eye offend thee." Malcolm's
observation (at the close of Act IV) that Macbeth "is ripe for shaking"
calls up Nahum's vision of the ruin of Nineveh.

One can hardly do justice in a brief comment to the subtlety, ingenuity, learning, and imagination Walker displays. His analysis of many
of the individual scenes is excellent. His conclusions, however, depend for
their conviction on the force with which one is impressed by the analogies
adduced. They frequently appear strained and elaborated beyond all

prudent limits—and yet his general position has been alluded to with respect by Kenneth Muir (E5) and G. Wilson Knight (28) among others, and finds support in the similar approach of G. R. Elliott (56). For alternative views, see Charlton (44) and Roland M. Frye, *Shakespeare and Christian Doctrine* (Princeton, 1963).

46. Stauffer, Donald. *Shakespeare's World of Images: The Development of His Moral Ideas* (New York, 1949).

Stauffer's book, like that of Caroline Spurgeon (31), uses the imaginative worlds of the plays as an index to the character of the playwright. Unlike Miss Spurgeon, however, Stauffer is not interested in reconstructing the daily life of the poet, but follows a more philosophical object: the growth of the poet's moral ideas. His interest in *Macbeth* is connected with the fact that, as one of the great tragedies, it reveals through its own unique pattern of images an aspect of Shakespeare's attempt to bring to harmonious reconciliation the earlier (partial) themes of "trust in man's godlike qualities" and the discordant note of "disease . . . animality and disorder." This new third vision rises to tragic heights in its conflicting grasp of man's great possibilities and his self-destructive weaknesses. *Macbeth* is analyzed as a version of the theme found in *Othello* and *Lear* of the ramifications of personal crime in the political and cosmic orders—a version, however, in which the emphasis is on the individual mind, the "personal moral drama."

Stauffer's analysis has the great merit of being free from preconceptions and of confining itself to the internal relationships of imagery within the play, and (its strongest point) to comparisons among the plays.

47. Farnham, Willard. *Shakespeare's Tragic Frontier* (Berkeley and Los Angeles, 1950).

The essay on "Macbeth" (Chapter III) is a discursive analysis of the main critical stumbling-blocks in the play, growing out of Farnham's conception of it as "a morality play written in terms of Jacobean tragedy." A lengthy discussion of the precise nature of the "Weird Sisters," turning over much contemporary literature on the subject, leads to the conclusion that they are "demons of the fairy order" with the power to delude man but not to interfere with his free will. Inspection of a number of late-sixteenth-century plays shows *Macbeth* to be in the tradition of plays about "conscience-stricken tyrants," but to be far superior to the others by the very imaginativeness of the hero's "recalcitrance in evil-doing." After discussing the question of the alternating fits of cowardice and bravery in the hero, Farnham proceeds to the relationship of the action of the play to human considerations of justice and concludes that the action illustrates the way in which "the mills of justice can grind exceedingly small."

Farnham's extensive familiarity with literary and dramatic traditions provides a useful perspective from which to view the play, as does his better-known work, *The Medieval Heritage of Elizabethan Tragedy*. Other critics, however, less strongly oriented toward historical interpretations, are more reluctant to reduce Shakespeare's drama to the dimensions of a morality play, even with the broadest of qualifications.

48. Booth, Wayne. "Macbeth as Tragic Hero," *Journal of General Education*, VI (1951). Printed in revised form in Lerner, pp. 180–190.

Booth's essay explains the techniques employed by Shakespeare in illustrating Macbeth's moral degradation without alienating the sympathies of the audience. He does this in several ways: through actions and the testimony of other characters, Macbeth's nobility is made convincing at the outset; his crimes are so represented that we do not respond to them as acts of unrelieved viciousness (that is, they take place offstage, or in Macbeth's absence); Macbeth and his wife suffer paroxysms of self-torture after each of the murders. In short, "wickedness is played up in the narration but down in the representation." What is more, we are unable to turn our sympathies against a man of such sensitivity as Macbeth's poetic gift reveals him to be. Macbeth's personal greatness of soul retains its lustre because he is shown as a victim of "tragic error"—his misunderstanding (for that is what it is) of the Weird Sisters and of his wife's importunities. In its "total impression of the play" an audience, knowing (as Macduff and the others for whom he is a "dead butcher" do not) the great potentiality of Macbeth, responds with pity for the waste of greatness and for the misjudgment visited upon him.

Booth's study is an excellent example of painstaking analysis of the play along traditional (Aristotelian) lines. Particularly effective is his constant appeal to the inferential nature of the scenes as presented—to the conclusions an audience is led to in spite of the narrative logic of the play.

49. *Fergusson, Francis. "*Macbeth* as the Imitation of an Action," in *English Institute Essays* (New York, 1951); repr: in his *The Human Image in Dramatic Literature* (New York, 1957). Anchor Books (A 124).

Fergusson's analysis of *Macbeth* is based upon the application of Aristotle's understanding of drama as "the imitation of an action." This is elaborated upon in Fergusson's well-known book *The Idea of a Theatre*, in which he analyzes *Hamlet* from the same standpoint. Basically, the action of a play can be expressed by an infinitive phase, in this case the phrase (actually uttered at one point by Macbeth) "to outrun the pauser, reason." The various individual actions, speeches, and images mirror this "action" in different ways. The play, in short, is not conceived in terms of sequential logical steps, but as an analogical system conveying meaning through juxtapositions and parallels. This "paradoxical striving beyond reason" is reflected, for instance, in the bleeding sergeant's report of the irrational encounters between the armies, and even in the Drunken Porter's paradoxes. Like the Witches, the porter "tempts [people] into Hell with ambiguities." The Macduff–Malcolm–Ross scene, so difficult to understand and to act, can be seen, from this standpoint, as the *peripeteia* in which the good characters, blindly groping at first, eventually make "an act of faith beyond reason," and thus participate finally in the central action of the play.

Fergusson's brilliantly reasoned book (to which this essay is an adjunct) has been extremely well received, with only occasional queries about the advisability of applying the same standards of judgment to the Greek theatre (so heavily dependent upon common mythic and ritual experience) and to Shakespeare's Elizabethan stage.

50. Harrison, G. B. *Shakespeare's Tragedies* (London, 1951).

This essay is worth reading as a minority report by a foremost Shakespearean scholar on the artistic merits of *Macbeth*. For Harrison, the play is filled with interpolations, "wooden" in characterization, sketchy

in plot construction—in brief, a failure. This can be explained on the
assumption of hasty composition for performance before the King—
composition, probably, with the aid of a collaborator. Nor is it a true
tragedy, since its hero is far from being a sympathetic figure, and his
downfall leaves us without the catharsis tragedy ought to provide. As for
the characters, Macbeth is weak and a "wanton murderer"; his wife is
utterly lacking in principle, but a woman of strong practical shrewdness.
Macduff is never fully explained as an "instrument of vengeance," nor is
his personality at all well developed. With all of its shortcomings the play
has some fine poetry and some magnificent scenes (the Banquet scene, for
instance). But it remains finally a product of "slap-dash and careless" work.

Harrison's view is obviously not the prevailing one; yet, at the same
time, it must be carefully weighed. All of these objections have appeared
before, but never in such an extreme form, nor arrayed together in such
impressive numbers.

51. Lucas, F. L. *Literature and Psychology* (London, 1951); repr. Ann
Arbor Paperbacks (AA 11).

Lucas discusses *Macbeth* at some length in Chapter 1 and again in
Chapter 4. Basing his observations on the studies of the Freudian analyst
Wilhelm Stekel, Lucas notes that Lady Macbeth's compulsive hand-wash-
ing finds its parallel in studies of obsessional neurotics—tortured souls
whose suppressed guilt transforms itself into compulsive ritual behavior.
As for Macbeth himself, he is "a murderer who drags . . . retribution on
his own head" because of his guilt feelings over the death of Duncan. The
Witches are symbols of hidden psychological forces that make men
"court the ruin" that satisfies their sense of guilt. This interpretation
enables Lucas to classify *Macbeth* as a tragedy of "self-destruction" rather
than one of "ruin brought by outside enemies."

Lucas is open to the same charges that may be urged against Coriat
(16) and Freud (19) himself, though his comments, compared to Freud's,
seem not so much wrong as superficial. At best they go little beyond what
common sense would suggest, and at worst create the impression that it
is enough to demonstrate parallels. Macbeth becomes simply an extraordinarily vivid depiction of a type of "psychopath" well known to analysts.

52. Jekels, Ludwig. "The Riddle of Shakespeare's *Macbeth*," in *Selected Papers* (London, 1952); repr. *Psychoanalysis and Literature*, ed. H. M. Ruitenbeek (New York: Dutton Paperbacks, 1964), pp. 142–167.

Jekels offers his views as a corrective to the interpretation which emphasizes ambition as the keynote of Macbeth's character. He stresses the fact that the play was written for James I and that the opposition between sterility and fecundity is one its major themes. The King (Duncan at first, and later Macbeth) is a father symbol. In the first phase, Banquo and Macbeth are respectively "good son" and "bad son"; Lady Macbeth is the "demon woman" who inspires Macbeth to parricide; and the Weird Sisters, from a psychological standpoint, are the "three forms into which the image of the mother is cast for a man in the course of his life": the actual mother, the beloved, and Mother Earth. In the second phase of the action, Macbeth is the "father" and Banquo and Macduff the "sons." The idea that "a bad son will become a bad father" explains such episodes as the appearance of Banquo's ghost (Macbeth fears the confrontation because it will bring requital for his evil deeds) and Macduff's seemingly callous abandonment of his family (since he must play the role of bad son to Macbeth, he first appears as bad father).

The parallels between Macbeth and Macduff, according to Jekels, underline an unsuspected truth: that Macduff, rather than Macbeth, is the real hero. The puzzling emphasis on Macduff's son can be explained by reference to the facts of Shakespeare's own life. He too was a son in conflict with his father, and a husband who had abandoned his family. Queen Elizabeth was herself a "bad child" like Shakespeare, Jekels declares, and was probably the model for Macbeth and Lady Macbeth, by a process which involved the "splitting of a psychic personality" and the dramatist's imaginative identification with the barren Elizabeth.

Lionel Trilling's "Freud and Literature," in his *The Liberal Imagination* (New York, 1950), issues valuable cautions against psychological criticism when it confuses the author's intention with the work of art itself, and when it substitutes psychoanalysis of the author for literary analysis of the work. Jekels has clearly stepped far out of bounds in this regard, and yet, as Norman Holland points out in his essay "Shakespearean Tragedy and the Three Ways of Psychoanalytic Criticism" (*Hudson Review*, XV [1962], his suggestion that the Macduff plot represents a "socially acceptable" version of the wish to kill the king–father is a convincing one.

53. Speaight, Robert. *Nature in Shakespearean Tragedy* (London, 1955).

Speaight's book grows out of the author's conviction that in Shakespeare's plays, despite their lack of a formal doctrinal content, there is to be seen a reverential, indeed a sacramental attitude toward nature, a *pietas* toward created things. Macbeth and his wife become "unnatural"; the witches are "subnatural"; superstition and "moral obliquity" supplant faith and goodness. A paramount example is Lady Macbeth's "Come, you spirits" speech, which is in effect a "theology of evil." The constant identification of *diablerie* with the unnatural, and of grace with nature, create, as Speaight sees it, a metaphorical ambience in which single details can be pressed for an underlying spiritual content. Thus, while Lady Macbeth walks in her sleep, "the shadows of the castle prefigure an eternal darkness," and in no other play of Shakespeare's is there an ending "more profoundly theological."

Speaight's essay is in the line of criticism established by Spencer (38) and Walker (45), and taken up later by Elliott (56), though his emphasis upon the sacramental character of Shakespeare's natural world and refusal to be drawn into overspecific identifications give it a commendable balance.

54. Stirling, Brents. *Unity in Shakespearean Tragedy* (New York, 1956).

Chapter IX, "Look, How Our Partner's Rapt," deals with *Macbeth*. Stirling's perceptive analysis of the inner structure of the play is an ingenious and detailed examination of the imagery. He attempts to show how the themes of darkness, sleep, raptness, and contradiction appear in varying poetic and dramatic forms in the play. Macbeth's surrender to the forces of darkness is seen to be obsessive and to involve a pattern of contradictions. Sleep is murdered, and Macbeth's raptness, in the course of the drama, turns into an awareness of reality, while Lady Macbeth's grasp of apparent reality gives way to the "raptness" of sleep-walking. Various scenes combine these in different ways and with alternative emphases—the Drunken Porter, for instance, being the "perfect embodiment of contradiction," and the Old Man's blessing another example of the same. The play is based, according to Stirling, on the idea of compulsive sin and self-destruction.

Stirling's analysis, by beginning where the Freudian approach usually terminates (in the idea that Macbeth is compelled toward self-destruction), serves to clarify the relationship between the two. The literary critic is concerned with the artistry with which the dramatist realizes his conceptions; Stirling's demonstrations of the manifold interrelations of the four themes identified at the outset unquestionably add to the depth with which one can respond to the play.

55. Kirschbaum, L. "Banquo and Edgar: Character or Function?" *Essays in Criticism*, VII (1957), 1–21.

Noting that modern criticism no longer regards characters in drama as "portraits" of real-life figures, Kirschbaum observes that Shakespearean characters sometimes appear as "realistic" and sometimes as "symbolic," though a more satisfactory term to describe the status of characters in a play is to say that they have a dramatic function. This allows for a discussion of a character's individualism at the same time that it permits treatment of his "meaning" (a better term than "symbolism" because it allows for different "ideational" purposes at different moments in a play). Banquo is not a real person, but a foil to Macbeth. In I, iii, he is seen to have a "free" soul, as Macbeth does not; in I, vi, his deeply religious vision points up the contrast with the "devil-haunted castle of actuality"; his "husbandry in heaven" speech suggests the overriding justice and omniscience of heaven, which will eventually triumph.

Kirschbaum's essay is a useful antidote to the still virulent strain of character-realism criticism, though it adds little to L C. Knights' (30) conception of the priority of "dramatic function" except to particularize it in the case of Banquo.

56. Elliott, G. R. *Dramatic Providence in "Macbeth"* (Princeton, 1958).

Elliott's book essays to prove that *Macbeth* is the supreme statement of Shakespeare's tragic vision, which is in essence the idea that infernal evil will overcome the natural goodness in man unless it is supported by "supernal Grace" (sometimes called supernatural, or preternatural, goodness). His argument leans heavily on the not unreasonable predication that Shakespeare consistently puns on the word "grace" in its ordinary and in its theological sense, and it is strongly implied that a similar ambiguity haunts the word "heaven." Thus, figures of "graciousness" like Duncan, and "heavenly" acts such as the "husbandry in heaven" which puts "their candles . . . all out," are read as theological symbols calling Macbeth (humankind) back from the paths of pride and ambition to those of righteousness. Elliott provides an extraordinarily detailed analysis of the play in the light of his controlling conception, arriving at such conclusions as that "the main source of Malcolm's resoluteness and all his other royal virtues is his Christian faith," and that Malcolm's closing speech underscores the waste of Macbeth's great human qualities through pride. "Christian self-esteem," instead of pride, would have made Macbeth a faithful servant of his country and his king, precisely what Macduff has become.

Any quarrel with Elliott's theory would unquestionably concern the matter of emphasis—of how far in the forefront of the play's dramatic texture the antithesis between infernal pride and Christian self-esteem really stands. The difficulty here is that Elliott's argument depends heavily on inferences concerning the strength of verbal nuance and symbolic overtone for Shakespeare's contemporary audience, and not all students would be willing to grant the specifically Christian suggestion of many of the details Elliott relies upon.

57. Ribner, Irving. "*Macbeth:* The Pattern of Idea and Action," *Shakespeare Quarterly*, X (1959), 147–159.

Ribner also discusses *Macbeth* in his *Patterns of Shakespearian Tragedy* (London, 1960), and repeats a good deal of the material in the *SQ* article. He stresses the "thematic functions" of the characters in opposition to the Bradleyan view, and opposes G. Wilson Knight's (28) conviction that Shakespeare does not present evil in terms of an ethical system. Evil, Ribner feels, operates on different levels and generates forces of good, until harmony is finally restored. Macbeth's sin is ambition—prideful rejection of the laws of nature. The witches, symbols of the unnatural, are rejected by Banquo, but endorsed by Lady Macbeth, all of which reflects the structure of the typical morality play. Individual scenes suggest such themes as the physical universe thrown out of harmony, the political reverberations of Macbeth's crimes, and the deteriorating relationships within the family. Macbeth sinks into despair, though he retains his vivid, imaginative grasp of reality. His imagination, however, is not the cause of his downfall, but simply a means of indicating his "strong moral feelings"; and his so-called fear is no more than "a dramatic device to stress his human ties," and thus enter into the major pattern of meaning. At the end, the reemergence of good out of evil provides us with a feeling of reconciliation (for Ribner, the "test of tragedy").

Ribner is fundamentally a historical critic, strongly inclining toward the positions taken by Stoll and Schücking, whose notions of conventional dramatic representation he has nicely reconciled with the newer "functional" approach of critics like Knights and Traversi.

58. Driver, Tom F. "The Use of Time: The *Oedipus Tyrannus* and *Macbeth*," Chapter VII of *The Sense of History in Greek and Shakespearean Drama* (New York, 1960).

Driver discusses Sophocles' play and Shakespeare's as part of a general analysis of the difference between the Greek and the Elizabethan attitudes toward history. The Greek is essentially a timeless, circular view, the Elizabethan a providential, linear view. In *Macbeth*, Shakespeare presents us with three kinds of time—ordinary chronological time (and Shakespeare is most skillful at suggesting the reality of passing time), historical or "providential" time, and Macbeth's own time. The conflict, in the beginning, is seen in terms of the opposition between the hero's sense of time and the unfolding vision of the future as seen, for example, in Duncan's speech about the succession. The murder of Duncan is Macbeth's way of making "his own history," and the play shows the working out of that history in the ironic light of his ultimate subordination to providence.

Oedipus Tyrannus is composed from the conceptualized Greek viewpoint of time as a determining thing—the past containing the future —unlike the Shakespearean outlook in which the possibility of free choice remains. The irony in Sophocles is the result of time itself, of man's ignorance of the nexus between past and present, whereas in *Macbeth* the irony resides not in Shakespeare's representation of time but in Macbeth's vain hope that he can "remake time into something which it cannot be." One reason the plays endure, Driver asserts, is that each embodies an entire culture's understanding of its relationship to time.

This book is an important contribution to the problem of the degree of Shakespeare's Christian orientation, since Driver's erudite and original approach to a particular problem of dramatic structure leads him to reaffirm the importance of the English mystery cycles and their medieval vision of a providential world order in the development of the dramatist's art. The corollary to this is to see Shakespeare emphasizing the matter of personal responsibility and sin, as opposed to the concept of *hybris*.

59. Lawlor, John. *The Tragic Sense in Shakespeare* (New York, 1960).

Chapter IV of Lawlor's book, "Natural and Supernatural," is devoted to *Macbeth;* there he takes up the matters of theme, characterization, action, and philosophical implications of the play. Macbeth, like other tragic figures, is caught, as Lawlor sees it, in a process of reduction from the status of agent to that of patient in a cosmic drama. In the beginning he is introduced as a character whose imagination can be played upon, but who vacillates. He is worked upon by demoniacal suggestion, however, and the importunities of his wife, until he no longer has freedom of choice. He must seize the crown by murder or cease to be a full man (in whom "act and valor" match desire). The tragic element in Macbeth is his development of an "insensibility to all natural feeling," and this, according to Lawlor, leads to the central conception of the play. Macbeth in his isolation is an "actor" facing a "potentially dangerous world of observers." Macbeth's overstepping of the limits of nature is mirrored in his choice of a dramatic image in which life appears to him (wrongly) as "a tale/ Told by an idiot, full of sound and fury / Signifying nothing."

Although Lawlor's agent–patient antithesis seems at times to be a Procrustean bed into which he is bent upon squeezing all the tragedies (and *Hamlet* seems a better subject for it than *Macbeth*), his critical acumen allows him to triumph over his own metaphor and to produce a very perceptive analysis of Macbeth's relationship to the natural.

60. Holloway, John. *The Story of the Night* (Lincoln, Neb., 1961).

Holloway's book, while a series of separate essays on the great tragedies, is written from a position which conceives of literature as a form of ritual, and which sees in Shakespeare's tragic heroes various versions of the ritual "scapegoat." Macbeth can be seen as a kind of "Lord of Misrule

—and image of revolt" who eventually succumbs to the "restorative forces of life" symbolized in the soldiers carrying branches (a suggestion of the folk-ritual May procession) as Birnam Wood moves to Dunsinane. Images of anti-nature and disorder prepare for an eventual definition of Macbeth as a monstrous figure who must be destroyed if society is to have its harmony reestablished. Holloway stresses the emblematic treatment of character and the ritual form of many of the speeches in support of his contention that interest centers more on a pattern of experience represented in the play (to which an audience responds as a concrete image of their collective experience) than on representations of nature or on realistic characterizations which ultimately call for a kind of philosophical analysis.

Although not an entirely novel approach, Holloway's book carries the idea further than it has ever been done with Shakespeare, and, despite the disagreement in principle which it will undoubtedly provoke, elucidates many passages in *Macbeth* which have always been obscure. It also calls attention to the importance of previously unnoticed patterns of imagery in the play (that of "horses and riders," to name just one).

61. Rossiter, A. P. *Angel with Horns* (London, 1961).

Rossiter's essay on *Macbeth* (Chapter 11) studies the powers which move human minds and society, ignoring "the passionate collision of human energies" (the Bradleyan approach to drama as "condensed psychology, illustrated with tense and vivid scenes") in favor of the "inner structure, . . . the main emotional forces in the play." The characters are seen as parts of a pattern, aspects of the motivations working in all moral conflicts. Macbeth and Lady Macbeth are the two halves of Shakespeare's conception of "self-assertive force" which disrupts order on all levels of existence. For Rossiter, *Macbeth* is a tragedy of success, in which the chief character is the embodiment of willful antagonism and of the emptiness which characterizes it. The rest of the *dramatis personae* are not individual figures but make with Macbeth "one event in a poem," with the Weird Sisters, for instance, symbolizing our ambiguous feelings about the shadowy aspect of nature which law tries to regulate and philosophy to understand.

Rossiter's extremely convincing argument resembles in its emphasis upon analogical features of plot—the most significant analogy being that between the brevity, speed, and vehemence of the play and the turbulence of a "soul at war"—the approach of Fergusson (49), except for the former's more naturalistic bias. They should be read together for comparison.

62. Toppen, W. H. *Conscience in Shakespeare's "Macbeth"* (Groningen, 1962).

Toppen's book is in one sense a polemic against the trend (as he sees it) in modern Shakespearean criticism to divorce literature from life —to ignore the psychological substance of dramatic characters in favor of an examination of patterns and themes. This is particularly reprehensible when the major meaning of the play is distorted, as by G. Wilson Knight (28), for whom Macbeth emerges a triumphant hero. The author's arena for his point of view is the question of conscience in Macbeth and his wife. First of all, Toppen finds ample evidence in Elizabethan literature and moral philosophy to warrant the supposition that Shakespeare would have found it a viable subject for the stage. He then proceeds to revitalize the "character-and-plot" approach of the older critics against the attack of Fluchère and Knights (30), with the result that conscience is to be seen not as a theme but as a universal human characteristic magnified in the stage life of Macbeth. He is a man "tormented by his conscience, which tells him, at times darkly, that he is wrong."

The witches (the subject of a chapter) are not to be taken as symbols of Macbeth's inner temptation, but as objectively real creatures "whose pernicious influence insinuates itself from the start into their victim's conscience." Stoll's (27) theory that Macbeth's conscience is an external thing, a way of creating a dramatic contrast between the murders and the original nobility of the murderer, fares little better. Conscience, as Shakespeare presents it, is a matter of psychological motivation rather than of theatrical effect. Toppen then attacks Charlton's (44) rejection of Shakespeare's Christian understanding of conscience, and goes on to an analysis of two scenes from the play, in which, among many similar comments, he takes Macbeth's "we have scotch'd the snake" speech as "an insight into his real spiritual state, at a moment when he is committing what seems tantamount to the unforgivable sin."

Toppen's book is one of the more massive artillery pieces in the current rebellion against the "school of Knight," but he aims as well at other critics whose influence has tended toward a depreciation of the importance of the Renaissance Christian understanding of human character with its psychological equipment. Although the author's excursions into theoretical criticism take away from its value as a study of a single play, there is much sensible commentary in the book.

63. Dyson, J. P. "The Structural Function of the Banquet Scene in *Macbeth*," *Shakespeare Quarterly*, XIV (1963), 369–378.

Dyson suggests that this scene is crucially important both because it is a mirror of the imagery and action of the play as a whole and because it is the scene of crisis (it is here that Macbeth goes beyond the point of salvation and realizes his tragic vision). The world has passed beyond his control. Banquets, Dyson argues, are traditionally symbols of harmony and fellowship, but here Macbeth's subversion of order turns against him. His defeat is metaphysical rather than political (symbolized by his remark about murdered men pushing us from our *stools*). The ghost's visit represents chaos, for Macbeth's sins are sins against the "whole order of things." The Banquet scene is thus a kind of watershed moment in the play, clearly representing the disruption of the "martlet setting" by the "raven world."

Though he rides details hard, Dyson's general estimate of the Banquet scene accords well with critical comment about the importance of similar "ceremonial" scenes in Shakespeare's other plays.

64. Kantak, V. Y. "An Approach to Shakespearean Tragedy: The 'Actor' Image in 'Macbeth,'" *Shakespeare Survey*, XVI (1963), 42–52.

Kantak's article is a contribution toward a reconciliation of the "new critical" emphasis on theme and imagery with the emphasis on "character-in-action." The greatest plays obviously do reveal complex patterns of imagery, but just as obviously move audiences to an apprehension of the speaking figures as simulacra of real people involved in real emotional and intellectual acts. As an example, the famous "Tomorrow" speech brings to a new level of awareness the images of time, sterility, borrowed robes, and darkness, giving "unity to all the various strands of meaning." On the assumption, however, that the "poetry" of the speech is a psychological

habiliment of Macbeth and not just a reflection of Shakespeare's own virtuosity, the choice of the image of the stage actor expresses Macbeth's
sense of what, by his crime, he has become. It "arises from Macbeth's
poetic power and his radiant self-knowledge to the last."

Considering the melancholy record of charge and countercharge
over the last sixty-odd years in the matter of naturalistic characterization
as opposed to various "conventional" interpretations of the elements of
drama, it is unlikely that Kantak's generally sensible suggestions will quell
controversy. Certainly some concession has to be made to the conventional
aspect of the verse spoken by a dramatic character, and it is a matter of
extreme delicacy to decide how far one can go with it as an index to the
mind of a particular figure.

65. Walton, J. K. "Macbeth," in *Shakespeare in a Changing World*, ed.
Arnold Kettle (New York, 1964).

Walton's essay is a contribution to a collection of Shakespearean
pieces most (though not all) of which are written, as the editor frankly
admits, from a viewpoint sympathetic to Marxism. Walton finds the basic
conflict in *Macbeth* in the opposition of individualism and the communal
spirit—between feudal and bourgeois ideas. Macbeth's inner anguish, as
he nerves himself for the murder of Duncan, takes the form of a struggle
between two antithetical views of man—"as an individualist whose primary
loyalty is to his own interests, and . . . as a member of society whose
primary loyalty is to the interests of his fellow men." Individualism wins
out and leads finally to isolation and bestiality. Macduff, in assembling
rebellious forces, represents the community interest. As they approach
Dunsinane in their "leavy screens," so Walton feels (following Holloway's
hint that they would remind an Elizabethan audience of a May procession), the forces achieve the culmination of their social unity. The leading
images of the play support this reading—fertility, for example, being associated with the united community, and sterility with Macbeth; clothing
imagery points up Macbeth's decreasing manhood as he pursues his individual ways. The play, according to Walton, is the most optimistic of the
great tragedies because the "united people overcome the tyrant." (The
fact that the old feudal order is restored with Malcolm's ascension to the
throne is explained in part by the fact that James I exercised a good deal
of control over the stage.)

It is hardly necessary to insist upon the drastic reduction of Shake-speare's meaning that this essay makes. For one thing, the neat dichotomy between man as individual and as member of society ignores such impor-tant alternatives as "man as religious creature," or "man as loyal subject," either of which leads to a totally different reading of the play.

66. Rogers, H. L. *"Double Profit" in Macbeth,* Australian Humanities Research Council Publications, No. 11 (Melbourne, 1964).

Rogers' interesting monograph studies the various aspects in *Mac-beth* of the "profit" theme and the "doublenesse" theme, with their con-nections, in the light of the quotation from Holinshed that probably prompted Shakespeare to use them. (Holinshed reports of Macbeth's mur-der of the nobles that "he wan double profit [as he thought] thereby"—that is, removed his enemies and confiscated their wealth.) Rogers suggests that the "paltering" or doubleness of the Witches, the "equivocation" scene, the lying of Malcolm, and a number of other references to doubt, illusion, fairness and foulness, appearance and reality, hoped-for success and actual defeat, and so forth, all enter into a general complex of sym-bolism which, while it may not be central in the play, does alter our re-sponse. Macbeth's final speeches, particularly, reveal a concern with the difference between what is and what is said to be, and even the fact that "he dies as a man free of illusion" determines part of our response to his ending.

Rogers' position is, on the whole, well argued and amply set forth, though many readers will find unconvincing his suggestion (on functional grounds) that Act III, Scene v, which almost all editors declare to be spurious, is in fact by Shakespeare.

67. Heilman, Robert. "The Criminal as Tragic Hero," *Shakespeare Sur-vey,* 19 (1966), 12–24.

Heilman argues that the play's "complexity of form" has created ambivalent responses in the audience. The problem is that the play is structured so that we experience what Macbeth experiences. Thus, in the course of the play we assume a number of roles: murderer, bereaved hus-band, defiant warrior. But the problem is that these specific experiences are not presented developmentally. As a result, the range of the play is too narrow to partake of tragedy of the first order. To do that, we—and Macbeth—would have to experience the "soul's reckoning," not merely the "world's judgment."

Heilman's essay is interesting and provocative, but it appears to be more a series of impressionistic judgments, rather than conclusions verified by the language and action of the play.

68. Rauber, D. F. "Macbeth, Macbeth, Macbeth," *Criticism*, 11 (1969), 59–67.

Rauber's essay identifies the triadic and diadic elements in Macbeth, and attempts to demonstrate how the conflict between them actualizes the themes of the play. There is clearly a perceptible pattern of threes in the structural, relational, and magical aspects of the play. The play has three parts (with a murder in each), and each part is identified by a different kind of political stability. The three parts of the cosmos are reflected in the idealized England (heaven), "bleeding Scotland" (earth), and realm of Hecate (hell—with its three Weird Sisters). The parts of the play separate Macbeth's life symbolically into Youth (virility, heroism), Middle Age (sterility), and Old Age ("appropriate symbols of old age"). In general, Rauber indicates, three is the realm of the numinous, two that of the logical. Structure is triadic, action diadic. Their interplay generates the "tensional vitality" of the play.

As the author realizes, number symbolism is a tricky affair. Some of the trinities seem a bit forced, but on the whole the essay makes a modest and plausible case for the importance of these structural elements in the plot.

69. Jorgensen, Paul. *Our Naked Frailties: Sensational Art and Meaning in Macbeth* (Los Angeles, 1971).

Despite its title, this book is concerned primarily with sensation as the inner world of sensible experience; "sensational" elements, in the sense of "spectacular"—such things as the Weird Sisters and Macbeth's vision of the dagger—are analyzed as external correlatives to states of feeling and perception in the characters. These states of feeling are in turn related to Shakespeare's dramatic identification of the process by which

Macbeth simultaneously earns and experiences his damnation—a damnation which is characterized by that "sense of pain" and "sense of loss" alleged in traditional theology. Thus, Macbeth's "pestered senses" (of vision and hearing, especially) are at once pictured as guilty *and* tormented. Sounds and sights, horrifying though they may be in themselves, "speak to something evil in Macbeth." Jorgensen pursues his analysis by means of a judiciously eclectic method, balancing "new critical" analysis (of image patterns, for instance) with thorough attention to tradition and contemporary ideas. His treatment of blood imagery not only shows how blood becomes for Macbeth a "symbol of evil and guilt" (at the same time pointing out the analogy between Macbeth's bloody hands and the "bleeding land" of Scotland), but also relates Shakespeare's practice to similar themes in Senecan tragedy, in the Bible and in Biblical commentary, and in contemporary homiletical literature.

Jorgensen follows his theme through eight chapters, each devoted to a single kind of sensationalism—some more successful in penetrating to a profound aspect of the play's total meaning, others more helpful in defining matters of dramatic technique and audience response. Thus, Chapter X, "Torture of the Mind," discusses the stages in Macbeth's sense of loss leading to "a blasphemous negation of life robbed of meaning." Chapter VIII, "The Rest Is Labor," although indicating in some detail the association with evil of "futilely applied" effort, is concerned to demonstrate how response is produced in the audience—how sensation can bring about an extraordinary tension, as in a restless sleep, "that accounts for our exhaustion and for whatever acquiescence we finally feel in Macbeth's sense of futility."

Sources and Date

INTRODUCTION

The principal source of the play is Holinshed's *Chronicles of England, Scotlande and Irelande* (1577). Holinshed's source in turn was Hector Boece's *Scotorum Historiae* (1526), translated into English by John Bellenden as *The Hystory and Cronikles of Scotland* (1535). The Porter scene may have been derived from the Harrowing of Hell episodes in medieval mystery plays. Shakespeare's knowledge of the writings and interests of James I has been well documented by Paul (S1). A detailed summary of the play's sources is given by Muir in his *Shakespeare's Sources, I* and in his Arden edition (E5).

Date

The play's allusions to the Gunpowder Plot and the related controversy over equivocation and the arguments of Paul (S1) support the theory that the play was written in 1606.

ENTRIES FOR SOURCES AND DATE

S1. Paul, Henry. *The Royal Play of Macbeth* (New York, 1950). Excerpt in Halio.

Paul's book attempts, in effect, a reconstruction of the mental life of Shakespeare during the months in which he was occupied in writing *Macbeth*. He accepts, and sets out to prove with even greater force and precision, the traditional theory that the play was written specifically for a performance before King James and King Christian of Denmark in

August, 1606 (August 7, as Paul believes). The particular form of the play (notably its brevity and compression) is accounted for in terms of the author's conception of the King's interests and intellectual sophistication, and the various important as well as subordinate aspects of its theme are referred to James' interests or to contemporary political or cultural events. Thus, not only does Shakespeare cater to the King's concern about witches and demonology, and about Scottish history and the royal succession, but his treatment of conscience in the play stems directly from his familiarity with James' own *Basilicon Doron*. The Bible, too, is a source, and so is Ovid's *Metamorphoses* (though perhaps indirectly); "Montaigne was an influence but not a source." Paul pictures Shakespeare sitting at his desk and writing each scene so as to conform to the interests and sensitivities of his sovereign.

The book provides a great deal of historical information about such things as witchcraft and the Gunpowder Plot, which is extremely helpful in realizing the intellectual climate of the play, but it suffers from a confusing arrangement and excessive repetition. The main points of Paul's argument are not to be denied, but then they are not really new. Its chief limitation is the extraordinary reliance upon circumstantial detail to fit the author's preconception of the kind of working playwright Shakespeare was—much more of a "court poet," with all the conventionality that implies, than most students of Shakespeare would be willing to allow. But that should not be allowed to obscure the great value of the work for its energetic accumulation of historical detail, the sweet reasonableness of Paul's rhetoric, and the sometimes brilliant conjectures that he makes.

S2. Bradbrook, Muriel C. "The Sources of *Macbeth*," *Shakespeare Survey*, IV (1951), 35–48.

Miss Bradbrook rehearses certain of the well-established facts about the use of sources in *Macbeth*, and analyzes in particular the significance of the cauldron scene (the pageant of James VI's ancestors) and the scene in England (Malcolm and Macduff). She decides that because of their political overtones they belong to the upper level of meaning (the topical) in the play, and were probably written first; the latter scene, treated at length in Holinshed, may have given Shakespeare his original suggestion for the play. Among other sources, Miss Bradbrook feels that an account of the customs of Scottish women prefixed to Holinshed's *Chronicle* may have provided the fundamental idea for the character of Lady Macbeth. She reviews the material on witchcraft available to Shakespeare, emphasizing the Christian doctrinal points evoked by the preternatural imagery of the play, and concluding that one cannot finally decide whether it is Divine or Natural justice which triumphs. A reference to Tarquin (II, i) suggests the comparison with Shakespeare's own *Rape of Lucrece*, and the author examines the roots of Macbeth's character in Shakespeare's earlier poem. The close similarity between them (Macbeth being more skillfully done) points to the prevailing unity in Shakespeare's art and the increasing mastery of characterization he displays.

Even though more elaborate analysis of the sources for *Macbeth* is to be found in Paul's book (S1), Miss Bradbrook's study remains valuable both for its sensible observations on the relationship between topical reference and general meaning, and for its insistence upon the importance not only of "external sources" but of the poet's own earlier work as a "source" for the "deepest levels of the play."

S3. *Harcourt, John. "I Pray You Remember the Porter," *Shakespeare Quarterly*, XII (1961), 393–402.

An important discussion of the medieval tradition of the Harrowing of Hell as enacted in the mystery plays and its relationship to the Porter Scene and to the importance of Macduff.

S4. *Jack, Jane. "*Macbeth*, King James and the Bible," *ELH*, XXII (1955), 173–193.

A study of the contribution of James' *Basilicon Doron* to the atmosphere of the play, specifically to the pervasive sense of evil.

Textual Criticism

INTRODUCTION

The only extant version of the play is that found in the First Folio (1623). This is almost surely an abbreviated text shortened for performance. The text also contains interpolations probably added by Thomas Middleton, although the range and extent of abridgment and interpolation have been disputed (see T3).

ENTRIES FOR TEXTUAL CRITICISM

T1. Flatter, Richard *Shakespeare's Producing Hand: A Study of His Marks of Expression To Be Found in the First Folio* (New York, 1948).

Four of Flatter's thirteen chapters deal specifically with *Macbeth*. He first claims the entire "bleeding sergeant" scene for Shakespeare, with all of its metrical irregularity, precisely because it is the sort of breathless, incoherent recital we should except from the wounded messenger. Next, he corrects several mislineations, resulting from a failure on the part of earlier editors to appreciate the dramatic effectiveness of pauses and the need for understanding some lines as being delivered simultaneously. Finally, the great number of four-stress lines in the play is explained by the fact that the speeches of the witches have influenced Macbeth's own language, particularly in the antitheses, which tend to produce a four-stress line. All of these considerations work against the long-standing opinion that the text is relatively corrupt. Dramatic considerations alone help to disprove this.

Flatter's very conservative reading of the text has, with reservations, found a good deal of favor (Muir [E5], for one, is generally in agreement with it). As an approach to the establishment of a text, however, it frequently becomes very subjective, as in the conception of the speech pattern of one character being influenced by that of another.

T2. Spencer, Christopher. *Davenant's Macbeth from the Yale Manuscript: An Edition, with a Discussion of the Relation of Davenant's Text to Shakespeare's* (New Haven, 1961).

Davenant's *Macbeth* is important not so much in itself, but because it is a document of Shakespearean criticism (by being a record of what a later poet saw in *Macbeth*), and because it may be the means of recovering textual readings of Shakespeare's play which the Folio text has garbled. Spencer's introduction discusses the changes made by Davenant and their possible reasons; the character of Lady Macduff, for example, is developed as a foil to Lady Macbeth because there was more opportunity for women actors in the Duke's Company. After discussing the printed versions and the manuscripts of the Davenant version, Spencer analyzes the probable method followed by Davenant. This very likely took the form of crossing out and adding on to a text of Shakespeare's *Macbeth* other than that of the First Folio, most likely a pre-Restoration manuscript of the play. Among a number of corollaries to his thesis is the probability that as much as ten lines of a Witches' song preserved only in the Davenant version may in fact have been written by Shakespeare.

Although he himself does not regard his case as demonstrated beyond all doubt, it is, what Spencer is willing to settle for, a "reasonable" conclusion. Both Davenant's possession of a pre-Wars manuscript and Shakespeare's authorship of the lines of the song have been questioned.

T3. Nosworthy, J. M. *Shakespeare's Occasional Plays* (New York, 1965), pp. 8–53

Nosworthy believes that the Folio text represents the original tragedy of *Macbeth* with "such alterations and additions as were necessary to bring the play into line with the theatrical taste prevalent in or about 1612 . . . ," the alteration of the text being done by Shakespeare himself. Nosworthy's is the most persuasive and coherent presentation of the case for the integrity of the text as it is given in the Folio.

Editions

E1. *Furness, Horace Howard, Jr. *A New Variorum Edition of Shakespeare: Macbeth*, 5th ed. (Philadelphia, 1903); repr. Dover Books (T 1001).

The Furness Variorum is a mine of information about the play. It contains, in the form of footnotes, a substantial amount of prior interpretation and emendations. An appendix contains additional scholarly material concerning date and sources, as well as the Witch scenes from Midleton's play (two songs are thought to have been interpolated from another play, *The Witch*, by the dramatist Thomas Middleton, 1570?–1627), and the relevant extracts from Holinshed's *Chronicle* and Wyntoun's *Cronykil*. There is also a copious selection of English, German and French criticism of the play and of the characters, and comments on various performances. The appendix concludes with the full text of D'Avenant's version of *Macbeth*, and some discussion of musical accompaniment and musical versions. The Index, which is very sketchy, is far more helpful as a guide to the appendix than to the notes on the text.

E2. Liddell, Mark Harvey, ed. *The Tragedie of Macbeth*, The Elizabethan Shakespeare, Vol. I (New York, 1903).

Except for its irritating format (sections of text, surrounded—above, below, and beside—by notes and commentary), Liddell's edition is a valuable work, with a very helpful Introduction. Regarding the First Folio text as substantially accurate, with a few "obvious interpolations," he detects a remarkable unity and continuity of thought development in the play. Liddell stresses the reality of the Witches, and conceives of Macbeth's dealings with them as a Faust-like bargain, and of the hero as a figure of epic and Homeric stature—another "Hercules furens," for, in the light of Elizabethan psychology, Macbeth is seen to be mad and to come to his senses only at the last moment of his existence. Liddell makes an excellent analysis of the play's aesthetic unity of action—the merits of its unconsecutive unfolding of details—and of the aptness of its poetic rhythms.

The author's most questionable theory is his conception of Macbeth's "madness," which is simply one of the extreme forms of the "character realism" approach, and which, though it continues to find adherents, also continues to provoke violent disapproval. Liddell's notes to the text, however, contain a wealth of illustrative quotation (linguistic and literary) from Shakespeare's other work and other Elizabethan literature, are invaluable.

E3. Adams, Joseph Quincy, ed. *Macbeth* (Cambridge, Mass., 1931).

Although an edition of the play, Adams' book boasts a nearly two-hundred-page study, in the form of a scene-by-scene commentary, and separate analyses of text, interpolations, occasion, and sources. He takes a firm position on several disputed points: the witches are by no means destinal forces; the chief elements in Macbeth's character are ambition and conscience; he is physically courageous but a moral coward; Lady Macbeth is "distinctly feminine in nature"; the Hecate lines are definitely an interpolation. The brief discussion of the occasion of the play and the possible performance before King Christian IV of Denmark in the summer of 1606 is excellent, as is the highly speculative reconstruction of the manner in which a prompt-book of the play might have been injured in the Globe fire of 1613, causing just those aberrations that we find.

Although Adams' analysis of character tends to continue the highly impressionistic strain in Shakespeare criticism, his discussion of the design of the play anticipates much of the best modern criticism. Frequently he strikes off an inspired comment, as when he notes of Macbeth's death that it "was not a physical defeat, but a sacrifice to the eternal cause of righteousness."

E4. Wilson, J. Dover, ed. *Macbeth*, The Cambridge Edition of the Works of Shakespeare (Cambridge, Eng., 1947).

Wilson, in his treatment of sources, occasion, text, and meaning of *Macbeth*, is extremely liberal and speculative. He claims, for instance, that the figure of Lady Macbeth owes a great deal to Stewart's *Buik of the Croniclis of Scotland*, that the play as we have it is a later adaptation of a cut version probably made by Shakespeare himself for the performance honoring the King of Denmark, and that there are numerous interpolations and obvious lacunae in the text. Wilson suggests, with diffidence to be sure, that an original *Macbeth* may have been performed in 1602 in Edinburgh, and that Shakespeare may even have visited Scotland. He may then have modified this play in the summer of 1606, adding such details as the "equivocation" scene, Malcolm's self-indictment, and the episode of the King's Evil. As we have it the play is an adaptation by a botcher, probably Middleton, to whom we owe the Hecate scenes and a good number of the rhyming couplets, as well as the mutilations—notably that of I, ii.

Wilson builds upon his theory of an earlier version in explaining even the character of Macbeth himself; the lines in which Lady Macbeth taunts her husband with a reminder of his earlier courage in planning the murder destroy the idea of a noble soul suddenly beset by temptation, if they must be taken to mean that the deed has been plotted before the play begins, but not if they refer to an earlier *scene* coming between the Witches' prophecy and the present one.

Wilson's theories are respected, although not generally accepted. (Muir [E5], for instance, rejects the notion of a wholesale revamping of the text), but his argument purely from the standpoint of logical consistency is a good one. The difficulty is that it requires too many suppositions for which actual evidence is lacking.

E5. Muir, Kenneth, ed. *Macbeth*, The [New] Arden Edition of the Works of Shakespeare (London, 1951).

Muir's approach to the text is conservative. He tends to agree in the main with Richard Flatter's theory (T1) that the Folio text is very close to Shakespeare's original, and shows comparatively little editorial interference. He believes the play to have been written in 1606, the "equivocation" references certainly a result of Shakespeare's interest in Garnet's part in the Gunpowder Plot, and he rejects most of the proposed interpolations. The Porter Scene, *pace* Coleridge, is Shakespearean in style, notably in the use of verbal antitheses, and closely related to the dominant themes and imagery of the play. Muir accounts for Shakespeare's treatment of his sources (mainly Holinshed) in terms of his desire to denigrate even further the character of Macbeth, the murderer of James' ancestor. Agreeing with Charlton that the play is Shakespeare's "most profound and mature vision of evil," he emphasizes the fact that it is a play about damnation, in which the good which Macbeth sacrifices is presented not only in such characters as Duncan and the Macduffs, but in a pattern of "imagery, symbolism, and iteration."

Muir has stern words for those who are misled by the great poetry spoken by Macbeth and Lady Macbeth into thinking that their positions are justified by the play. The famous "Life's but a walking shadow" soliloquy, for example, is simply poetically convincing that life has become meaningless for Macbeth, not for Shakespeare. Macbeth, though a tragic hero, is a criminal and belongs to the company of the damned. Muir wisely admonishes the reader to remember that the play is a poem as well as a drama, and that the characters are based on ideas as well as on the facts of individual human psychology. In calling *Macbeth* "the greatest of morality plays" we must not forget the unique poetry of its vision of the universe. (Appendices contain the relevant excerpts from Holinshed's *Chronicles* and Stewart's *Buik of the Croniclis* of Scotland, as well as parallel passages from Shakespeare's *Rape of Lucrece, 2 Henry VI*, and *Richard III*.)

Muir's text is one of the best modern scholarly editions, and his introduction probably the sanest general statement available concerning the meaning of the play. He respects modern critical approaches to patterns of imagery and language, admits the value in psychological analysis of character, and yet insists upon exacting historical reconstruction of the text and of Elizabethan interests and conventions.

Staging

INTRODUCTION

Stage histories of the play are given in G. C. D. Odell's *Shakespeare from Betterton to Irving* (2 vols., London, 1920), in William Winter's *Shakespeare on the Stage* (3vols., New York, 1911–16), and in *The Reader's Encyclopedia of Shakespeare*, ed. O. J. Campbell and Edward Quinn (New York, 1966). J. C. Trewin's *Shakespeare on the English Stage, 1900–1964* (London, 1964) surveys twentieth-century productions.

ENTRIES FOR STAGING

St1. Bartholomeusz, Dennis. *Macbeth and the Players*. Cambridge University Press, 1969.

The most detailed and comprehensive stage history of this play, Bartholomeusz' study provides a vivid account of productions ranging from the 1611 performance at the Globe, witnessed by Simon Forman, to the 1964 production at the Mermaid in London. This account of the plays, reconstructed from prompt-books, playbills, memoirs, and reviews, not only brings clarity and insight to our knowledge of early productions but enables us to appreciate the degree to which performance and criticism are interrelated activities.

General Works Related to Shakespeare

Bibliographies

The most complete annual Shakespeare bibliography is published in the summer issue of *Shakespeare Quarterly*. Annual summaries of work also appear in *Shakespeare Survey* and *Shakespeare Jahrbuch* (Heidelberg). More selective summaries are given in *The Shakespeare Newsletter* and *Shakespeare Studies*.

Twentieth-century Shakespearean bibliographies include Ebisch and Schucking's *A Shakespeare Bibliography* (Oxford, 1931), covering the period from 1900 to 1930. There is a supplement for the years 1931–1935 (1937). By far the most extensive modern bibliography is Gordon Ross Smith's *A Classified Shakespeare Bibliography, 1936–1958* (Pennsylvania State University, 1963). A selective, briefly annotated list is given by Ronald Berman in *A Reader's Guide to Shakespeare's Plays: A Discursive Bibliography* (Chicago: Scott, Foresman, 1965).

Reference Works

Onions, C. T. *A Shakespeare Glossary*. Oxford University Press, 1911.

A handy-sized dictionary of obsolete words in Shakespeare. Convenient and detailed, it indicates the origins of the words as well as their meanings.

*Granville–Barker, Harley and G. B. Harrison, eds. *A Companion to Shakespeare Studies* [1934]. New York: Doubleday Anchor Books, 1960. 390 pp.

A collection of essays on many aspects of Shakespeare's life, art, and times. Each essay is written by a distinguished contributor. The result is a comprehensive handbook and guide.

Campbell, Oscar James and Edward G. Quinn, eds. *The Reader's Encyclopedia of Shakespeare*. New York: Thomas Y. Crowell, 1966. 1014 pp.

An attempt to provide an exhaustive survey of Shakespeare's life and works. It contains over 2,700 entries alphabetically arranged, an extensive chronology of the most significant dates in Shakespeare's life and a 30-page bibliographhly. The book is handsomely illustrated with photographs and line drawings.

Muir, Kenneth and Samuel Schoenbaum, eds. *A New Companion to Shakespeare Studies*. Cambridge University Press, 1971.

A sequel to the 1934 *A Companion to Shakespeare Studies*, this compilation updates certain categories and replaces others. Its contributors—lacking the "star" status of the original which included T. S. Eliot, Granville–Barker, and A. W. Pollard—are nevertheless competent and readable contemporary experts.

Biographies

Rowe, Nicholas. *Some Account of the Life . . . of Mr. William Shakespeare* [1709]. Reprinted in *Eighteenth Century Essays on Shakespeare*, ed. D. Nichol Smith. Oxford University Press, 1903; 2nd edition 1963. 340 pp.

> Rowe's is the first formal biography of Shakespeare. It was written as an introduction to his edition of the plays in 1709. Although inaccurate by modern standards, it incorporates much valuable information, including many local traditions and legends of Shakespeare's life in Stratford.

Lee, Sidney. *A Life of William Shakespeare*. London, 1898, rev. 1925. 476 pp.

> Lee's biography summarized nineteenth-century scholarship on Shakespeare's life. Long regarded as the standard work, it has been superseded by subsequent studies.

Adams, Joseph Quincy. *A Life of William Shakespeare*. Boston: Houghton Mifflin, 1923. 560 pp.

> Adams' study is a reliable and readable full-length treatment of the poet's life and work, but it needs to be updated in the light of more recent scholarship.

Chambers, E. K. *William Shakespeare: A Study of Facts and Problems*. 2 vols. Oxford University Press, 1930.

> The standard reference for all biographical and scholarly material, Chambers' study is indispensable. This two-volume work discusses not only biographical material but the fundamental problems concerning the text, printing, authenticity and chronology of the plays. It also includes reprints and excerpts from early documents relating to Shake-

speare. The care, learning, and lucid objectivity of this work mark it as one of the great achievements of modern literary scholarship.

Hotson, Leslie. *Shakespeare Versus Shallow*. Boston: Little, Brown, 1931; *I, William Shakespeare*. London: Cape, 1937; *Shakespeare's Sonnets Dated*, Oxford University Press, 1949; *The First Night of "Twelfth Night,"* New York: Macmillan, 1954; *Mr. W. H.*, New York: Knopf, 1964.

Hotson has devoted the major part of his life to the intense scrutiny of Elizabethan documents and records. He brings to his task the skill of the professional and the zest of the amateur. The result has been a series of books which are lively and imaginative as well as informative. Each of his books deals with the information contained in previously un-discovered records: *Shakespeare Versus Shallow* is based on the discovery of a document naming Shakespeare in a court order; *I, William Shake-speare* traces the life of Thomas Russell, Shakespeare's friend and the overseer of his will; *The First Night of "Twelfth Night"* reconstructs from contemporary evidence what may have been the first performance of Shakespeare's comedy; *Mr. W. H.* is an attempt to identify the "friend" of Shakespeare's sonnets as William Hatcliffe. Not all of Hot-son's conjectures, particularly those in *Mr. W. H.*, have been accepted by scholars, but all of them have proved challenging and provocative.

Fripp, Edgar I. *Shakespeare, Man and Artist*. 2 vols. Oxford University Press, 1938.

Fripp's work contains a wealth of valuable material about life in Strat-ford during the Elizabethan age. The weakness of the book lies in its lack of coherent organization.

*Chute, Marchette. *Shakespeare of London*. New York: E. P. Dutton, 1949. Dutton Paperback. 397 pp.

Miss Chute's book is an admirable popular biography. Readable and lively, it evades admirably the temptation of most popular biographies to engage in fanciful speculation.

*Eccles, Mark *Shakespeare in Warwickshire*. University of Wisconsin Press, 1961. 182 pp.

A very reliable description of Shakespeare's family, friends and neighbors in and around Stratford. Rigorously accurate, based upon original docu-ments, it is designed more as a collection of data than as a narrative account of Shakespeare's environment.

*Bently, Gerald Eades. *Shakespeare: A Biographical Handbook*. Yale University Press, 1962. 256 pp.

> Like Eccles, Bentley scrupulously avoids conjecture, concentrating exclusively on the known facts of Shakespeare's life as revealed in contemporary documents. Bentley's work judiciously incorporates the findings of later scholars such as Hotson while retaining much of the material in Chambers.

*Rowse, A. L. *William Shakespeare*. New York: Harper & Row, 1963. 484 pp.; New York. Pocket Books, 1965. 511 pp.

> This well-known book promises a good deal more than it delivers. The author claims to have "proven" that Shakespeare's friend in the Sonnets is the Earl of Southampton. However, he offers no really new evidence to substantiate his claim. The case for Southampton as the friend has always been a fairly impressive one; Rowse has not made it any more so.

Schoenbaum, Samuel. *Shakespeare's Lives*. Oxford University Press, 1970. 838 pp.

> Schoenbaum provides an exhaustive account of Shakespearean scholarship, focusing on the biographers, editors, forgers, anti-Stratfordians who have contrived to provide us with a significant body of facts and an ocean of conjecture. This is a work of considerable value, both in itself and as a prologue to a projected biography by Schoenbaum that will update and expand the work of Chambers.

The Elizabethan Theatre

Greg, W. W., ed. *Henslowe's Diary*. 2 vols. London: Bullen, 1904: *Henslowe's Papers*. London: Bullen, 1907.

> Philip Henslowe was a theatre owner and manager of one of the leading acting companies in Elizabethan London. His records and accounts have provided an unequalled source of information about theatrical conditions of the time. A new edition of the *Diary* has been edited by R. A. Foakes and R. T. Rickert (Cambridge University Press, 1961).

Chambers, E. K. *The Elizabethan Stage*. 4 vols. Oxford University Press, 1923.
> A monument of scholarship, this four-volume work contains histories of the Elizabethan acting companies and of the Elizabethan theatres, biographies of every known Elizabethan actor and playwright, reprints or excerpts from all the relevant documents, and an account of every extant Elizabethan play up to the year of Shakespeare's death in 1616. All of this material is brought together with extraordinary objectivity and meticulous scholarship. Only slightly less impressive is the author's companion study, *The Medieval Stage* (2 vols. Oxford University Press, 1903).

Baldwin, T. W. *The Organization and Personnel of the Shakespearean Company* [1927]. New York: Russell and Russell, 1960.

> An ingenious attempt to reconstruct the history of Shakespeare's acting company and to assign the particular roles played by various members of the troupe. Some of the conclusions are overly ingenious, but many others are plausible and quite valuable.

Greg, W. W. *Dramatic Documents from the Elizabethan Playhouses*. 2 vols. Oxford University Press, 1931.

> Greg has collected here facsimiles of the major theatrical documents of the age. An invaluable aid.

Bentley, Gerald Eades. *The Jacobean and Caroline Stage.* 7 vols. Oxford University Press, 1941–68.

> Bentley's massive work is a continuation of Chambers'. Covering the years 1616 to 1642, it completes the histories of the acting companies and provides accounts of the playwrights of all the plays written during the period. An admirable, scholarly work, it is designed to be used, as are the Chambers volumes, as a reference work. A more readable account of Shakespeare's relationship to the theatre of this time is the same author's *Shakespeare and His Theatre* (University of Nebraska Press, 1964).

*Harbage, Alfred. *Shakespeare's Audience.* Columbia University Press, 1941; Columbia University Press Paperback. 1966. 201 pp.; *Shakespeare and the Rival Traditions.* New York: Macmillan, 1952.

> *Shakespeare's Audience* is a perceptive and original attempt to reconstruct the attitudes and interest of the majority of Elizabethan theatergoers. It has helped to dispel the popular but inaccurate notion of them as a band of rowdy, colorful illiterates. *Shakespeare and the Rival Traditions* is a provocative attempt to see a radical division within the Elizabethan theatre between the public and the private theatres. Both books are written with Harbage's customary stylish wit.

*Beckerman, Bernard. *Shakespeare at the Globe, 1599–1609.* New York: Macmillan, 1962. 254 pp.

> Beckerman's book provides a detailed study of the activity of Shakespeare's company at the height of his career, from the opening of the Globe Theatre in 1599 to the purchase of the private Blackfriars Theatre in 1609.

PLAYHOUSE STRUCTURE

The attempt to reconstruct the size and structure of the original Elizabethan playhouses, and the Globe Theatre in particular, has been one of the most interesting developments of modern Shakespearean scholarship. Although there are large areas of agreement about the general structure of the playhouses, there is considerable dispute over certain major details. One of these, for example, is the often debated question as to whether or not there was an "inner stage" situated at the rear of the larger stage. The answer to this question provides an important key to our understanding of the staging of the original plays. The most important studies are the following:

Adams, John Cranford. *The Globe Playhouse*. Rev. edn. New York: Barnes & Noble, 1961. 420 pp.

> Adams argues that the Globe was an octagonal, Tudor-style building. Its stage contained a large inner stage at the rear, used for all the indoor scenes in the plays. This inner stage is the forerunner of the modern picture-frame stage.

Hodges, C. W. *The Globe Restored*. New York: Coward–McCann, 1953 199 pp.

> Hodges sees the Globe as a 16-sided polygonal building, ornately decorated in baroque style. He rejects the idea of an "inner stage" in favor of the view that the rear of the stage contained a curtained booth used for some special occasions when stage directions call for a "discovery."

Hotson, Leslie. *Shakespeare's Wooden O*. New York: Macmillian, 1959. 335 pp.

> The most radical of the reconstructionists, Hotson conjectures that the Globe was a theatre-in-the-round, the audience seated on all four sides of the stage with curtained areas on the sides. Hotson's view has met with very little acceptance by scholars.

*Nagler, A. M. *Shakespeare's Stage*. Yale University Press, 1961. 117 pp.

> Nagler accepts Hodges' hypothesis of a curtained booth as against an inner stage, but rejects the idea that the stage contained two pillars upholding the roof.

Hosley, Richard. "The Discovery Space in Shakespeare's Globe," *Shakespeare Survey*, 12 (1959); "The Origins of the Shakespearean Playhouse," *Shakespeare Quarterly*, XV (1964), 29–39.

> Hosley argues that the Globe was a round building, similar to the bear-baiting rings. He rejects both the "inner stage" and "curtained booth" theories, suggesting instead that a curtain was hung at the rear of the stage about two feet from the tiring house wall and that "discoveries" took place by drawing back this curtain. From the standpoint of simplicity and coherence, Hosley's arguments are the most convincing that have thus far been advanced.

Smith, Irwin. *Shakespeare's Blackfriars Playhouse: Its History and Its Design*. New York University Press, 1964. 577 pp.

Occupied by the King's Men in 1609, the Blackfriars and its audience had a considerable impact on the style and substance of Shakespeare's last plays. Smith recounts the history of this former monastery and attempts to reconstruct the dimensions and structure of that part of the building that came to be used as an interior playhouse. Much of his work—particularly the enormous detail—is impressive: however, his conjectures as to the design of the playhouse remain open to question.

King, Thomas J. *Shakespearean Staging, 1599–1642*. Harvard University Press, 1970.

King examines the stage directions and other sources of information contained in every extant play and prompt-book of the period. His conclusions support in general the thesis advanced by Hosley.

Elizabethan Literature, Life, and Thought

Lee, Sidney and C. T. Onions, eds. *Shakespeare's England*. 2 vols. Oxford University Press, 1916

> A wide-ranging collection of essays on every aspect of Elizabethan life treated in Shakespeare's plays. The book contains chapters on sports, social customs, professions, handwriting, education, and numerous other subjects, all written by experts in the field. For an updated treatment of many of these topics, see *Shakespeare Survey*, 17 (1964).

*Byrne, Muriel St. Clair. *Elizabethan Life in Town and Country* [1925]. New York: Barnes & Noble, 1961.

> A valuable social history of the period. Miss Byrne's volume casts considerable light on the social relationships in Shakespeare's plays.

Craig, Hardin. *The Enchanted Glass: The Elizabethan Mind in Literature*. Oxford University Press, 1936.

> Craig's work is an important account of the Elizabethan's idea of man and the universe. A less complete but more readable account is given in E. M. W. Tillyard's *The Elizabethan World Picture* (New York: Macmillan, 1943).

Wilson, F. P. *Elizabethan and Jacobean*. Oxford University Press, 1945.
> A small but admirable book, *Elizabethan and Jacobean* contrasts the life and literature of the two eras in which Shakespeare lived. The last chapter deals with the "Elizabethan" and the "Jacobean" Shakespeare.

Lewis, C. S. *English Literature in the Sixteenth Century. Oxford History of English Literature*. Oxford University Press, 1954. 696 pp.

> Although Lewis' volume does not treat dramatic literature, his stimulating comments on Elizabethan prose and poetry provide important

insights into the drama of the period. The same is true of the companion volume in the Oxford series, Douglas Bush's *English Literature in the Early Seventeenth Century* (Oxford University Press, 1945).

*Haydn, Hiram. *The Counter-Renaissance* [1950]. New York: Grove Press, 1960

Haydn's work deals with the development of skepticism and its impact on the literature of the early seventeenth century. His thesis is particulary relevant to *Hamlet*.

Cruttwell, Patricik *The Shakespearean Moment* [1954]. New York: Modern Library Paperback, 1960. 262 pp.

A provocative and interesting attempt to postulate a "poetic revolution" in the 1590's that was the source both of the achievements of Donne and the poetic diction Shakespearean tragedy. Written with liveliness and vigor, its chief weakness is its fondness for generalization.

Wilson, F. P. and G. K. Hunter. *The English Drama, 1485–1585*. Oxford University Press, 1969. 244 pp.

This volume, part of *The Oxford History of English Literature*, deals with pre-Shakespearean drama and provides an illuminating view of the groundwork which fostered the great Elizabethan dramatic achievement.

General Criticism

*Traversi, D. A. *An Approach to Shakespeare* [1938]. New York: Anchor Book, 1956. 304 pp.

> Traversi's book is a good representative of the application of "new criticism" to Shakespeare's plays. Close analysis of the language and verse, and a subtle probing of ethical values, distinguish the work.

*Van Doren, Mark. *Shakespeare*. New York: Holt, 1939. Doubleday Anchor Books, 1953. 302 pp.

> Brief, eloquent essays on each of the plays characterize this excellent example of impressionist criticism. The reader is repeatedly delighted by Van Doren's low-keyed, sensitive appreciation of Shakespeare.

Sewell, Arthur. *Chaacter and Society in Shakespeare*. Oxford University Press, 1951. 149 pp.

> This book is representative of a recent attempt among some critics to view Shakespeare's characters not as psychological entities but as expressions of, and exponents for, a complex pattern of world-views that is the artist's final vision. Not recommended for beginning students.

*Harbage, Alfred. *William Shakespeare: A Reader's Guide*. New York: Farrar, Straus, 1963; New York: Noonday Press, 1965. 498 pp.

> Harbage's book provides an excellent scene-by-scene commentary on the major plays. The opening chapter on the "components" of the plays is easily the best available brief introduction to the reading of Shakepeare.

Holland, Norman, *The Shakespearean Imagination*. New York: Macmillan, 1964. 388 pp.

> An excellent book for the general reader or the student beginning his study of Shakespeare. The book provides a summary account of Shake-

speare's life and theatre, a brief history of his reputation, and a balanced and sensible analysis of the plays, skillfully synthesizing the conflicting claims of modern critical schools.

IMAGERY AND LANGUAGE

Whiter, Walter. *A Specimen of a Commentary on Shakespeare* [1794]. London: Methuen, 1967; New York: Barnes & Noble, 1967.

> Based upon the principles of John Locke's associationist psychology, this remarkable eighteenth-century study anticipated by over a hundred years many of the insights of modern imagery studies of Shakespeare. Whiter examined passages in the plays in order to demonstrate a chain of association triggered in the poet's mind by a particular image.

*Spurgeon, Caroline. *Shakespeare's Imagery and What It Tells Us*. Cambridge University Press, 1935. Chicago University Press, 1960. 408 pp.

> This book is justly famous as the pioneer systematic study of the image patterns in Shakespeare. Part I deals with the imagery as revelations of the character and mind of the poet. Part II, considerably the more valuable section, considers the major images in each of the plays and their relation to the play's theme.

Sister Miriam Joseph. *Shakespeare's Use of the Arts of Language*. Columbia University Press, 1947.

> An extended, comprehensive survey of the use of rhetorical figures in Shakespeare's plays. Shakespeare, as did all Elizabethan writers, received extensive rhetorical training, adding considerable breadth and flexibility to his use of language. Sr. Miriam's book provides ample evidence of Shakespeare's rhetorical skill.

*Empson, William. *The Structure of Complex Words*. London: Chatto and Windus, 1951. 451 pp.

> With subtlety and ingenuity Empson focuses on the significance of key words in some of Shakespeare's plays, such as "honest" in *Othello* and "fool" in *King Lear*. His analysis makes clear the multiplicity of levels on which Shakespearean language operates.

THEMES

Spencer, Theodore. *Death and Elizabethan Tragedy*. Howard University Press, 1936.

Spencer traces the idea of death as it altered from the Middle Ages to the Renaissance, and the incorporation of that idea in Elizabethan drama. Although not dealing exclusively with Shakespeare, his study throws a great deal of light on the workings of this fundamental concept in the great tragedies.

*Harbage, Alfred. *As They Liked It*. New York: Macmillan, 1947. 234 pp.

Harbage treats Shakespeare's "moral artistry," the ethical values underlying the dramas. He argues that the moral outlook of the plays is essentially that of the majority of the Elizabethan audience; that Shakespeare was neither an innovator nor a rebel; and that this ethical orthodoxy, rooted in an essentially Christian world view, is the shared assumption of Shakespeare and his original audience.

*Righter, Anne. *Shakespeare and the Idea of the Play* [1962]. Penguin Books, 1967. 200 pp.

The first and most comprehensive treatment of a subject of growing interest among critics and scholars: the idea of the theatre and the metaphors of the play and the actor as Shakespeare handles them. Miss Righter explores this development up to and including its conclusion in *The Tempest*, where the distinction between illusion and reality is erased: "Life has been engulfed by illusion,"

Vyvyan, John. *Shakespeare and the Rose of Love*. London: Chatto and Windus, 1960.

Vyvyan explores the themes of love in the early plays, up to and including *Romeo and Juliet*—and argues that Shakespeare is drawing on the three conceptions of love: medieval, courtly love; Renaissance neo-Platonic love; and the Christian doctrine that identifies God as the source of love.

West, Robert. *Shakespeare and the Outer Mystery*. University of Kentucky Press, 1968

West deals with the nature of the supernatural in the tragedies. He concludes that the "pattern of human morality" in these plays is a reflection of the outer mystery of the universe. The resolution of this mystery requires not necessarily a Christian nor a theistic belief but a faith in a transcendent power that tolerates evil as well as good.

Turner, Frederick. *Shakespeare and the Nature of Time*. Oxford: Clarendon Press, 1971.

A critical examination of the differing conceptions of time reflected in the *Sonnets, Romeo and Juliet, As You Like It, Twelfth Night, Hamlet, Troilus and Cressida, Othello, Macbeth,* and *The Winter's Tale*.